The Hittites

THE HITTITES
People of a Thousand Gods

Johannes Lehmann

TRANSLATED BY
J. MAXWELL BROWNJOHN

COLLINS
St James's Place, London
1977

William Collins Sons & Co Ltd
London · Glasgow · Sydney · Auckland
Toronto · Johannesburg

Originally published in German under the title
DIE HETHITER
Volk der tausend Götter

First published 1976
ISBN 0 00 216314-4

Set in Monotype Plantin
Made and Printed in Great Britain by
William Collins Sons & Co Ltd Glasgow

Contents

Illustrations

Introduction

This is the story of a people wrapped in oblivion for 3000 years. Although they once conquered Babylon and put the Pharaoh Rameses to flight, nothing was known of them a century ago except their name. Our great-grandfathers had no precise idea where they lived or where their capital city lay buried.

After holding sway for half a millennium, their empire crumbled and collapsed under the onset of foreign invaders. Their traces were scattered, and only the Bible preserved a recollection of the 'Chittim', whom we call Hittites.

Today, we can stroll among the massive walls of the Hittite capital, admire Hittite art treasures in museums and draw upon tens of thousands of inscribed clay tablets for an insight into the history and customs of those who styled themselves 'the Nation of a Thousand Gods' and differed from their neighbours in many important respects.

We now know that the Hittites were Indo-Germans – or, to use the more up-to-date and accurate term, Indo-Europeans – whose laboriously inscribed cuneiform texts embody words still current among the Germans of today. They were migrants from the north, and archaeological research has recently brought to light a Stone Age town inhabited 7000 years ago by the legendary autochthons from whom these Indo-European settlers took their name: Çatal Hüyük, the world's earliest-known town apart from Jericho – perhaps the earliest of all.

What follows is the story of a people who built palaces like that of the fabled Cretan Minotaur in the rugged Anatolian highlands of Asia Minor, who sold Abraham a tract of land still regarded as sacred soil by the Jews and Arabs of modern times, and whose royal line once came close to acquiring the throne of the Egyptian Pharaohs.

I THE QUEST

A surprise for King Suppiluliuma

'I have never encountered such a thing in all my life,' wrote Suppiluliuma, who ruled the Hittites 3600 years ago. If he had been less disconcerted, the history of the world might have taken a different turn. The king had just received a letter borne by courier for two whole weeks across desert and mountain. It read:

'My husband is dead. I have no son. But you, so they say, have many sons. Were you to send me one of your sons, he would become my husband. I shall never take one of my servants and make him my husband. That I should find too abhorrent.' The letter had been sent from the land of Egypt by Ankhesenamun, daughter of Nefertiti and widow of Tutankhamun, a young woman less than twenty years old.

The Hittite king, who was besieging the city of Carchemish on the Euphrates, scented a trap. He summoned his council of elders and debated the proposal. Why should the Pharaoh's widow have chosen to make one of *his* sons ruler of Egypt? It might be a stratagem designed to harm his people. Two Hittite generals had just invaded the Egyptian-dominated area between the Lebanon and Anti-Lebanon mountains, and the Egyptians – to quote a contemporary document – 'were afraid'.

So how did Ankhesenamun come to ask her country's enemies for a royal consort? Although the Pharaohs often imported their wives from abroad, the Pharaoh himself had always been an Egyptian. Finally, young as Ankhesenamun was, she must surely have produced some offspring who could succeed her late husband.

We do not know the text of Suppiluliuma's reply, but his misgivings can be gauged from a second letter delivered by an Egyptian envoy.

'Why do you say "they are trying to deceive me"?' wrote Tutankhamun's widow. '. . . I have written to no other country, only to you. They say you have many sons. Give me one of your sons and he will be my husband and lord of the land of Egypt.'

It was one of those moments when history is governed less by political expediency, by the will of a ruler or nation, than by the human element – in this case, the feelings of a young and beautiful widow who declined to marry her own grandfather and make him Pharaoh simply to provide her country with a king.

We know little about Ankhesenamun, who is the subject of much scholarly controversy. Her parents – Amenophis IV, also called Akhenaten, and the celebrated Nefertiti – married her as a ten- or twelve-year-old child to Tutankhamun, who could scarcely have been much older. He was the same Tutankhamun whose tomb was discovered in the Valley of the Kings in 1922 and whose immense hoard of funerary treasures has conferred world-wide renown on an otherwise insignificant Pharaoh.

Although Tutankhamun was duly installed on the throne after Akhenaten's death, it is probable that Ay, Nefertiti's father, who was high priest and court chamberlain, ruled on the young couple's behalf. Ay also bore the title 'Fan-bearer at the King's Right Hand', was superintendent of the royal stables and modestly permitted his inferiors to address him as 'Divine Father'.

When Tutankhamun died a few years later – possibly assassin-ated, as some have deduced from the condition of his mummy – sixty-nine-year-old Ay devised an eminently practical solution. Even though he already ruled the country, he would combine business with pleasure by marrying the young widow and be-coming king in name as well as fact.

Such were the circumstances under which Ankhesenamun hurriedly wrote to the Hittite king that she was reluctant to marry 'one of her servants', a category which included Ay. She had little time to spare – only the regulation 70 days set aside for the embalming of her husband's body – and couriers took a fortnight to complete the journey from Thebes in Egypt to Carchemish on the Euphrates.

Suppiluliuma wasted precious time by hesitating, the more so because he himself sent an envoy to Egypt with the following brief: 'Go, bring me trustworthy information. They may be trying to mock me – perhaps they already have a successor to the throne, so bring me back information worthy of credence.'

The wary Hittite was finally convinced by his envoy's response and Ankhesenamun's second missive. He chose one of his sons and sent him to Egypt with a retinue. If the projected marriage had actually united Suppiluliuma's dominions with those of the Pharaohs, the Hittites would have controlled an area bounded by the Nile and the Black Sea, the Euphrates and the Mediterranean.

But Zannanza, Suppiluliuma's son, never reached his destination.

A Hittite cuneiform text of subsequent date informs us that 'they killed him as they were conducting him to Egypt', and we may assume that fate was given something of a helping hand by high priest Ay. At all events, it was he who married his own grand-daughter when the 70 days were up and installed himself on the pharaonic throne.

Had Ankhesenamun's plan succeeded and a Hittite ascended the Egyptian throne backed by the military strength of the Hittite Empire, there might never have been a Rameses II. If a Hittite prince had become Pharaoh, history might well have followed a different course. It is fascinating, in any case, to speculate on what would have happened if a union between the queen and the prince had encouraged Indo-European Hittites and Hamitic Egyptians to know each other better and gradually commingle. The Hittites were no better than their contemporaries, but they were certainly different.

All these matters, including the Ankhesenamun-Zannanza episode, have come to light only in the past few decades. It is one of the enigmas of history that the Hittite Empire, which was one of the great powers of its day, should have lapsed into such utter oblivion that no reference is made to it even by the historians of the ancient world.

The story of the Hittites must therefore be prefaced by an account of their rediscovery, in which chance played as great a part as dogged spade-work and flashes of inspiration.

Only then can an attempt be made to reconstruct a picture from the separate fragments of mosaic that have been found.

Abraham bows to the Hittites

Meyers Neues Konversationslexikon (1871) summarized all that was known about the Hittites in a scant seven lines. Although the encyclopedia was not to blame, their content was fundamentally erroneous.

Headed 'Hittites', the entry read: 'Canaanite tribe encountered in Palestine by the Israelites, resident among and alongside the Amorites in the region of Bethel. They were pressed into service by Solomon. Still later, however, an independent and monarchically governed Hittite tribe existed nearer Syria.'

On checking the source of the encyclopedia's pearls of wisdom, we soon spot that every reference stems from the Bible, which, although a historical work, presents history solely from an Israelite standpoint.

The notion that the Hittites were a Canaanite tribe can be found in *Genesis* x, 15–16: 'And Canaan begat Sidon his firstborn, and Heth, and the Jebusite . . .' A total of eleven tribes are attributed to Canaan in this way.

The Hittites are mentioned again when God promises the land of Canaan to Abraham and his descendants. Another long list of tribes is given, but these inhabited an area larger than Canaan proper, which corresponded roughly to modern Israel, including the occupied territories. The tribal area referred to in *Genesis* xv, 18, extended from 'the river of Egypt unto the great river, the river Euphrates'.

According to the Biblical account, therefore, the Hittites lived somewhere in the tract of land between the Nile and Mesopotamia.

Rather more precise information was supplied by the scouts whom Moses sent to spy out the land of Canaan at the conclusion of his trek through the desert: 'We came unto the land whither thou sentest us, and surely it floweth with milk and honey; and this is the fruit of it. Nevertheless the people be strong that dwell in the land, and the cities are walled, and very great: and moreover we saw the children of Anak there. The Amalekites dwell in the land of the south: and the Hittites, and the Jebusites, and the Amorites, dwell in the mountains: and the Canaanites dwell by the sea, and by the coast of Jordan' (*Numbers* xiii, 27–9).

This implies that the Hittites lived in the centre of modern Israel. One of the former Jebusite mountain strongholds captured by King David and proclaimed 'the city of David' was Jerusalem. The Bible never defines the extent of the Hittites' territory, but we do at least have a clue to where they *also* resided, namely south of Jerusalem at Hebron, a fact mentioned in the same context by Meyer's encyclopedia.

It was in Hebron that Abraham's wife Sarah died at the Biblical age of 127, and it was there that Abraham, having duly mourned and lamented her passing, wished to bury her. The land belonged to the Hittites, however, so negotiations were instituted. The patriarch adopted a 'low-key' approach and asked if he might purchase a burial-place. The Hittites generously offered to give him the land outright, but Abraham insisted on payment and a deed of sale.

For more than 2000 years, the story of Abraham's acquisition of a family grave at Hebron remained the sole document in which the Hittites were not only mentioned as a people but represented as animate and articulate members of the human race. This being so, and because the passage typifies the leisurely style of such accounts, I quote it in full:

And Abraham stood up from before his dead, and spake unto the sons of Heth, saying, I am a stranger and a sojourner with you: give me a possession of a burying-place with you, that I may bury my dead out of sight. And the children of Heth answered Abraham, saying unto him, Hear us, my lord: thou art a mighty prince among us: in the choice of our sepulchres bury thy dead; none of us shall withhold from thee his sepulchre, but that thou mayest bury thy dead.

And Abraham stood up and bowed himself to the people of the land, even to the children of Heth. And he communed with them, saying, If it be your mind that I should bury my dead out of sight; hear me, and intreat for me to Ephron the son of Zohar, that he may give me the cave of Machpelah, which he hath, which is in the end of his field; for as much money as it is worth he shall give it me for a possession of a burying-place amongst you. And Ephron dwelt among the children of Heth: and Ephron the Hittite answered Abraham in the audience of the children of Heth, even of all that went in at the gate of his city, saying, Nay, my lord, hear me: the field I give thee, and the cave that is therein, I give it thee; in the presence of the sons of my people give I it thee: bury thy dead.

And Abraham bowed down himself before the people of the land. And he spake unto Ephron in the audience of the people of the land, saying, But if thou wilt give it, I pray thee, hear me: I will give thee money for the field; take it of me, and I will bury my dead there. And Ephron answered Abraham, saying unto him, My lord, hearken unto me: the land is worth four hundred shekels of silver; what is that betwixt me and thee? Bury therefore thy dead. And Abraham hearkened unto Ephron; and Abraham weighed to Ephron the silver, which he had named in the audience of the sons of Heth, four hundred shekels of silver, current money with the merchant.

And the field of Ephron, which was in Machpelah, which was before Mamre, the field, and the cave which was therein, and all the trees that were in the field, that were in all the borders round about, were made sure unto Abraham for a possession in the presence of the children of Heth, before all that went in at the gate of his city. And after this, Abraham buried Sarah his wife in the cave of the field of Machpelah before Mamre: the same is Hebron in the land of Canaan. And the field, and the cave that is therein, were made sure unto Abraham for a possession of a burying-place by the sons of Heth (*Genesis* xxiii, 3–20).

To this day, the spot is a 'holy place' to pilgrims of three religions, and Christians have some difficulty in doing right by the Jews and Mohammedans who likewise venerate Abraham as a patriarch. A synagogue requires you to cover your head and a mosque to remove your shoes, but at Hebron the visitor has to do both: don a skull-cap and leave his shoes at the door . . .

Esau, Abraham's grandson and Jacob's brother, formed even closer links with the Hittites. He married 'Judith the daughter of Beeri the Hittite, and Bashemath the daughter of Elon the Hittite. Which were a grief of mind unto Isaac and to Rebekah' (*Genesis* xxvi, 34–5). The Old Testament makes two more references to the Hittites. On one occasion they are listed with other peoples as forced labourers engaged in constructing the Temple at Jerusalem for King Solomon (I *Kings* ix, 20), or about a thousand years before our era. Another time – and this is quite incompatible with forced labour in the Temple – they are mentioned by the Syrians as allies of Israel on a par with the Egyptians – indeed, they actually come first in the list: 'Lo, the king of Israel hath hired against us the kings of the Hittites, and the kings of the Egyptians . . .' (II *Kings* vii, 6).

For thousands of years, this was the sum total of written references to the Hittites apart from the disreputable story of King David, who 'in an eventide . . . arose from off his bed, and walked upon the roof of the king's house . . . and saw a woman washing herself; and the woman was very beautiful to look upon.' He sent for her and seduced her, with the inevitable result. Bathsheba was 'the wife of Uriah the Hittite', as the Bible expressly states, so David proceeded to do something that 'displeased the Lord'. He wrote to his general, Joab, as follows: 'Set ye Uriah in the forefront of the hottest battle, and retire ye from him, that he may be smitten, and die.' Uriah was killed, David took Bathsheba into his house, 'and she became his wife' (II *Samuel* xi).

We now know that all these Bible-based references in nineteenth-century encyclopedias were misleading because the kingdom of the Hittites had long been sought in the wrong place. Even their name was only vaguely known from the Bible. The Hebrew text gives it as Chet, plural Chittim, though the vowels are a more or less arbitrary addition because Hebrew script is written without any. The Hebrew scriptures were not vocalized by means of a simple dot-system until much later on.

The King James Bible renders the name as 'sons of Heth' or 'Hittites'. Luther, using the dotted text transliterated into Greek, which invariably wrote 'h' for 'ch', referred to the 'Ch-t' as 'Hethiter', though 'Chettiter' would have been more apt.

The Germans have stuck to 'Hethiter', though they could (and occasionally do) write 'Hettiter', 'Hetiter', 'Hittiter' or 'Chetiter' without actually misspelling the name. The Hittites 'called' the area in which they lived 'the land of Hatti' or 'Chatti', an appellation which also occurs in Assyrian texts. Egyptian records 'speak' of 'Cheta'las', though here too the vocalization is arbitrary because hieroglyphs likewise express consonants but not vowels. Only the consonants 'h' and 't' are supplied, and one can again choose between a pure aspirate and a palatalized 'ch' as in the Scottish 'loch', which is the more likely. The French used to write 'Héthéens' before they adopted 'Hittites' from the English. Just to render chaos complete, German representatives of the major Christian denominations resolved in 1971 to use 'Hetiter' in Bible translations, whereas German orthography still favours the Lutheran 'Hethiter' but sanctions other spellings as well.

This, for good or ill, was all we knew about the Hittites a century ago. Nothing more transpired until 1888, and then only by chance.

Like so many oriental tales, the present one exists in two different versions. Some relate that an Egyptian peasant-woman rooting around in a heap of rubble beside the Upper Nile, far from Cairo, found some inscribed clay tablets which she sold to a friend for ten piastres (about 35p). The consequence of this transaction was that other fellahin started digging because antiquities were already regarded as a good investment.

The more attractive but less plausible version is that the same poor peasant-woman angrily pelted some inquisitive foreigners with clay tablets to drive them away, thereby achieving the opposite effect: the tablets were the reason for their presence.

All we know for certain is that at least 200 pieces came on to the Cairo black market late in 1887, the export of antiquities being already prohibited. An honest and legal attempt to sell the inscribed tablets to an official of the celebrated Cairo Museum had previously failed because he considered them to be common-or-garden fakes and turned the offer down. Jules Oppert of the Louvre also pronounced them spurious, but the Austrian collector Theodor Graf accepted their authenticity and bought some. Wallis Budge acquired 82 whole and fragmentary tablets for the British Museum.

In the course of time, the lion's share – 160 pieces – of these 'fake' tablets of 'unprecedented size' was acquired in Cairo and from the Graf Collection by Berlin Museum. Thorough scrutiny disclosed that they were not only genuine but a sensational find of the first magnitude.

What had been discovered was Egypt's largest and most important collection of clay tablets: the government archives of the heretical king Akhenaten, who broke with the old religion and introduced a cult strictly dedicated to the sun-god Aten. In about 1350 BC, beside the Upper Nile 200-odd miles from Cairo, he built a new capital named 'Horizon of the Globe' (Akhetaten) where he could devote himself entirely to the sun-god's worship. The city, which was abandoned after Akhenaten's death, fell into decay and was buried by the sands. The most popular and celebrated find made there more than a century ago was the bust of Nefertiti, now in Berlin Museum.

Today we know the city by its archaeological name, Tell el Amarna, and the clay tablets are succinctly referred to as the Amarna letters. They consist of correspondence between the Pharaohs Amenophis III, his son Amenophis IV (Akhenaten) and son-in-law Tutankhamun, and the rulers of the contemporary world, and include letters from Babylonia, dispatches from

Assyria and treaties with other Near Eastern countries. Together, they constitute a government archive which sheds light on international relations in the fourteenth century BC and provides the world of scholarship with a rich store of treasure.

It would, however, be wrong to suppose that the Amarna letters are dry-as-dust communications which conceal as much as they disclose. Egypt having become the civilized world's major gold producer, thanks to its Nubian possessions on the Upper Nile, they are larded with forthright and unabashed requests for consignments of precious metal.

As Tushratta, King of Mitanni, ingenuously writes to Amenophis III: 'You maintained a very, very close friendship with my father. Now that we are friends, it is ten times greater than with my father. So I say to my brother, let my brother apportion me ten times as much as my father. Let my brother send me an abundance of gold. Let my brother send me more gold than my father.'

Amenophis III must have sent some statues of gilded wood instead of the requisite number of gold statuettes, because Tushratta's next missive embodied the following complaint: 'Yet gold is as dust in the land of your son. Is this friendship?'

This begging letter was no isolated phenomenon. Whoever the royal correspondent, the customary preamble in which monarchs addressed one another as 'brother' and exchanged protestations of friendship was immediately followed by a reference to gold.

Amenophis, King of Egypt, has thus been addressed by Burnubariash, King of Babylon, your brother: prosperity attends me. May great prosperity attend you, your house, your wives, your children, your country, your noblemen, your horses and chariots. From the time when my father and your father talked of friendship together, they sent one another handsome gifts, nor did either of them ever withhold any fine thing for which the other asked. But now my brother has sent me only two minae of gold as a gift . . . Why did you send only two minae of gold?

Elsewhere, reference is made to gifts of a less impersonal kind.

Another Babylonian king writes: 'As to the maiden, my own daughter, whom you wrote that you wished to wed, she is full grown and fit for a husband. Send hither. Let her be fetched.' Gifts being preservers of friendship, he requests an Egyptian princess for his harem in return but is haughtily rebuffed: 'No daughter of an Egyptian king has ever been given to anyone from time immemorial.' The Babylonian's shrewd rejoinder: 'Then send me some beautiful woman or other as if she were your daughter. Who will deny her to be daughter of a king?'

These begging letters also included a communication in Babylonian cuneiform from a Hattian king whose name the Egyptians wrote 'Sapalulu' (Suppiluliuma). Written to congratulate the heretic-king Akhenaten on his accession to the throne, it was couched in the language used by one ruler to another of equal rank.

At long last, scholars had identified a Hittite king who could be dated: Suppiluliuma must have reigned *ca.* 1370 BC.

Other letters mention a Hittite invasion of Syria, and the chronicles of Egyptian Pharaohs of the New Kingdom likewise refer to encounters with the Hittites.

These documents from Amarna suddenly conjured up a new picture of the Hittites – one that corrected the sparse information given by the Bible.

Quite obviously, these Hittites could not have been a petty tribe resident round Jerusalem in the mountains of Judaea. It was even doubtful whether the Hittites mentioned in the Bible were identical with those of the kingdom of Hatti. The new documentary evidence implied that they were pushing southwards into Lebanon, and Egyptian temple inscriptions actually disclosed that they got as far as the Orontes. But the Biblical Hittites lived far to the south, so anyone in search of the kingdom of the Hittites would have to look for it north of Kadesh, in Syria or beyond. In that case, what of the so-called Hittites of Palestine?

Kadesh, situated in the northern foothills of the Lebanon range, contributed to the assessment of the Hittites in yet another important respect. Egyptian temple inscriptions claimed that Rameses II had inflicted a crushing defeat there on 'the wretches of Hatti'. This could not be correct, however, because the reportedly annihilated Hittites soon afterwards joined the Egyptians, as partners of equal status, in concluding a treaty of 'perpetual peace'.

All these factors gradually reinforced scholars in their supposition that the Hittites, like the Egyptians, were one of the great powers of the second millennium BC, even though they had been mysteriously effaced from the minds of posterity.

By 1900, our grandfathers could glean rather more from Meyer's encyclopedia than it had offered their fathers thirty years earlier:

Hittites (Egyptian: Cheta): the third great civilized people of the Near East, the others being the Egyptians and Babylonian-Assyrians; referred to in Egyptian records of Tuthmosis III to Rameses (fifteenth to twelfth century BC.)

Ca. 1350 BC, destroyed the neighbouring kingdom of Mitanni on the Upper Euphrates, whose king, Tushratta, had conducted the recently discovered correspondence [of El Amarna] with Amenophis III. In the fifth year of his reign (or *ca.* 1295 BC), Rameses II fought a battle with the Hittites near Kadesh [in northern Syria] which he extolled as a great victory, but which was not decisive because he and the Hittite king Chetasar concluded a treaty of peace and alliance *ca.* 1280.

Relics of the Hittites extend approximately from Hamath to Carchemish, but these Syrian Hittites form only one branch of a large ethnic group of which similar relics are scattered throughout Asia Minor as far as the Aegean . . . Their nationality is still in doubt because attempts to decipher the peculiar Hittite pictography do not, as yet, appear to have been wholly successful.

Before saying something about these 'peculiar' Hittite pictograms, which have resisted full elucidation to this day, I ought to stress one thing: whatever was known about the Hittites at the turn of the century, the central problem remained unsolved.

Nobody had yet located the Hittites' capital and, thus, the hub of their empire.

If the Bible had given the impression that the Hittites resided mainly in the region of modern Israel, the Amarna letters and Egyptian temple inscriptions prompted archaeologists to seek them further north, or, in modern terminology, in northern Lebanon and Syria as far north as the Euphrates. In fact, this area had also yielded 'relics' which were attributed to the Hittites, though not with complete certainty.

It was an unfruitful quest because none of these finds could be classified. Archaeologists came across unfamiliar signs belonging to a pictographic script which they could neither read nor interpret. They found strange figures whose attributes were unknown. The culture was neither Babylonian nor Assyrian nor Egyptian. Could it be that the objects which defied classification stemmed from that strange race known as the Hittites, who had yet to be identified?

In search of Arzawa

It all began, as befits an oriental tale, with a sheikh named Ibrahim. The sheikh was a merchant, or so he claimed. He had visited the holy city of Mecca as a pilgrim – that much was certain – and was so well versed in the Koranic code that he confounded a pair of Arab lawyers who tested him on the subject. He roamed hither and thither, to and fro, from Arabia to the Holy Land and from there to the Euphrates, spending part of his time in Syria and part in Egypt.

Just as he was about to embark on another journey, Sheikh Ibrahim died in Cairo at the age of thirty-three and was laid to rest in a Mohammedan cemetery with the ceremony proper to a hajji, or Mecca pilgrim. The year was 1817.

Sheikh Ibrahim had led a colourful life, but the crux of the story is that he belonged to an old patrician family from Basle – one that has continued to produce eminent diplomats and historians in our own century. The sheikh's real name was Johann Ludwig Burckhardt.

At twenty-five Burckhardt had donned oriental dress and travelled to Syria to acquaint himself with the country and its inhabitants. When Cambridge University inherited his library and literary remains – 350 volumes including original oriental manuscripts and his own traveller's diaries – the material was considered interesting enough to merit publication. One of these volumes, entitled *Travels in Syria and the Holy Land* (London, 1922), described a strange stone embedded in a house corner in the bazaar of Hamath. It bore a number of small figures and symbols which appeared to be hieroglyphs, 'although they in no way resembled those of Egypt'.

No one took any notice of this rather vague description, and fifty-eight years elapsed before two Americans, a consul and a missionary, rediscovered this stone in the bazaar of Hamath (modern Hama, a Syrian provincial capital on the Orontes) together with a pair of similar stones. They, too, could only talk of 'small figures and symbols' because as soon as they approached the stones to examine them or make sketches the local inhabitants warned them off. It seemed that the strange inscriptions were credited with miraculous properties, above all the power to cure rheumatism.

Another year went by before the miraculous stones were rediscovered for a third time by an Irish missionary named William Wright. Wright had more luck than his predecessors. Earlier that year – 1872 – the rigidly orthodox and xenophobe Turkish governor of Syria had been replaced by Subhi Pasha, a man of more liberal disposition and founder of the Istanbul archaeological museum. At the missionary's request, the new pasha sent some soldiers to rip the stones out of the wall and, heedless of the ensuing pandemonium, transport them to his rest-house. The latter became the target of demonstrations by outraged believers who would rather have stormed the pasha's abode and destroyed the therapeutic stones than abandon them to the infidel.

Wright, who was in an awkward predicament, hurriedly promised that the pasha would pay for the stones next morning. Nobody believed him, of course. Experience had taught the Arabs what a pasha's promise was worth, so they were doubly surprised when they actually got their money. But even that failed to pacify them. As bad luck would have it, there had been a big shower of meteorites in the night, and dervishes ran excitedly through the streets proclaiming to all and sundry that this celestial omen was proof positive that the stones should not have been removed.

The pasha himself was forced to intervene. He did what can always be done with signs and portents: he interpreted them in a diametrically opposite way. On the contrary, he said, the shower of falling stars was proof positive that the heavens had signalled their unqualified assent.

The stones could at last be transported to Istanbul, but not before Wright had taken impressions of the figures and symbols for the British Museum.

But neither Istanbul nor London could make anything of the inscriptions. No system of reference existed. Two travellers had reported seeing some peculiar inscriptions in Syria shortly after 1700, it was true, but that meant little. Whatever the field of study, interrelationships always take a while to grasp because many common features discerned by later observers appear quite unrelated, chronologically or intrinsically, to their original discoverer.

Such was the case here. Moreover, the attention of scholars and public was currently focused on an altogether different discovery. Nineveh had been unearthed a few years earlier, and only months after the 'healing' stones were removed from Hamath a certain George Smith of London rocked the foundations of Christendom by publishing a text found there. Inscribed on a cuneiform tablet from Nineveh, he had discovered a story that struck him as oddly familiar: it was the story of the Flood, hitherto known only from the Bible.

Although the account was not identical, one thing became clear. Since the Mesopotamian story of the Flood was older than the Biblical account, the Bible must have 'copied' it. In other words, that which had previously been regarded as a divine truth and revelation was demonstrably part of an age-old store of popular legend. We may find it hard to comprehend the flurry this caused among orthodox believers, genuine and pharisaic, but we can well understand why it made Smith world-famous overnight.

George Smith was no archaeologist or Assyriologist, nor even an erudite man, simply a copperplate engraver who had been commissioned to illustrate a work on the cuneiform inscriptions of the Near East and Nineveh in particular. On reading the book, he became so enthralled that he used it as a primer to help him learn the language and script of Assyria. Before long he was making scholarly discoveries of his own and succeeded in proving that four of the kings of Judah or Israel mentioned in the Bible were contemporaries of the Assyrian king Tiglath-pileser III, a fact which supplied new clues to Biblical chronology. The British Museum thereupon appointed the former copperplate engraver its expert on Assyrian cuneiform inscriptions.

In 1876, having additionally discovered the Gilgamesh Epic, another Ninevite text in which the legend of a great flood occurs, Smith set off in quest of the Biblical city of Carchemish. His employers were more interested in this venture than in the Hamath stones whose impressions had been gathering dust in the British Museum for the past four years – understandably, because Assyrian texts disclosed that Carchemish had once been an important centre with a colony of foreign hieroglyphers.

The only question was, where had the city stood? The prophet Jeremiah (xlvi, 2) placed it 'by the river Euphrates', but the Euphrates was long and nobody had yet found the site. Smith was in luck. He rode up to an expanse of ruins beside the Euphrates, now in the Syro-Turkish border area, announced that it was the ancient city of Carchemish, and proved to be correct. Preliminary excavations there brought to light some peculiar hieroglyphs like those at Hamath.

This put quite another complexion on the matter. The British Museum excavated Carchemish for three years (1878–81), though Smith did not live to see the results. A few months after discovering the place he died of plague.

But the impetus had been given, and in 1880, when the thirty-four-year-old archaeologist A. H. Sayce found similar inscriptions in Smyrna and the Taurus Mountains of Anatolia, hundreds of miles from Hamath and Carchemish, he was bold enough to theorize that the strange pictograms and monuments discovered during recent years in Syria and Asia Minor belonged to the vanished kingdom of the Hittites.

Although he could not prove his claim, this did not deter him from promptly publishing an article with the unequivocal title 'The Hittites in Asia Minor', and his lectures on the subject earned him the reputation of being the 'discoverer' of the Hittites.

The Hittites made headlines in the British Press, and in 1884 London witnessed the inauguration of 'Hittitology' when William Wright published a book entitled *The Empire of the Hittites, with a decipherment of Hittite inscriptions by Prof. A. H. Sayce.* It could not be said that the texts had really been deciphered, nor was there any firm evidence, only an assortment of clues and conjectures which were frequently at variance with accounts given in the Bible. Sketchy as it was, however, the very audacity of the theory stimulated serious research into the vanished Hittites.

Three years later, when letters from the Hittite king Suppiluliuma and other information about the Hittites came to light at Tell el Amarna – like a miracle made to order – the sensation was complete.

All the Amarna letters were written in Babylonian cuneiform and all were decipherable by scholars save two, which could be read but not understood. They were likewise written in finest cuneiform, but in a totally unintelligible language which bore no relation to the pictograms found in Syria and Smyrna. The only fact to emerge was that they were addressed to a hitherto unknown king of 'Arzawa'.

For every pointer to the Hittites supplied by the Amarna letters, a new query arose. No sooner had the Hittites been discovered than another unknown people, the Arzawans, demanded identification.

And yet it was the Arzawa correspondence which, more than anything else, led to the discovery of the Hittite capital and kingdom.

Because we shall often meet the terms 'hieroglyph' and 'cuneiform' in the pages that follow, it may help to clarify the principles underlying these two 'picture-languages' if we devote one chapter to a brief explanation of both forms of writing.

Cuneiform and hieroglyphs

Wherever in the dawn of history men began to write, they did not use separate characters for individual sounds but drew a picture of what they meant to convey. This pictorial writing, in which a wavy line signified water or a painted duck signified a duck, had nothing at all to do with the sound of the spoken language. Nobody had to learn such a 'script' because he grasped its meaning even if he had no command of the appropriate tongue. Thus the early pictographic scripts had the great advantage of combining extreme simplicity with 'international' intelligibility.

The wider the range of ideas and activities and the more abstract the processes to be expressed, however, the more numerous and complicated became the symbols that had to be devised and, ultimately, committed to memory.

This was the development undergone by written Chinese, which comprises thousands of characters whose meaning is intelligible to the literate person and can be traced to early pictograms such as that for 'quarrel', which shows two women under the same roof.

We, who habitually dissect a word into separate sounds and syllables, find it hard to conceive that a person can write and understand Chinese script perfectly without being able to speak a single word of the language or comprehend it by ear.

Most of us are unaware that this comprehension of symbols functions independently of the spoken language and that we still use a picture-language system in many fields, even today.

For example, Roman numerals are purely pictographic. I, II and III represent raised fingers, V symbolizes the splayed hand and X two hands crossed. We do not need to know that III is *trois* in French and *kolme* in Finnish: irrespective of the sound of a language, we grasp the meaning of III just as we do of Arabic numerals which are equally international and independent of sound.

Our road signs are another purely pictographic script. Without these modern hieroglyphs we should go hopelessly adrift in foreign countries. As it is, we immediately grasp their pictorial message and can express it in our own tongue. We also encounter picture-writing where ignorance of words like *Andres* and *Gynaikes*, *Hommes* and *Femmes*, *Señores* and *Señoras* could result in an embarrassing mistake – in fact we use far more pictography in our daily lives than many of us realize.

Although pure picture-writing has great advantages, most pictographic systems developed unlike Chinese because the vast number of characters proved a deterrent. People began to convert pictograms into phonetic symbols. Although Egyptian hieroglyphs still consisted of pictures which could, and can even now, be instantly recognized as 'man', 'woman', 'eye', 'water', and so on, they did not always – and this is the crucial point – signify what they portrayed. A bull's head no longer meant 'bull' but conveyed the sound 'A' because the word for bull, *alef*, began with an 'A'. A house stood for the letter 'B' as in *bait*, or house. Putting the two together, we get the 'alphabet' which was eventually handed down to us by the Phoenicians.

We find it quite natural to use separate characters for individual sounds. This automatically reduces the number of characters in a script but has the disadvantage of tying it to a spoken language and restricting its comprehensibility to those who can also speak that language. In the case of *trois* or *kolme*, for instance, we must learn what the words mean.

We should not liken the reading of hieroglyphs to the decipherment of a complicated rebus, or pictorial riddle. The process is far more intricate because the Egyptians were inconsistent. One pictogram could have different functions in the same text. Sometimes it was a straightforward picture of the object in question. In many cases, however, the picture also served as a phonetic symbol conveying individual consonants or combinations of the same. The symbol for 'hoe', for example, could actually mean hoe but might equally mean 'to love' because the word for hoe, like the word for love, consisted of the consonants m-r.

In addition to pictograms and phonetic symbols, so-called determinatives or ideographic signs were devised as an aid to reading. Written but not pronounced, they served to prevent confusion between words composed of the same consonants. The word m-n-h, for instance, can have three meanings: papyrus-plant, young man, or wax. Depending on what m-n-h was intended to convey, the scribe clarified his meaning by prefixing it with the hieroglyphs for plant, man or mineral. The same pictogram can therefore signify the object it represents, act as a phonetic symbol or, in its determinative role, remain mute.

Until this realization dawned, hieroglyphs were considered to be as unintelligible as the familiar usage of the term still implies. It was Champollion who in 1822 succeeded with the aid of some bilingual inscriptions (notably the Rosetta Stone) in identifying the names Ptolemy and Cleopatra, a discovery which led to the gradual decipherment of the hieroglyphic script.

So much for the Egyptian picture-writing which Clemens Alexandrinus (ca. AD 215) christened *grammata hieroglypha* or 'sacred carved writings'.

Cuneiform, which evolved in Mesopotamia during the third millennium BC, was also based on picture-writing, though this is no longer apparent to the eye.

It was the picture-writing of Uruk, the earliest-known script in the world, which gradually became reduced to angular shapes so that characters could be more easily impressed into moist clay with a split reed. This produced the characteristic 'wedge-shape' from which the script derives its Latin name.

Structurally, cuneiform bears a strong resemblance to the hieroglyphs of Egypt. It, too, employed the same characters as pictograms, phonetic symbols and (mute) determinatives, but with this difference: cuneiform could reproduce syllables as well as consonants. In other words, it also expressed vowels.

Although similar in principle to hieroglyphs, cuneiform took longer to decipher. A first key was discovered in 1802 by the German philologist Georg Grotefend, who managed to identify a few kings' names, but it was not until 1860 that scholars were able to read all the various languages written in cuneiform. Sumerians, Akkadians, Elamites, Hittites, ancient Persians and other peoples employed cuneiform just as most modern languages are written in the Roman alphabet.

This so-called Babylonian-Akkadian cuneiform never developed into a fully fledged alphabetic script despite some progress in that direction, whereas Persian cuneiform ultimately became – though not until *ca.* 500 BC – a combined alphabetic and syllabic script which made do with 41 characters (36 phonetic symbols and 5 determinatives). It was the only thoroughbred Indo-European language to be written in cuneiform.

Because of their inconvenience, cuneiform and hieroglyphs were both superseded in the course of time by purely phonetic symbols. The last extant letter in hieroglyphic handwriting (demotic cursive) dates from *ca.* AD 470, or long after the Phoenicians had 'reinvented' writing by adopting a wholly alphabetic script.

The Hittites had a picture-writing of their own which was used primarily for ceremonial and formal purposes, that is to say, on monuments (like the stone of Hamath) or seals, but they also employed Babylonian-Akkadian cuneiform to record texts in their own tongue.

We do not know the source of hieroglyphic Hittite. Since the Hittites knew and used Akkadian cuneiform almost from the first and would scarcely have evolved a pictography of their own thereafter, they are assumed to have adopted it from somewhere during the third millennium BC and to have retained it for religious purposes. Another theory is that the Indo-European settlers brought it with them. It is certainly noteworthy that pictograms of similar appearance have been found on cylinder seals in India and that isolated Hittite pictograms seem to have been used in

conjunction with the Cretan hieroglyphs on the still undeciphered
Phaistos Disk.

Hieroglyphic Hittite being unrelated to Egyptian hieroglyphs
and Sumerian-Akkadian scripts alike, it has still to be fully
deciphered in spite of the considerable strides made since the
1930s.

II THE DISCOVERY

The bookworm turns a page

It is all too easy for a narrator to convey the impression that certain discoveries come about in accordance with a fixed scenario devised by a celestial dramatist endowed with infinite and unfathomable sagacity.

In fact, as we have already pointed out, posterity can perceive interrelationships of which those involved were totally unaware. There even seems to be a law of series which dictates that different people do or seek the same things independently of each other, the subsequent effect being to conjure up a purposefulness and consistency that never actually existed.

During the last century, and particularly towards its close, there was a veritable craze for reading about ancient places and, more than that, for discovering and excavating them. Johann Ludwig Burckhardt, alias Sheikh Ibrahim, who roamed the Near and Middle East in oriental garb, was symptomatic of an attitude which declared itself at all levels, profound and superficial.

Emulating illustrious figures such as Napoleon, who showed an interest in the Pyramids at the beginning of the century, and Kaiser Wilhelm II, who visited Jerusalem in state a hundred years later, archaeologists began to explore ruined sites from Cairo to Mount Ararat, where Noah's ark was said to have landed. Few of them were archaeologists in the modern sense. They can best be described as excavators, if not straightforward treasure-hunters, because nobody yet had any experience of how to dig or what a site might yield.

Johann Joachim Winckelmann (1717–68), who is regarded as the founder of modern archaeology, did no more in his *Geschichte der Kunst des Altertums* (1764) than point out that students of the ancient world are not limited to written sources but can also enlist the aid of cultural relics. Before these relics could be located and systematically explored, however, it was necessary to find the proper ways and means.

The process began with Nineveh, discovered in 1820 but not excavated until twenty years later. In 1871 Heinrich Schliemann found Troy. Having blithely taken Homer's account at its face value, like the layman he really was, Schliemann turned out to be right. Three years later he excavated Mycenae and discovered that its shaft-graves contained a hoard of gold which he at first assumed to be Agamemnon's treasury, but this time he was wrong.

In 1878 a railroad engineer unearthed the Pergamum Altar, and 1887-8 saw the discovery of the pharaonic archives at Tell el Amarna, which focused attention on Asia Minor and brought the Hittites into view. Further excavations were carried out at Troy in 1893-4, and in 1895 a start was made on Babylon. Finally, in 1899, Arthur Evans began to excavate the legendary Labyrinth, or palace of the Cretan Minotaur.

All these great names and civilizations aroused widespread public interest for decades as they emerged in ever swifter succession from the millennial dust and rubble that had hidden them from view.

Only the Hittites were excluded from this revelatory process. A few more digs and discoveries in Asia Minor and southern Turkey made it increasingly clear that they were a people of some importance, but it was not until eighteen years after the discovery of the Amarna letters that anything decisive occurred.

Then, after a lapse of time which might well have sufficed to reinter the Hittites in oblivion, the stage was claimed by one Dr Hugo Winckler from Gräfenhainichen in Saxony, an enduringly unlikeable character but one who – if only by chance – discovered the Hittite capital.

Dr Winckler was a cuneiform expert and unsalaried lecturer at Berlin University. Twenty-five years old when the Amarna letters were published, he had then been engaged on a two-volume work devoted to 'the cuneiform texts of Sargon' which appeared in 1889. Three years later he published a book entitled *Keilschrift-*

THE BOOKWORM TURNS A PAGE

liches Textbuch zum Alten Testament. He also translated the laws of Hammurabi of Babylon and wrote a two-volume history of Israel.

Winckler was the typical backroom academic who buries himself in his books and writes for a very limited circle of fellow-experts. One can picture him carefully donning his oversleeves every morning, arranging his needle-sharp pencils at ninety degrees to the leading edge of his desk, and, with narrowed eyes, reading his cuneiform texts as another man might read a newspaper.

He was a lone wolf, and the years had transformed him into an insufferable malcontent 'filled with rancour for all who were more successful than himself', to quote a contemporary description. This covered virtually all the colleagues who had become well-established professors while he, being a lecturer without a fixed income, waited year after year for a professorial chair to come his way.

Winckler was also the type of person who finds it easy to make enemies on every occasion. He was intolerant of his colleagues' opinions but took the deepest umbrage whenever someone showed a reluctance to concede, promptly and unreservedly, that every invention, every flash of inspiration – in short, everything great and good – had come straight from Babylon. For him, only Babylon existed. The world had begun with Babylon and would end with Babylon. In Winckler's eyes, anyone who failed to see this was a dead letter.

Toiling away at his cuneiform texts, the frustrated Saxon did not take long to become a first-class Assyriologist. No sooner have we chalked up a point in his favour, however, than it has to be cancelled by another black mark. Despite his status as an orientalist and expert on Semitic languages, Winckler was a rabid anti-Semite. That this did not in any way deter him from persuading wealthy Jews to finance his early expeditions may serve to show, if nothing else, what an ambivalent character and difficult man he was.

In 1903 Winckler got one of his pupils, Baron Wilhelm von Landau, to defray the cost of an expedition to Sidon in southern Lebanon, where he proposed to look for texts in the Arzawan language.

He launched his excavations under the aegis and supervision of an official from the Ottoman Museum in Constantinople, because at that time the whole of the Near East belonged to Turkey. It would be tempting but unfair to assume, in the case of a man like Winckler, that he found nothing. Although he found nothing that interested him, such is the fate of many an expedition. This is all too easy to forget because historians of archaeology place an understandable emphasis on its successes and seldom report its failures.

Winckler had no luck with his Arzawan texts, but he would never have discovered the Hittite capital had it not been for his trip to Sidon.

Back in Berlin, he found at least a crumb of consolation awaiting him: he was appointed an associate professor. Being so clearly unsuited to field-work, he prepared to spend the rest of his life among books.

Then, one morning, a parcel arrived from Constantinople. Not unnaturally, since the addressee was a cuneiform expert, it contained a cuneiform tablet. Winckler read the tablet through but could not understand a word. He stared at it in bewilderment. What he had failed to find in Sidon, someone had sent him by mail: a tablet in the language of Arzawa.

The parcel from Constantinople was, in fact, a direct product of his expedition to Sidon. Macridy Bey, Winckler's escort from the Ottoman Museum, had been reminded of the luckless German when an unusual cuneiform tablet came his way, and had sent it from Constantinople to Berlin. Winckler's dig at Sidon had, after all, brought him closer to his objective.

One can well imagine what this meant to a scholar who had been acquainted with the two Arzawan letters from Amarna for fifteen years and cherished a natural ambition to solve the riddle they posed. Winckler decided to pay an immediate visit to Constantinople, which he did in the autumn of 1905, hurriedly and without any kind of preparation.

Once there, he asked Macridy Bey where the tablet had been found and was surprised to learn that it came from Anatolia, not Syria. Although it had sometimes been conjectured that the Arzawans lived in southern Anatolia, this information came as a shock. Still more surprisingly, the clay tablet did not come from southern Anatolia but from a northern village situated roughly 100 miles or five days' journey beyond Angora, an unimportant town whose only claim to European fame was the angora cat. (It has since become the Turkish capital, Ankara.)

Winckler and Macridy Bey prepared to set out for Angora. Winckler was back in his element, grousing about everything under the sun. Nothing oriental met with the orientalist's approval. The days were too hot and the nights too cold, and the fact that it took three whole days to purchase three wretched nags and a little basic equipment sent him into transports of fury. He later complained of the frightful horses and saddles, refusing to acknowledge that, in the East, good bargains can only be struck after protracted and laborious haggling.

They finally rode off on 14 October. The scholar from Gräfenhainichen took offence at every last bug he encountered in their lodgings en route, as if bed-bugs were something alien to the time and place. Adventurous as trips through Turkey can still be, travellers early in the present century were inured to conditions which we should more readily associate with the depths of the Middle Ages.

Winckler was doubly delighted when he reached his destination, the village of Boğazköy, and found that the local landowner, Zia Bey, had lent the party some silk quilts: they were back among civilized people at last! This time, Winckler noted gleefully, Macridy Bey was the first to jump up and start scratching. The bemused servants were roused in the middle of the night and ordered to swap the infested quilts for others. No sooner had

Winckler lain down again than he discovered that, like their predecessors, the replacements were universally infested with *tahtabitleri*, or bed-bugs.

19 October 1905 dawned at last. Winckler made a preliminary reconnaissance of the neighbouring ruins, but the mountainous terrain and rocky ridges looked relatively unpromising. Then, just at the south-east entrance to the village, he came upon a site roughly 100 yards square and subdivided into dozens of narrow chambers by stone walls. A little higher up the slope were cyclopean walls, huge blocks of stone, a gate guarded by stone lions, a whole fortress – a town. It was a spacious site extending to a conical summit nearly 3600 ft high and enclosed by a wall which appeared to be miles long: a town nearly three-quarters of a mile across – by ancient standards, a city.

But where was the spot that had yielded the clay tablet bearing the Arzawan text? The villagers smiled at the question and shrugged – similar fragments were strewn around everywhere. Winckler eventually succeeded in locating the main site of discovery, only to find that others had dug there before him. The place showed signs of aimless rummaging rather than systematic excavation, however, so the normally discontented scholar was gracious enough to note that 'it did not arouse our ire in the slightest'.

Three days later the first heavy autumn rains set in and Winckler had to discontinue his search if he wanted to reach Angora before the tracks became impassable. But he was satisfied. His saddlebags contained 34 tablets in Arzawan – an immense haul considering the time at his disposal.

Winckler was so excited that he did something quite uncharacteristic on the return journey. Unable to sleep while lodging overnight at Nefesköy, he went outside to ponder on the future and – as he noted in his diary – gaze at the stars!

Once back in Berlin, he moved heaven and earth to organize a Boğazköy expedition. He negotiated with the Deutsches Archäologisches Institut and the newly founded Deutsche Orientgesellschaft, whose avowed aim was 'to promote the study of oriental antiquity', pestered bankers and called on the directors of the national museums. Within a few months he had amassed sufficient funds to enable him to excavate the ruins at Boğazköy the following year.

Boğazköy

Boğazköy (gorge-village) stands at an altitude of about 3000 ft in the central Anatolian Plateau. Some 100 miles east of Ankara as the crow flies, it is situated in the great bend of the Kizilirmak (the river Halys of antiquity). Being a village with barely a hundred buildings and less than a thousand inhabitants, it is only to be found on large-scale maps under the name Boğazkale. Today, the 130 miles of well-laid road between Ankara and Boğazkale can be covered in half a day.

Although Boğazköy ceased to be the official name of the place after it was rechristened in 1937, the old appellation is still generally used in a Hittite context because it has become established in specialized literature. Boğazköy is often taken to include the ruined city itself, which the Hittites knew as Chattusa or Hattusa.

Hugo Winckler was not the first to visit Boğazköy. He had a predecessor in Charles Félix-Marie Texier (1802–71), who had gone in search of the ancient Roman city of Tavium. Reaching Boğazköy, he learned that there were ruins on the mountainside behind the village.

In his book *Description de l'Asie Mineure* (Paris, 1839), Texier gave an account of the long walls enclosing the city, 'as large as Athens in its prime', of the two massive gateways, one adorned with a sphinx in relief, the other with stone lions, and of the spacious temple complex outside the city. 'Wholly dominated by the idea that I had to find the Tavium of antiquity, I was tempted to regard these ruins as a temple of Jupiter complete with the sanctuary mentioned by Strabo,' Texier wrote, 'but I was later compelled to abandon this view.'

Texier did not know what he had discovered. 'No building here could be attributed to any Roman period. I was extraordinarily disconcerted by the grandiose and singular nature of the ruins as I

46

sought to give the city its historical name . . .'

Apart from these ruins, Texier also discovered on the plateau opposite (now only half an hour away) the rocky sanctuary of Yazilikaya (English: inscribed rock) with its 66 stiff and solemn deities carved into the walls of two communicating chambers. Some of them were winged while others held objects in their hands or stood on the shoulders of other figures.

Shortly after Texier, the British antiquary William Hamilton likewise visited Boğazköy and assumed it to be Tavium. He also found another ruined site thirteen miles north-east of Boğazköy near the village of Alaca Hüyük. Other travellers visited Boğazköy over the years, among them the French archaeologist Ernest Chantre, who unearthed some fragmentary clay tablets there as early as 1893 but failed to impress their significance on the world of scholarship.

The 420-acre site at Boğazköy was excavated under the supervision of Hugo Winckler and the archaeologist Otto Puchstein in 1906–7 and 1911–12. Digging continued between 1931 and 1939 under Kurt Bittel, who resumed his labours after World War II and pursued them from 1952 until the 1970s under the auspices of the Deutsches Archäologisches Institut.

The results of this work have been published by the Deutsche Orientgesellschaft (DOG) of Berlin in the series entitled *Wissenschaftliche Veröffentlichungen*.

City in the gorge

So July 1906 saw Hugo Winckler back in Constantinople. To quote the memoirs of his new assistant, Ludwig Curtius: 'I had been greatly looking forward to working with an orientalist whom I could not picture as other than a widely travelled and sophisticated personality. I was not a little surprised, therefore, to find on reaching Constantinople that Winckler was an insignificant-looking gentleman who, with his unkempt brown beard, sports shirt . . . and a petit bourgeois manner which seemed incongruous in the authentic East, lacked every attribute proper to a man of the world.'

Curtius pronounced just as unfavourably on Theodore Macridy Bey, who was once more in attendance: 'Macridy Bey was a strange combination of the semi-erudite dilettante and the ardent enthusiast, the civil servant loyal to his superior, Halil Bey, and the secret trafficker, the restless explorer and the abruptly irresponsible hedonist; magnanimous and charming one day, cynical and scheming the next . . .'

Such was the ill-assorted team destined to make the crucial discovery.

Reaching Boğazköy on 17 July 1906, they were greeted like old friends by the landowner Zia Bey, who disregarded the injunctions of the Prophet Mohammed sufficiently to accept, with gratitude, a bottle of good brandy.

The ensuing process of excavation would have horrified a modern archaeologist. Instead of carefully removing each layer in turn, staking out areas and listing every find, however small, according to its location and level, Winckler paid the villagers a piastre a day to shovel away as the fancy took them.

He himself sat in a leafy shelter in the middle of the Büyükkale, or castle mound. Hat on head, neck shielded by a cloth and both hands encased in gloves, he sat there grumbling to himself. He couldn't stand the heat, he couldn't stand the food, he couldn't stand the whole business . . .

Winckler was largely indifferent to what the villagers unearthed. They could have dug up gold plate for all he cared – clay tablets were his sole concern. These he assembled in the hut and catalogued. Three weeks passed in routine activity, unenlivened by any occurrence of note. Nothing turned up that might have excited Winckler's interest.

It should be remembered that, being a classical philologist and cuneiform expert, Winckler could tell at a glance whether there was anything exceptional on the tablets that were found – always provided they were not inscribed in the still undeciphered language of Arzawa. All the other texts were written in the Babylonian language and in Akkadian-Babylonian cuneiform.

Then, on 20 August, one of Winckler's labourers brought him yet another tablet. Not only could he read and understand it at sight – he had been familiar with its contents for years.

Winckler must have thought he was dreaming, but it was true: the object in his hand was a missive from Pharaoh Rameses II of Egypt to a Hittite king. It was written confirmation of the peace treaty which both parties had concluded after the battle of Kadesh and which had long been known to scholars from the hieroglyphic inscriptions at Karnak:

The covenant of Rameses, Beloved of Amun, Great King of the land of Egypt, hero,

with Hattusili, Great King, King of the land of Hatti, his brother, providing for good peace and good brotherhood in the relations of the Great Kingdom between them for ever, runs thus:

Rameses, Beloved of Amun, Great King, King of the land of Egypt, hero of all lands, son of Sethos the Great King, King of the land of Egypt, hero, grandson of Rameses the Great King, King of the land of Egypt,

to the King of the land of Hatti, hero, son of Mursili the

Great King, King of the land of Hatti, hero, grandson of Suppiluliuma the Great King, King of the land of Hatti, hero . . .

Winckler wrote of this moment:

'All my lifetime's experience dwindled to nothing. Here was something that might perhaps have been yearned for in jest, as a vain hope: Rameses writing to Hattusili on the subject of their joint treaty. Although recent days had yielded more and more small fragments referring to the pact between the two countries, here alone was confirmation that the celebrated treaty familiar to us from hieroglyphic records on the temple wall at Karnak was destined to have light shed on it by the other treaty partner. Rameses, with his titles and lineage specified exactly as in the text of the treaty, was writing to Hattusili, who was designated in like manner, and the contents of the letter tallied verbatim with the clauses of the treaty.'

But Winckler's discovery could mean only one thing: many weeks' journey from Egypt, this place where the copy of the famous Egyptian-Hittite treaty had lain must also be the capital of the Hittite Empire. Treaties of this importance were never stored haphazardly but kept in the capital's 'records office'. Thus the countless clay tablets and fragments bearing cuneiform texts must be the Hittite government archives, and the spot where Winckler had erected his hut of branches was the Hittite royal palace in which the kings referred to by the treaty – Hattusili, his father Mursili and grandfather Suppiluliuma – had once resided.

But if Boğazköy was the long-sought capital of the vanished Hittites, why had so many Arzawan texts been found alongside texts in Babylonian? Could it mean that the Arzawan language, also written in cuneiform but unintelligible, was really the language of the Hittites? After all, the 'Arzawan' letters had only been so called after their discovery at Tell el Amarna because they were addressed to someone in 'Arzawa'. They had to be called something, but their name conveyed nothing about the language in which they were written. In other words, that which had hitherto been called Arzawan, for want of a better term, was really Hittite!

Thus, the quest that had taken Winckler to Sidon and Boğazköy was rendered doubly fruitful by his discovery of the Egyptian-Hittite peace treaty: he had not only found the Hittite capital but rediscovered the Hittite language which, though unintelligible, had long been known as Arzawan.

Years later, Winckler reviewed the emotions that gripped him on that August day in 1906. The following account was found among his papers:

It gave me, of all people, a curious sensation to be able to set eyes on such a document. Eighteen years had passed since I examined the Arzawan letter from El Amarna in the Bulaq Museum and familiarized myself with the language of Mitanni in Berlin. Pursuing the facts inferred from the find made at El Amarna, I then voiced the supposition that the Rameses treaty, too, had originally been drafted in cuneiform. And now I held one of the communications referring to it in my hands – in finest cuneiform and good Babylonian!

It was indeed a rare coincidence to have occurred in one man's lifetime that what he had once deduced in Egypt, when he first set foot on oriental soil, should now find confirmation in the heart of Asia Minor.

Such a coincidence might seem as miraculous as a tale from the Arabian Nights, yet the following year was to bring something even more miraculous: the discovery of all the documents in which there recurred the figures who had so often preoccupied me during those eighteen years . . . It was indeed a rare conjunction of circumstances to occur in one human lifetime.

By now gravely ill and accompanied by a nurse, Winckler paid one more visit to Boğazköy in the winter of 1911–12. A year later he died at the age of fifty.

Perhaps we should slightly revise our verdict on the man. He may have been a disgruntled and intolerant person who found it hard to conceal his own shortcomings, but he accepted the fulfilment of a lifetime's scholarship with gratitude.

Picturing him at work, year after year, on a single project whose realization must have seemed far beyond his reach in some distant land of dreams, we can understand his amazement when everything so unexpectedly came true. We can also understand his pride at having found the Hittite capital while pursuing the riddle of the Arzawan letters. Arzawa receded from view, admittedly, but the Hittite language had been discovered instead.

Fresh mysteries

One has to check the position of the Hittite capital, Hattusa, with the aid of a map to understand the astonishment that greeted its discovery.

To judge by all that was so far apparent from excavations and written sources, the focal point of the Hittite Empire should have lain somewhere in the vast tract between the Mediterranean and Mesopotamia, the land of the 'Two Rivers' Tigris and Euphrates – in other words, south-east of the massive Taurus ranges.

Instead, the Hittite capital had been found beyond that mountain barrier in the area between the Mediterranean and the Black Sea which the Greeks had named quite simply after the direction in which it lay from their own geographical standpoint. The Greek word *anatole* means no more than 'east'.

Anatolia, now the Asiatic part of Turkey, is roughly twice the size of Italy and enclosed on all sides by mountains that shield the hinterland from the outside world.

In the south of Anatolia, stretching from Lycia in the west to the Euphrates in the east, the Taurus Mountains separate the Mediterranean coast from the Anatolian Plateau. With peaks that rise steeply from the sea to a height of over 12,000 ft, the Taurus Mountains form an almost insurmountable barrier which very few rivers have managed to penetrate. There is practically no southern access from Anatolia to the Mediterranean.

Further east, too, where Anatolia and Syria adjoin one another, the Taurus Mountains are passable only where rivers have carved out their beds over millions of years. Among these passes are the Cilician Gates through which the army of Alexander the Great marched on its way to India.

In the north, Anatolia is screened from the Black Sea by the Pontic Mountains, another natural barrier nearly 700 miles long and 100 miles deep, while a smaller mountain threshold separates it from the Aegean in the west.

In the east the Pontic and Taurus Mountains merge to form a steadily ascending range which for much of its extent attains altitudes in excess of 12,000 ft and is partly snow-covered or even glaciered all year round. Of 31 peaks in the vicinity of Lake Van, only six are under 9000 ft. Most of them are extinct volcanoes, the mightiest of them being Agri Dağ (the 'cloven'), known to us from the Bible as Mount Ararat.

In this immense mountain-girt basin lies the Anatolian Plateau, which never dips below 1500 ft above sea-level, rises at many points to 3000 ft or more, and is itself threaded with mountain chains and ranges.

The intervening plateaux have springs and rivers of their own but no outlets. This has created a series of lakes which, like Lake Van, lose a great deal of water by evaporation during the hot summers and are consequently so saline that few fish can live in them.

One example is Tuz Golü, the great salt lake in 'the dead heart' of Anatolia, whose 34 per cent salt content makes it considerably more saline than the Dead Sea and one of the most saline expanses of water in the world. Though only between three and six feet deep, it covers an area – when at its fullest – roughly three times that of Lake Constance. The water almost entirely evaporates in summer, so that by autumn it becomes a whitish 'snow-field' of glistening salt deposits many feet deep.

Few of Anatolia's rivers reach the sea and none is navigable. The meander, or pattern of lines that winds in and out, to and fro, without getting anywhere, takes its name from the west Anatolian river Menderes, called Maeander by the ancients.

Most rivers that have to eat their way laboriously through mountains carry immense quantities of alluvial silt which discolour their water. One such river bears the name 'red'. This is the Kizilirmak, which rises in the Pontic Mountains and flows south, only to double back in a sweeping northerly arc and debouch into the Black Sea. Known in antiquity as the Halys, the Kizilirmak was the river crossed by Croesus, who trusted the Delphic Oracle's prediction that he would destroy a great kingdom without guessing that the kingdom was his own.

In this bend of the Halys, situated nearer the Black Sea than the Mediterranean, in a highland valley open to the north and sealed by mountains in the south, lies Boğazköy.

The position and outlook of the place do not immediately suggest that the Hittites extended their dominions south and south-eastwards across the rocky ribs of the Taurus Mountains to Babylon and still further south to Palestine, especially as, even in the interior, the Anatolian ranges run in a predominantly east-west direction and block the route southwards with a succession of mountainous barriers.

This made it even more surprising that the Hittite capital should have been discovered in northern Anatolia, an area which not even the ancients had numbered among the centres of civilization.

Were the Hittites a race of Anatolian mountain-folk? Excavation had demonstrated singular links between them and a variety of cultures. Architectural complexes were unearthed whose foundations might have been mistaken for those of the Cretan Labyrinth, and similar finds were later made in India. A few of the Hittites' gods were traceable to Mesopotamia. It had also been ascertained that they wrote Babylonian-Akkadian cuneiform and knew Babylonian, but that they possessed a language of their own which seemed unrelated to any known tongue. This left one none the wiser.

It was now possible to venture ethnic inferences from the Hittites' physiognomy. Enough sculptures and reliefs had been found – quite apart from the long-familiar representations in Egyptian temples and tombs – to conjure up a picture of them.

Egyptian artists, who portrayed whole hordes of subjugated peoples to the greater glory of the reigning Pharaoh, evidently found that the feature most typical of Hittite prisoners was a high

55

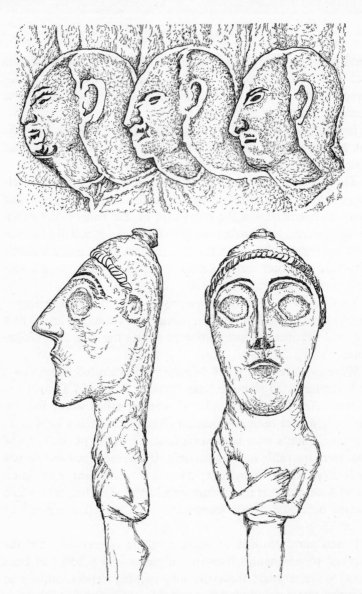

A 'Greek' profile. The Hittites were customarily portrayed with prominent noses that merged with their foreheads to form an unbroken line, also hair that hung down their backs. *Above:* an Egyptian impression of some Hittite prisoners (*ca.*1280 B.C.) *Below:* bronze statuette of a Hittite deity (Syro-Hittite, 15th century B.C.)

domed forehead which merged directly with the nose. This produced a strange combination of Greek profile and Semitic nose, though it should be stressed that, as a linguistic term, 'Semitic' defines members of the Semitic language family: the peoples who, in about 3000 BC, pushed northwards from the Arabian peninsula into Palestine, Syria and Mesopotamia, and down the African continent as far as Ethiopia. Thus, Arabs are as much Semites as Jews.

The same profile occurs in the Hittites' portrayals of their own race, though the domed forehead is far less common than the curved nose and the continuous Greek profile. No uniform picture emerges, however, because some sites have yielded other physiognomical types more reminiscent of Persian figures. We should in any case be wary of such portrayals, which may be based on current fashions or abstract ideals of beauty. Nefertiti also had a 'Greek' profile, but nobody would claim that she was Greek in consequence. Nevertheless, Hittites in effigy do bear a distinct resemblance to the peoples of Asia Minor.

Even though nothing specific can be inferred from their cast of feature, their hairstyle is characteristic. In contrast to the Egyptians and other peoples of Asia Minor, the Hittites did not crop their hair or shave their heads to facilitate the wearing of wigs. Paintings and sculptures make it clear that they wore their hair shoulderlength or even longer. An Egyptian inscription reads: 'I cast down the Hittite before you: he lies before you bound with his own hair . . .'

Fashions changed, however. Portrayals from other periods show Hittites with a kind of Chinese pigtail. Beards were 'in' or 'out' depending on period, one interesting fact being that they often alternated in conflict with the tonsorial fashions of other peoples. The Egyptians generally painted the Hittites' hair black, though some inscriptions refer to it as light brown.

The Hittites' clothing, too, displays certain peculiarities but no crucial differences. They wore a short-sleeved tunic of the sort found in Germanic art, but they also affected a short smock like the Philistines or like King David when, 'girded with a linen ephod', or priestly vestment, he danced before the Ark of the Lord.

Whatever comparisons were drawn by Winckler and his contemporaries, the picture they formed of the Hittites differed in no major respect from that of the Hittites' neighbours, nor did it furnish any definite clue to the origin and history of these Anatolian highlanders.

The only special feature that might have proved informative was the language of the Hittites as recorded on clay tablets. But, although thousands of these tablets and fragments had accumulated in museums, 'Arzawan' was the one language that continued to defy comprehension.

Its decipherment caused another public stir.

III THE SURPRISE

A startling revelation

To the layman, it must seem well nigh miraculous that anyone can decipher and read a language whose letters or symbols are as unknown as its vocabulary, yet there are many instances where such an equation has been solved in respect of scores or hundreds of unknowns, the best example being the decipherment of ancient Egyptian hieroglyphs.

To illustrate the special difficulties involved in deciphering the 'Arzawan' texts written in Hittite, I must first present a very general account of the decipherment principle.

There is no magic about the process, even though it often requires a flash of insight to discover the fixed point from which all else flows. Without such a starting-point, no amount of effort will bear fruit. If we have never heard a word of Arabic and are ignorant of Arabic characters, we can stare aimlessly at an Arabic inscription for years on end without extracting any kind of sense from it.

If enough text is available, however, certain things can be ascertained.

In the case of a totally unfamiliar script, we begin by mechanically totting up the number of characters. If there are no more than 30-odd, we may assume with some certainty that it is an alphabetic script like our own, which possesses one character for each vowel and consonant.

If the range of characters is larger but still reasonably limited in number, we are probably confronted by a syllabary or syllabic script. In this case, each character stands for a consonant plus a vowel. Because each consonant can be compounded with any one of five different vowels – e.g. ka, ke, ki, ko and ku – a syllabary will comprise roughly 100 different characters (20-odd consonants in five assorted combinations). We cannot, however, be certain of the precise number in the case of an unknown tongue because languages differentiate in varying degrees between sibilants or soft and hard consonants such as d/t and b/p, and therefore require more or less characters for their differentiation.

The second point to be ascertained about an unknown script is how it should be read, in other words, from right to left as in Hebrew, from left to right as in our own case, or – a far from infrequent phenomenon in ancient Greek – in each direction alternately. The flow of an unknown script is particularly hard to detect if every line runs from margin to margin and no word- or sentence-endings can be discerned.

Where hieroglyphic or pictographic scripts are concerned, their flow is often easier to discover than that of alphabetic scripts because certain pictograms are inherently directional. Feet, for example, which symbolize the concept of walking or movement, logically point in the direction of the sentence as a whole. If the same foot-symbol occurs reversed in the next line and alternates in regular succession, the text must be written in one of those alternating scripts termed boustrophedonic, from the Greek 'ox-turning', i.e. 'as the ox turns when ploughing'. With an alphabetic script, linear alternation can often be detected from the fact that the characters in every second line are carved in reverse.

The longest extant Greek inscription, the Cretan Code of Gortyn, written in the ancient Doric dialect and comprising no less than 17,000 characters, observes this alternation of line-flow and reversal. It is carved on twelve juxtaposed blocks of stone, so each line is nearly 28 ft long. This illustrates the point of the boustrophedonic mode of writing. To save the reader from having to walk eight or ten paces between lines, the stone-carver followed a route like the weft in a piece of cloth. Even so, since the Gortynian inscription runs to 62 lines, anyone planning to read it all must be prepared for a quarter-mile walk.

Apart from distinguishing between alphabetic, syllabic and pictographic scripts and ascertaining the direction in which they are written, we can often discover the length of individual words.

Not invariably, but in many scripts, words are separated by lines or ticks, word-spaces being omitted to save room.

This much we can deduce from the outward appearance of a script, but we are still ignorant of what the characters signify and what language lurks behind them. Unless we can discover the meaning of one or two characters through comparison with other scripts and languages, we grind to a halt.

This applies to another Cretan find mentioned in an earlier chapter, the so-called Phaistos Disk, a seven-inch disk spirally inscribed on both sides with pictograms representing easily identifiable objects such as heads, hands, flowers and axes. Since there are only 45 different symbols, they probably belong to a script which is not purely pictographic but a blend of the syllabic and alphabetic. The characters were imprinted with stamps and occasionally overlap, so their sequence is known. Even the word-divisions can be clearly discerned, yet scholars have been vainly trying to plumb the meaning of these characters for over 70 years because no comparison with any known language presents itself – reason enough for many people to regard the Phaistos Disk as a relic of vanished Atlantis.

What is needed at this stage is a so-called bilingual or text in two languages, for example a hieroglyphic inscription whose text is reproduced alongside in Greek. This at least conveys the thought-content but affords no clue to how the language is constructed or how the characters are pronounced. Even if we learn what is written in the Koran from a translation, we are very far from reading Arabic or recognizing a single word of that language.

Such was the problem that confronted Champollion when he tried to decipher the hieroglyphs of Egypt in 1822. He did have a bilingual, the famous Rosetta Stone which now graces the British Museum and bears a Ptolemy V inscription of the year 196 BC, but although the latter was written in Greek and Egyptian, both demotic and hieroglyphic, this proved of no immediate assistance.

Then Champollion had an idea so simple that, with hindsight, we cannot understand why it did not occur to everybody in the first place. He wondered why certain hieroglyphs were enclosed by a cartouche, or oval ring. These cartouches coincided roughly with the points at which Ptolemy's name appeared in the Greek text. Why shouldn't such an ornament have been used to pick out and emphasize the king's name, rather as if the scribe had distinguished the king from many other figures in a picture by putting a crown on his head?

If this were true, one had only to compare the eight hieroglyphs in the cartouche with the eight letters in the Greek version of Ptolemy's name to discover the sound of several hieroglyphs. Champollion did so and compared the result with another bilingual which also contained the name Ptolemy. Sure enough, the same eight hieroglyphs were enclosed by a cartouche. He had acquired his first reference-point.

Finding a cartouche on another stone, Champollion deduced from a Greek inscription that it might enclose the name Cleopatra. The names Ptolemy and Cleopatra had a few Greek letters in common: P, L, and O. If he were correct in his hypothesis, the same three hieroglyphs would occur in the appropriate position in each name – which they did. Champollion thus knew the phonetic value of several different symbols and had paved the way for the gradual decipherment of an unknown language.

Grotefend had earlier, in 1802, made a successful start on deciphering cuneiform in the same manner. By identifying the royal names Darius and Xerxes and the word for king, he too gained preliminary access to a pictographic script which, as it turned out, bore a close structural resemblance to the hieroglyphs of Egypt.

The position was rather different when it came to 'Arzawan'. Since the letters found at Amarna were written in cuneiform, whose phonetic values had since been established, their text could be read aloud. The sound of the language was known but the words were wholly unfamiliar. The problem here lay not in decipherment but in the language itself. There was no bilingual and, consequently, no means of drawing grammatical conclusions about the meaning of individual words.

Still, the cuneiform system did at least aid the decipherment of symbols such as those for 'fish' and 'father' because cuneiform embodied ideograms, or pictographic representations which could still be identified. A stylized fish meant 'fish', so the expert knew what the passage in question referred to. What he did not know was the word for fish in 'Arzawan'. Much the same happens when we meet the symbol '3' in a foreign-language text. We know that the writer is talking about a specific number but cannot enunciate the word for that number in the said language.

This was more or less the state of affairs in April 1914, when the Deutsche Orientgesellschaft sent a team of Assyriologists to the Ottoman Museum in Constantinople (now Istanbul) to classify and publish its collection of cuneiform texts from Boğazköy, Hugo Winckler having died in 1913 after his second full-scale expedition to Hattusa.

By now, twenty-six years had elapsed since the discovery of the 'Arzawan' letters at Tell el Amarna without any real progress having been made in the study of that language, even though the discovery of Hattusa in 1906 had made thousands of tablets available.

It now became evident, yet again, that advances in scholarship are not attributable solely to erudition and hard work. They can also stem from the spontaneous flash of insight which, by freshly combining two long familiar but seemingly unrelated factors, produces a startling solution.

Credit for this particular brainwave must go to a Polish-born Czech named Bedrich (also known as Friedrich) Hrozný, who had become Professor of Assyriology at Vienna at the early age of twenty-six.

To modify a well-worn phrase: Hrozný came, saw and comprehended. When World War I broke out and he had to leave Constantinople after five short months, later to serve in the Austro-Hungarian army, the thirty-five-year-old authority had the solution in his pocket.

It was over a year before Hrozný, now in uniform, found time to air his sensational discovery. A preliminary report published in *Mitteilungen der Deutschen Orientgesellschaft* in December 1915 proclaimed the 'solution of the Hittite problem'. Shortly beforehand, on 24 November, Hrozný had delivered a first public account of his discovery to the Vorderasiatische Gesellschaft in Berlin – in so far as experts can be accounted members of the public.

He had begun work in Constantinople with the usual comparisons of words to which it was possible to assign a constant and determinate meaning in different contexts. Even without knowing their sense, he had been struck by the fact that, in some contexts, certain words became modified in a strange and unexpected way. Above all, it was the present participle (giving, doing) which seemed to have a characteristic and oddly familiar form.

Hrozný's colleagues had, of course, noticed the same structural changes but, because they were looking in an altogether different direction, failed to grasp what they were reading. Scholars of all ages have been afflicted by an expectative attitude which decrees that the improbable cannot exist.

Having postulated the improbable, Hrozný struck oil. His Hittite grammar, published two years later, described the key experience that transformed his theory into an 'unshakable solution'.

Although I cannot recount every detail in this chapter (an indication of what was involved will appear in the next), I shall now try to reconstruct the thought-process that led Hrozný to his discovery.

It all began with a sentence which Hrozný, as he himself admitted, found 'wholly unintelligible' at first reading. If we reproduce the phonetic value of each cuneiform sign in Roman letters and separate each sign – and, thus, syllable – with a hyphen, this sentence read as follows:

'nu NINDA-an e-iz-za-at-te-ni wa-a-dar-ma e-ku-ut-te-n(i?).'

We are inclined to sympathize wholeheartedly with Hrozný's

inability to fathom its meaning.

However, the sentence did contain one cuneiform sign which advertised its derivation from the Semitic-Sumerian pictographic script. Hrozný therefore knew its meaning. It was the symbol for bread – the 'NINDA' which appears in small capitals above.

Well, Hrozný said to himself, if the writer was referring to bread, he may well have followed it with the appropriate verb: bread is eaten, just as water is drunk.

The more brilliant the idea, the more simple it sounds in retrospect. Any philologist worthy of the name can think of the word for 'eat' in a dozen assorted languages. 'Eat' is 'edere' in Latin, 'essen' in German, 'ezzan' in Old High German – and there it was: e-iz-za-te-ni! The resemblance may not seem so striking to our eye, but Hrozný spotted it at once because Akkadian cuneiform was a syllabary restricted to pairs of consonants and vowels. The scribe could not, to take an English example, split the word 'button' into separate letters of which each represented a single sound. The rules of Akkadian cuneiform demanded that he write it 'bu-ut-to-on', rather as children's code-language converts 'I like you' into 'Agi lagike yagou'.

Compressing the syllables required to write the Hittite word 'e-iz-za-at-te-ni' into speech, Hrozný got 'ezzateni'. This was definitely Old High German, but how had an Old High German word found its way to Anatolia?

So far, the sentence read 'bread-eat', NINDA being the Akkadian-Babylonian word for 'bread' and ezzateni the Old High German word for 'eat' – a bewildering combination.

But it went further than that. Anyone rereading this cuneiform sentence after what has just been said may hit upon the same idea as Hrozný, because certain fixed associations and paired concepts are common to almost all peoples: fire and water, night and day, man and woman, father and son. The first stimulus-word has only to be spoken and the second leaps into the mind, or vice versa. It would have been natural, having referred to the eating of bread, to talk of drinking water – and there it was again! Via the German 'Wasser' and English 'water', Hrozný arrived at the Old Saxon 'wadar'. He had now wrested meaning from a sentence that had at first been almost entirely incomprehensible. 'Nu NINDA-an e-iz-za-at-te-ni wa-a-dar-ma e-ku-ut-te-n(i)' meant 'Now shalt thou eat bread and drink water'.

Without expatiating on the grammatical considerations involved here, we may note another surprising fact: the word 'nu', which introduces numerous sentences in Saxon and Hittite, means 'now' (modern German 'nun') in both languages.

But what sort of language *was* Hittite? Akkadian, whose cuneiform script Hrozný was reading, was a Semitic tongue which had earlier been called Assyrian and was later displaced by Aramaic – the language spoken by Jesus. Anyone who knows Arabic or Hebrew can still recognize words transliterated from Akkadian inscriptions. The word for the sun-god Shamash in the Akkadian Gilgamesh Epic is almost identical with the modern Hebrew word for sun, 'shemesh', and is linguistically related to the Philistine name Samson.

So Akkadian cuneiform had been used to record words that suddenly turned out to be 'German' as opposed to Semitic. Because nobody had yet tumbled to the idea that 'Arzawan' could be related to German, nobody had yet been able to make sense of it. Expectation often obscures reality, even among scholars, and no such linguistic relationship had been looked for in the wilds of distant Anatolia.

But I must now qualify the word 'German'. Although the two words in the above sentence are genuinely related to Old High German, the ancient Greeks and Romans could with equal justification have claimed to be linguistically related to the Hittites.

Concentrating on sound, Hrozný now discovered a whole range of words familiar to him from various languages. The Hittites used 'uga' for 'ich' (I), the Romans 'ego'; 'kuis' and 'kuid' corresponded to the Latin 'quis' and 'quid' in sound and meaning, 'eszi' to 'est' (is), 'nash' to the Latin 'nos' (we), 'wi' to 'Wein' (wine) and 'vinum', 'memal' to 'Mehl' (meal) and 'asesta' to 'setzen' (set); 'pedan' (place) was related to the Greek 'pedon', German 'Boden', 'hwantes' to the word 'wind' and 'pedar' to 'Feder' (feather).

Thus, even though scholars may differ on this or that derivation, it is possible to draw up long lists of words that illustrate the affinity of Hittite to other languages.

The existence of such links between different languages had long been known, a discovery made – as sometimes happens – by a layman rather than a professional scholar. Sir William Jones, an eighteenth-century Calcutta high court judge, had noticed resemblances between Sanskrit and various European languages. In 1786, or nearly 200 years ago, he postulated a linguistic connection between India and Europe, and detailed proof of this Indo-European (formerly 'Indo-Germanic') language family was produced in the century following.

The term Indo-European should be construed in a purely geographical sense because it defines the easternmost and westernmost ambit of the family's diffusion. To be more precise, the line stretches from Sri Lanka to Iceland. So far, scholars have identified fifteen language groups which are demonstrably akin in respect of vocabulary and grammatical structure. They comprise (including languages now extinct): the Celtic group, the Italic group, notably Latin, which lives on in the Romance languages; the Germanic, Baltic and Slavic groups; Illyrian, Thracian, Albanian, Greek and Phrygian. The list continues with the Hittite, Armenian and Iranian languages until, right in the east, we come to the Indo-Aryan languages and the Tocharian of Turkistan.

The older the stages of development under comparison, the more these languages correspond in terms of phonetic system, vocabulary, formation and syntax. Thus it was that Hrozný discovered his first correspondence in the typically Indo-Germanic participial formation of Hittite.

The discovery of the Indo-European language family was not a matter that concerned philologists alone, even though Indo-

Germanic studies are themselves so complicated a subject that they can only be pursued by those armed with a philologist's academic and intellectual equipment.

The fact that a variety of languages spoken thousands of miles apart should so manifestly have derived from a common source was bound to be of the utmost interest to historians as well. Because languages do not spread of their own accord, historians had now acquired an aid to the closer study of ethnic movements. Where the history of the Hittites is concerned, we shall soon see in detail what this meant.

Hardly had Hrozný published his 'essay in decipherment' under the title '*Die Sprache der Hethiter – ihr Bau und ihre Zugehörigkeit zum indogermanischen Sprachstamm* (The language of the Hittites – its structure and membership of the Indo-Germanic language family), which appeared in 1917, two years after his preliminary report, than a lively debate arose over the question of where the Hittites came from and whether they might not, in fact, be ancient Germans. This notion intrigued the Kaiser himself, and His Imperial Majesty expressed profound annoyance that a copy of Hrozný's Hittite grammar had not been deposited on his war-lordly desk immediately after publication.

He can neither have read the 246 pages nor understood them, for men of greater intellectual capacity than Wilhelm II find it diffcult or impossible to thread their way through strictly academic works, and substantial sections of Hrozný's grammar are intelligible to the expert alone.

Before going on to relate what new realizations stemmed from the fact that scholars could now understand the Hittite language and evaluate cuneiform tablets bearing texts in 'Arzawan', I should like to interpolate, for the benefit of the interested reader, a chapter containing some information about the technique of reading Hittite cuneiform texts and its attendant problems.

Hittite cuneiform texts

It is unnecessary to have learnt to read and write cuneiform to take an interest in the Hittite language. Scholarly works naturally reproduce cuneiform tablets and fragments character by character so that Assyriologists can read them in the original, but specialized literature generally contents itself with transcription, or conversion into the Roman alphabet. Even in transcription, however, a passage of Hittite can look quaint enough. For example:

$\text{INa}^{\text{MAT}}\text{Mi-it-tan-ni}\ \ \text{e-es-ta}^{\text{m}}\text{Bi/Pi-ih-hu-ni-ia-as-ma}\ \ \text{AMEL}$
$^{\text{ALU}}\text{Ti-bi-ia} \ldots$

Even if we do not understand a word of Hittite, we can tell from this curious arrangement of lower-case letters and large and small capitals, some in a superior position, whether a word is Hittite (i.e. Indo-European) or a Semitic loan-word. Indeed, we can even tell whether the sentence incorporates certain terms such as man or woman, king, city or country, without knowing the Hittite word for them.

This may sound like a party trick but is quite simple once the system has been mastered.

I propose to explain the principle because it sheds an interesting light on the structure of Hittite and the pictographic system in general.

It has already been pointed out in the chapter 'Cuneiform and hieroglyphs' that hieroglyphic and cuneiform symbols can have three levels of meaning. They can be:

1. Pictorial symbols proper (ideograms), as when the representation of a fish actually means a fish;

2. Phonetic symbols, as when a house stands for 'B' because the word for house (bait) begins with that letter;

71

3. Determinatives, which are written but not pronounced and serve to preclude ambiguities. A character signifying 'man' or 'tool' indicates that the following word refers to a human being or inanimate object respectively.

In adopting cuneiform, the Hittites also adopted the three functions of the cuneiform character. For Indo-European words belonging to their own language they used cuneiform characters as phonetic symbols: in the case of our sample sentence, the words that have been dismembered into syllables separated by hyphens.

The Hittites also employed words from the Semitic language-area of Asia Minor, which were easier to write in cuneiform because language and script were better attuned: in our sentence, the words in large capitals.

Finally, they also adopted the determinatives, although these symbols were unnecessary in a syllabic script that spelt everything out: in this case, the words above the line.

We can therefore tell at a glance that our sample contains two non-Indo-European words and two specially defined Hittite words.

Because the determinatives (man, tool, city, etcetera) were the same as in Babylonian, which had already been deciphered, they afforded a welcome opportunity to narrow down the meaning of the Hittite word that followed them.

Let us try this out on our sentence. The Akkadian determinative MAT (printed in small capitals and raised) means 'land'. It should therefore be followed by a territorial designation – and it is: Mi-it-tan-ni is the land of Mitanni, whose name we already know. The second raised word is ALU, the determinative for city. We can therefore take it for granted that the Hittite word Ti-bi-ia refers to a city (even if we are unfamiliar with its name). The capitalized word on the line must be an Akkadian loan-word: in fact, AMEL means 'man'.

And now, strange as it seems, we can almost translate the Hittite sentence in its entirety. Of the two remaining words, one is the lower-case e-es-ta. Running the syllables together, we get

Anatolia's proto-Hattian population, from whom the Hittite settlers adopted many cultural assets, flourished during the Stone Age. This wall-painting from Çatal Hüyük shows gigantic vultures attacking headless human figures. Approximately 8000 years old, it is the earliest-known painting associated with Çatal Hüyük's peculiar death-cult. (Copy of an original found in a shrine in Level VII.)

Above: a 7000-year-old hunting scene from Çatal Hüyük (Level III) depicting hunters clad in leopard-skins and armed with bows. *Below, left:* Stone Age jewellery. *Right:* flint dagger with a neatly fashioned bone handle. These finds come from Level VI and are about 8000 years old.

Above: the oldest landscape painting ever found. It shows the town of Çatal Hüyük in the foreground and, beyond it, the volcano of Hasan Daǧ in process of erupting. *Below:* the inhabitants of Çatal Hüyük interred the dead in their sleeping-platforms, males below the men's beds and females below the women's.

Wood was an important building-material in Stone Age Anatolia. A fire at Çatal Hüyük preserved this example of half-timbering: the load-bearing beams burnt away, leaving cavities in the mud-brick and plaster walls (Level VI).

esta, which is the Latin 'est' and means 'is'.

To take the first word last, INA, printed in capitals, is another familiar Akkadian loan-word meaning 'in'. Now let us try to translate the whole sentence:

'In ^{LAND}Mitanni is Bihuniyasma MAN ^{CITY}Tibiya', or, a trifle more elegantly:

'Bihuniyasma, the man from Tibiya, is in the land of Mitanni.' This, in fact, is the correct translation.

There is naturally a difference between solving such a problem by ourselves and having the solution spelt out for us. Many a passage is considerably harder and its meaning less easy to extract, but we have at least clarified the basic principle.

A few more details remain to be touched on. The name of the man, for example, starts with a strange pair of alternatives: Bi and Pi. Here, the scholar making the transcription has offered a variant because he is uncertain whether the initial letter should be 'P' or 'B'. The same uncertainty exists in the case of 'T' and 'D' because it is still unknown how these consonants were pronounced, hard or soft. This accounts for the many b/p and d/t variations in spelling, which reflect scholarly preference rather than definite knowledge. (Much the same applies to the problem of whether the Latin word Caesar should be pronounced soft as in 'Caesarian' or hard as in the German 'Kaiser'.) Consequently, there are scholars who – with equal justification – spell the name of the Hittite king Suppiluliuma 'Subbiluliuma'. The same happens in the case of nouns and proper nouns incorporating the consonants 'd' and 't'.

While on the subject of Suppiluliuma, we may note that this name sometimes occurs with an initial 'Sh', i.e. Shuppiluliuma. This, too, is a matter of opinion. Hittite only had one sibilant, transcribed by scholars as 'š', but we do not know if its pronunciation inclined towards 'sh' or 's'. I have already commented on the pronunciation of the aspirate 'h' or 'ch'.

At this point, yet another problem arises. Many words in Indo-European Hittite were doubtless pronounced differently from the way suggested by cuneiform texts, but cuneiform characters adopted from a foreign language could not convey the true pronunciation because they only offered a particular set of syllabic compounds. To take an example which many a music hall or pantomime artiste has employed before now: if we want to write the word 'freedom' in Chinese, it becomes 'flee dum'. Assume that 'flee dum' turns up unexpectedly in a Chinese text, written in Chinese characters, and it is easy to see how hard even a British Sinologist would find it to recognize the English word in its new guise – just as it would not immediately occur to an Englishman or an American that 'neschen' is the German phonetic transcription of 'nation'.

This was precisely the difficulty that confronted all Hittitologists before Hrozný discovered the true sound of words dismembered into many syllables, even though patterns of speech and writing did not correspond.

And here lies one fundamental difference between the Indo-European and Semitic languages. Indo-European languages tend to construct their 'linguistic skeleton' out of consonants *and* vowels, whereas Semitic languages such as Akkadian and Hebrew base the recognizability of a word far more firmly on consonants alone.

If we write down the consonantal sequence 'l-b', the Hebrew-speaker has no alternative but to assume that we mean 'leb' ('heart'): the vowel is so unimportant that he omits it from the written word. If an Englishman writes 'l-b', his compatriots are left to guess whether he means 'lab(oratory)', 'lib(eral)' or 'lob'.

Again, if we write down the consonantal sequence 's-l-m l-ch-m', the Jew effortlessly reads it as 'shalom alechem' and the Arab as 'salām alaikum', simply because no alternative exists in either Hebrew or Arabic. Hieroglyphs and cuneiform characters were geared to this consonantal singleness of meaning. At best, consonant followed vowel or vice versa. Words with an accumulation of consonants, e.g. 'marksman', would according to this system of writing have to be dissected, producing the hyphenated 'Hittite' monstrosity 'ma-ar-ka-sa-ma-na'.

Thus the formal transcription of Hittite words tells us nothing about their actual pronunciation. 'Ha-at-ra-a-nu-un' is pronounced 'hatranun', for example, because cuneiform is devoid of a character for 'hat' but has one for 'ha' and another for 'at'. These are simply juxtaposed, but their juxtaposition does not entail that the 'a' be pronounced twice over.

It is not, therefore, as easy to read and understand Hittite as our sample sentence may have implied, especially as cuneiform scribes often made mistakes or tinkered with their system of speech and writing.

Here is one mind-boggling but far from rare example. The royal name 'Hattusili', whose pronunciation has been definitely established, can be written either Ha-tu-si-li in the hyphenated manner or, equally, $^{GIŠ}PA\text{-}ši\text{-}DINGIR^{LIM}$.

This rebus-like puzzle arises because scribes aurally associated the -ili ending of Hattusili with the similar-sounding Akkadian word 'ilu', meaning 'god'. The ideogram for god, pronounced 'dingir' in Akkadian, had a suffix appended, so 'ilu' was replaced by 'dingirlim'. And because the name of the city and land of Hatti sounded like 'hattu', the Akkadian word for sceptre, whose ideogram was pronounced 'gišpa', the name Hattusili could, as it were, be 'translated' into Akkadian by writing gišpašidingirlim where the reader was meant to understand Hattusili.

The study of every foreign language is an adventure which becomes even more hazardous when it provides our almost exclusive aid to the reconstruction of a people's history. Far from every Hittite word has been deciphered, and we have only to read how fiercely scholars still debate the meaning or nuance of this word or that to marvel at how much of the language already counts as firmly established.

Gone, for instance, are the days when assiduous scholars could invent a non-existent king because they thought they knew more about Hittite grammar than the Hittite scribes themselves, although – to be fair – this happened in the case of a Phoenician hieroglyphic script written without vowels. Four experts had been sent copies of a text relating to a King Asitawanda and were producing independent translations of the same. When the four versions were compared, three differed in minor details only whereas the fourth came up with a sensational new discovery. The first three Semitists had apparently overlooked the fact that the text referred not only to King Asitawanda but, in the fifth line, to a fellow-monarch named Anek. The fourth translator had his discovery checked by another two Semitic scholars. His reasoning was so ingenious that it banished all doubt: there was indeed a King Anek.

If only one translation of this text had been made, the king might still be lingering on. Thanks to the three check-translations, he was finally killed off.

What had happened? King Anek owed his conjectural existence to the characters 'n-k', written in unvocalized hieroglyphs. This is one of the first words learnt by a student of Semitic languages because 'n-k' simply means 'I' (vocalized in Biblical Hebrew as 'anochi'). Thus it was in the present text, and all four translators wrote 'I' whenever they read 'n-k'. Only the fourth had hesitated over the fifth line. This seemed to read 'for the sons and daughters of I', which was obviously nonsensical. If 'n-k' was taken to mean 'I' in every case, the same grammatical anomaly recurred a little later in the text.

Since it was to be assumed that a Phoenician scribe knew his own language well enough to distinguish between the nominative and other cases, 'n-k' must mean something else. The fourth translator had therefore proposed the well-turned phrase 'for the sons and daughters of Anek'.

The truth was far more prosaic. A footnote by another translator sufficed to settle King Anek's hash: 'The author of the inscription,' he wrote, 'has the barbarous habit of linking "n-k" – "I" – with the third person singular masculine of the perfect tense (instead of the first person singular).' In short, the Phoenician scribe was

guilty of that sin which the English-speaker still commits –
though in another context – when he idiomatically but un-
grammatically responds to the question 'Who is it?' with 'Me'
instead of 'I'.

Scholars now know Hittite better than the ancient Hittites
themselves – so much so that Johannes Friedrich was able to
preface his big Hittite dictionary, published between 1952 and
1954, with the following words: 'In a few rare instances, obvious
mistakes on the part of ancient scribes, a few erroneous or dupli-
cated determinatives and the like, have been *tacitly corrected . . .*'

The italics are mine!

Hittites from Hesse?

The realization that the Hittites belonged to the Indo-European language family brought historians into the picture. Till now, they had understandably taken it for granted that Asia Minor had been inhabited by Semitic peoples since the dawn of history. They were now compelled to acknowledge that, some 4000 years ago, it received an influx of Indo-Germanic migrants who succeeded in imposing their language and political authority over a wide area. The only question was, migrants from where?

There are countless theories about the Indo-Europeans' original home because this problem still awaits scientific elucidation. Since it was rather unlikely that the same vocabulary and grammar had evolved in different parts of the world, earlier authorities strove to find the 'proto-race' and 'cradle of our civilization', for reasons of varying merit, by more or less equating the Indo-European language family with the Indo-Aryans. This linking of language and race has, however, proved to be scientifically untenable.

All we can say is that numerous peoples share a common linguistic root. Considerations of ethnic prestige do not, therefore, dictate that the geographical source of Indo-European be located as close as possible to Europe. Certain discoveries suggest that its original home may have been Eastern or even Central Europe, though the bulk of expert opinion favours the Caucasus region. However, none of these theories can be refuted or verified beyond doubt.

Whatever the truth, this language family must have become diffused by migration. Even if it was not known where the Hittites began their move to Anatolia, it might at least be possible to identify the quarter from which they headed for Asia Minor an estimated 4000 years ago. Did they come from the west via the

Bosphorus, or had they pushed southwards from the east or north-east?

Once again it was philology that provided a clue. Oddly enough, the Indo-European language family can be divided into a 'centum' and a 'satem' group. All the West European branches of this family – in other words, the Greek, Italic, Celtic and Germanic – originally expressed the number 100 by variants of the word 'centum', whereas the others used 'satem'. The Hittites could be definitely assigned to the Western or 'centum' category. It was logically concluded that they had migrated to Anatolia from the area of the Danube.

On the other hand, many experts still cling to the view that the Hittites came via the Caucasus. The following prayer to the Sun-god by the Hittite king Muwatalli (*ca.* 1300 BC) seems to turn the world back to front:

> Sun-god of heaven, shepherd of mankind!
> Thou dost ascend from the sea, sun of heaven!
> Sun of heaven, my lord, thou dost mete out justice
> to man, to dog,
> to swine, to the wild beast of the field,
> O Sun-god, day by day.

This prayer does not seem particularly remarkable at first sight. Its inherent contradiction becomes clear only if we imagine ourselves in Asia Minor and then talk about the sun rising from the sea: there is no sea to the east of Anatolia, just thousands of miles of terra firma.

A people from the Western Mediterranean would have been entitled to say that the sun rose from the sea in the east, but the Hittites certainly did not come from there – in other words, they were not water-borne settlers.

Proceeding on the well-tried assumption that religious customs and conventions have great powers of survival and tend to perpetuate much that is ritually and linguistically archaic, we may take it that this invocation of the sun was already very ancient. It may even have hailed from a period preceding the Hittite settlement of Anatolia, for why else should anyone have composed a prayer whose content was so obviously at variance with the facts? In view of this, Friedrich Sommer postulated in 1921 that the Hittites had inhabited the western shores of the Caspian Sea prior to their migration and had consequently travelled via the Caucasus. This theory has much to recommend it, although the sun can equally be seen rising from the waves on the western shores of the Black Sea, which would support the western or Danube hypothesis.

Anyone wishing to combine the two theories has only to settle the Hittites beside the Black Sea, then get them to trek once round it to the Caspian and on to Anatolia. There is little to be gained from such a compromise, clearly, but this does not deter many scholars from assuming something similar in respect of the Indo-Europeans' original home. These authorities posit the existence of two centres, a 'cradle' further east and an area of diffusion further west, but this sounds suspiciously like an auxiliary construction.

Under such circumstances, and in default of any precise clue to where the Hittites came from, we are all the more grateful that a man like Tacitus should at least have told us something about their later movements. In his *Germania*, the Roman historian mentions some tribes that appeared between the Rhine and Weser during the centuries immediately preceding our era. Called the Chatti, they were a tough and warlike people who excelled their neighbours in the martial arts (*Germania*, xxix *et seq.*) These Chatti, whose name gradually became modified into Catti and, much later, Hassi, were the forefathers of the Hessians of central Germany.

This sounds so incredible that we are inclined to reject it out of hand. Why should the Hittites have embarked on a long Odyssey to the Rhine after the destruction of their empire? On the other hand, lengthy migrations of this kind were not only feasible but of frequent occurrence in the ancient world. After all, the Indo-European Hittites had already made one trek southwards into the bleak highlands of Anatolia while other Indo-European tribes pushed on into India.

No firm evidence can be deduced from this similarity between names, but we are not dependent on names alone. *Altanotolien* by Theodor Bossert, a leading Hittitologist, contains a map showing all the sites that have yielded divine effigies standing or seated on a bull. They run in a straight line from Syria to Boğazköy and from there along the Danube to the Rhine, with an offshoot veering left to Italy. This god mounted on a bull is the Hittite weather-god. A particularly fine example from the Roman period, portraying him complete with all his attributes (e.g. thunderbolts and double-axe) and riding a bull, was found at Heddernheim, now part of Frankfurt-am-Main, early in the present century.

Werner Speiser may have read too much into this when he declared in his book *Vorderasiatische Kunst* (1952) that the Hittites' heads and long, vigorous noses made them look positively 'Falian' – in other words, like (Nordic) Westphalians – but there is no harm in pondering on the basic theory once it has been accepted. After all, the Galatians of Asia Minor, to whom St Paul addressed one of his epistles, were related to the Celts of Northern Europe.

Attractive though this theory is, and much though it has to recommend it, one cannot help smiling at Friedrich Cornelius's claim (1973) to have discovered where the Hittites came from. Cornelius, whose main field of study was the ancient Germans, had been struck by the Hittites' habit of writing Suppiluliuma on some occasions and Subbiluliuma on others, that is to say, their propensity to confuse p and b in the same way as g and k. If the Hittites drew little distinction between hard and soft consonants, Cornelius argued, it must have been an age-old Germanic legacy 'brought with them from their homeland'. Richard Wagner the Saxon having found the alliteration of '*Brülle du Prahler!*' quite in order, it was not difficult for Cornelius to locate the Hittites' place of origin. His *Geschichte der Hethiter* duly informs us that it should be sought 'in modern Saxony or the Sudetenland', the somewhat rash presumption being that the Saxons were as lazy at articulating 4000 years ago as they are today.

On this basis, the Hittites were simply globe-trotting Saxons who missed their way home after 800 years and ended up in Leipzig. Cornelius's theory does at least have the merit of implying that the insufferable Hugo Winckler from Gräfenhainichen in Saxony had piously rediscovered his own forefathers at Boğazköy. Moreover, if Cornelius is right, the Hittite king's daughter Naptera – or Nabdera – whom Rameses II took as his chief wife must also have been a Saxon.

Stimulating to the imagination as all these theories about the Hittites' provenance and subsequent fate undoubtedly are, none of them can adduce definite proof. It may none the less be amusing to pursue them a little further because of their never-ending attempt to rediscover the mysterious Hittites in other peoples as well.

In 1923, for instance, the American authority Nora Griffith sought to prove that Tiye, mother of the Egyptian heretic-king Akhenaten, was a Hittite. It was allegedly through her that Hittite ideas and customs were introduced into the court of Amenophis III, so that all Akhenaten did, in essence, was to proclaim the Hittite sun-cult. Long-standing ties of kinship between the Hittite kings and the Pharaohs would also, according to Griffith, explain why Ankhesenamun requested the Hittite king Suppiluliuma for one of his sons after the death of her husband Tutankhamun.

This sounds quite plausible. The Hittites did indeed worship the sun, as we saw in the hymn of Muwatalli, and existing family ties would account for Ankhesenamun's approach to the Hittite king in her hour of need. Neat as it is, however, this theory will not hold water. Suppiluliuma would hardly have called such a request unprecedented and the Egyptians might well have refrained from killing his son en route. Besides, the Egyptians had no need to borrow from the Hittites when it came to sun-worship. From the dawn of their history, and long before Amenophis IV/ Akhenaten introduced the cult of Aten, they had revered the god

Re, and subsequently the god Amun, as sun-gods in their own right. Finally, the multiplicity of Hittite gods could scarcely have stimulated the monotheistic worship of Aten.

If Nora Griffith found that Queen Tiye looked Hittite – an extremely arbitrary view – it was inevitable that others would later pronounce Nefertiti to be typically Hittite too, and this reduced the whole thing to absurdity.

Of course, specialists such as anthropologists and art historians are also entitled to draw their own conclusions from resemblances and stylistic influences. But the more fortuitous the scope for comparison and the less precisely it can be said who was dependent on or influenced by whom, the more dubious the comparative process and the greater the scepticism with which it should be regarded. An additional factor is our invariable dependence on portrayals that are stylized in the manner of their period and seldom try to achieve a personal likeness. Unless corroborative evidence is forthcoming, therefore, comparisons of this kind can rarely be accepted as conclusive.

It is different when comparisons can be made between skeletons and skulls found in graves. Measuring techniques have become so accurate that racial characteristics are now distinguishable with a fair degree of certainty. The Hittites, too, can be studied from this aspect. In 1958 the Deutsche Orientgesellschaft devoted its 71st scientific publication to some Hittite graves discovered six years earlier in the immediate vicinity of the capital, Hattusa, below a spur of rock named Osmankayasi after the owner of the neighbouring field. Excavation of this burial-ground yielded 50 cremation burials and 22 skeletons.

Taken in conjunction with other finds made in Anatolia, these human remains enabled experts to distinguish the Hittites from other races. To quote the publication mentioned above: 'If we temporarily disregard the human types portrayed in Hittite art and focus our attention on shape of skull alone, the Hittites can be typologically classified in a manner which, at least at first glance, seems simple in relation to the generally confusing ethnic history of the Near East. During Anatolia's pre-Hittite period, or in the Chalcolithic and Early Bronze Ages, narrow-skulled types are found. In the Middle Bronze Age, or *ca.* 2000 BC, brachycephalic types occur in the central Anatolian region. After 1200 BC – and the collapse of the central Hittite Empire – these gave way to dolichocephalics who were later (in Greek and, more particularly, Roman times) succeeded by the brachycephalics who still predominate in our own day. The likely inference is that Hittite settlers introduced these brachycephalic skulls into central Anatolia *ca.* 2000 BC.'

These remarks confirm two things. In the first place, they place the arrival and decline of the Hittites precisely within the 800-year span computed by archaeologists and historians, and, secondly, they imply that the Hittites were indeed an alien people, not an autochthonous Anatolian tribe risen to unprecedented heights of power and glory.

If it were possible to trace the migratory route of these brachycephalics, we might unearth a 4000-year-old skull marking the Hittites' original home – an eerie thought.

It is something of a relief to learn that science cannot help us here. Brachycephalic types occur in many places. The Hittites' round or short skull-formation points to membership of the alpine race, while the toughness of the skull, low sinciput and bony brow-ridges are more reminiscent of numerous finds made near the Caspian (above whose waters the sun rises in the east!)

Perhaps we shall one day know whence the Hittites came when they emerged from the mists of time to found an Anatolian empire comparable with that of the Pharaohs. Perhaps, too, we shall one day be certain of where the sun rose for them before they set off into the unknown.

As long as this remains obscure, we must be content with the knowledge that only 4 per cent of 258 Hittite teeth were carious, that over 30 per cent were excessively worn by stone-dust from the grinding of corn, and that the worn teeth of old people displayed less caries than teeth found in younger graves. The older the graves, the smaller the incidence of caries. However, susceptibility to caries was, on average, 3.5 per cent higher among the Hittites than among their contemporaries in Europe, where it affected only 2 per cent of a sample of approximately 4000 teeth.

It seems almost grotesque that modern science can elicit such details while events that have genuinely changed the world – conquests and migrations included – leave us playing blind man's buff with a multitude of 'ifs' and 'buts' or putting forward theories and hypotheses of varying merit and utility.

But, even though the Hittites' starting-point and final destination cannot be precisely determined, one interrelationship is worth pursuing because we shall encounter it on several future occasions.

While other scholars were probing the origins of the Hittites and combing cuneiform texts for personal and geographical names, the Swiss Hittitologist Emil Forrer came across some names which steered his thoughts in quite another direction.

The Hittites made reference to a people called the Ahhiyawans, who lived somewhere in the west. Forrer equated these Ahhiyawans with the Achaeans – and the Achaeans were Greeks.

Did Hittite cuneiform texts really contain allusions to the Greeks? If so, this was extremely interesting because names from the Greek sagas might also turn up – names familiar to us from the *Iliad* or *Odyssey*. Moreover, since Homer's *Iliad* was not recorded in writing until late in the sixth century BC, references to Greeks in cuneiform texts would authenticate the later Greek tradition.

Homer, who seldom used the appellation 'Hellenes' as a name for all Greeks, referred to them generally as Achaeans and less commonly as Argives (men from Argos) or Danaeans. The Achaeans inhabited various places in the eastern Aegean, including the island of Rhodes, which lies off the south-west coast of Anatolia. It would, therefore, have been quite possible for the Hittites to have known their Greek neighbours by the name Achaeans. After all, Troy (ancient Ilium) was itself situated on the western shores of Anatolia.

Forrer did, in fact, discover a number of names mentioned in the same context by Homer. Because cuneiform's syllabic system could not reproduce foreign names except in an approximate form and had to insert additional vowels, and because Greek used to have a character for 'W' which later disappeared, Forrer had to undertake various philological detours – omitted here – in order to arrive at the Greek originals.

The result of Forrer's detective work was illuminating, however. He identified 'Attarsiyas' of Ahhiyawa with Atreus of Achaea, father of the Agamemnon and Menelaus who fought at Troy. As if that were not enough, cuneiform inscriptions mentioned an 'Alaksandu' who hailed from 'Wilusa'. The name Alexander leaps to the mind, and Forrer equated Wilusa with ancient Ilion, earlier spelt 'Wilion', thereby resurrecting Alexander (Paris) of Troy. Eventually, he found a reference to Troy itself. The land of Assuwa had a city named Taruisa which Forrer transcribed into Greek and read as 'Troisa'. Because a sibilant between vowels disappears in Greek, this would make it an etymological precursor of the name we know as Troy.

What helps to support this interpretation is the name Assuwa itself, which has evolved, via the usual phonetic modifications, into Asya and then Asia – precisely that part of the world which Homer himself called Asia (the area south of Troy, subsequently known as Lydia). The term for this province of Asia was later extended to cover modern Asia Minor and ultimately became the appellation of an entire continent which Homer never saw.

Forrer unearthed various other names, e.g. 'Lazpas', which he identified with Lesbos, as well as some more debatable ones. Illuminating though Forrer's 1924 report on 'pre-Homeric Greeks in the cuneiform texts of Boğazköy' may seem, it found little immediate acceptance among other scholars even though, conversely, a reference – or possible reference – to the Hittites had been found in Homer. Precisely in the right context (*Odyssey* xi, 521), Homer lists some 'Ceteians' as allies of the Trojans. Ceteians could easily be a Greek garbling of Hattians (the change

between Ch/H and K is not uncommon, as we saw in the case of
the Chatti/Catti). If so, the Hittites took part in the fighting
round Troy and the cuneiform scribes had good reason for
knowing and mentioning 'Alaksandu of Wilusa'. This would
weaken the objection that Forrer took the names of totally unrelated people and applied them to Greeks.

Even so, Emil Forrer and his colleague Johannes Friedrich
became embroiled in a war of words which, though waged at a
snail's pace, left nothing to be desired in the way of malice and
mutual accusation.

Forrer's first 22-page article, published in the spring of 1924,
was countered a mere 19 months later, in autumn 1926, by a
broadside from Friedrich alleging that Forrer's Greek hypothesis
seemed 'mistaken in its main conclusion'. Other recurrent
epithets in Friedrich's paper were 'unproven', 'false' and 'misleading'.

Forrer was stung by this, and barely a year passed before he
wrote a rejoinder which was promptly – two years later, in January
1929 – published in a scientific journal. By now the debate had
lasted five years, although the participants had given tongue three
times in all.

On his side, Forrer spoke of 'assertions' by Friedrich which
were 'erroneous' and 'rashly advanced on the basis of insufficient
knowledge'. The remainder of his riposte is so littered with
charges of inaccuracy and misinterpretation that a layman might
be forgiven for wondering how two experts could have made as
many blunders as each of them alleged.

It is a sad fact, and one to which we must become inured, that
scholars can be aspirants to fame and reputation as well as seekers
after truth. Much of what passes for scholarly debate is mere
hair-splitting, as countless examples could be adduced to show,
and the establishment or refutation of a theory often depends on
which party outlives the other.

Forrer's theory that the Greeks figure in Hittite cuneiform
inscriptions is frequently represented as 'dubious', but the same

judgement can be passed on many findings in the field of scholarship. One has only to be on nodding terms with specialized literature to know that, right or wrong, and however cogent the 'evidence' cited in their favour, very few theories hold undisputed sway.

But Forrer not only proved right in the end. He was one of those scholars who, because of their capacity for seeing things with new eyes, are apt to play havoc with established ideas. He was a man who saw the fulfilment of his life's work, not in copying down individual hieroglyphs, but in seeking interrelationships and general perspectives with the aid of extraneous stimuli.

For the 'cuneiform Greeks' were not Forrer's first outrage. Years earlier, in 1919, he had thrown the world of Hittitology into confusion and proved right yet again.

But that is worth a chapter on its own.

Not Hittites at all

Two years after the publication of Hrozný's Hittite grammar, Emil Forrer proclaimed a startling fact: the Hittites were not Hittites at all.

He put it so mildly that the implications of what he had said might well have escaped the likes of us.

'A survey of all the Boğazköy fragments,' wrote Forrer, 'has elicited that no less than eight different languages occur in them: apart from Sumerian, Akkadian, the language hitherto described as 'Hittite' but, as we shall see, more aptly termed Kaneshite, and Old Indic, Hattian, proto-Hattian, Luwian and Palaic.'

Such is scholarship! Our first temptation when faced with Forrer's rather convoluted syntax is to tot up the languages and see if there really are eight. There are, but Hittite isn't one of them.

So now, with the Hittite texts finally deciphered, somebody had come along and claimed that there were eight languages instead of one Hittite language proper. This was bad news indeed, except that two languages predominated while the rest occurred in fragmentary form and were of no importance. It was rather as if a city like London or New York had been dug up after 3000 years of oblivion. Archaeologists would doubtless marvel at the multilingualism of its inhabitants because notices in French, German and Spanish would be found in banks, museums and railway stations. To pursue the analogy still further, it would be necessary to assume that, in addition to modern English, a Chaucerian idiom had survived in written form.

Thus the really explosive feature of Forrer's pronouncement lay less in the multiplicity of the languages he listed than in the tortuous sentence containing the parenthesized word 'Hittite' and the assertion that what had hitherto been regarded as Hittite should really be termed Kaneshite.

It may be argued that the name of a language is irrelevant – the main thing is to know who speaks what. The language spoken in New York remains the same whether we call it English or American.

Unfortunately, for reasons that have long been known, the Hittite problem is not so simple. The Hittites were not a uniform and homogeneous people but comprised autochthonous Anatolians as well as Indo-European settlers. The settlers were the stronger of the two groups. They assumed power in Anatolia and gradually built an 'empire' with a language of its own – one they brought with them and imposed on the original population.

Since the Indo-Europeans called themselves 'Hattians', lived in the capital, Hattusa, and were ruled by kings of whom several bore the name Hattusili, it was naturally assumed that the original appellation derived from the victors' language – naturally but erroneously.

The cuneiform texts of Boğazköy proved – and this was Forrer's major contribution – that all references to the language of the 'Hattili' related to the non-Indo-European tongue of the original inhabitants.

Forrer's assertion, which has never been disputed, bore upon fundamental questions of historical research and ethnic psychology as well as philology. It ran counter to all experience that victors should adopt the name of the vanquished. When the Romans conquered and ruled Germania, they did not adopt the Germanic tongue and call themselves Germans: on the contrary, the ancient Germans adopted words and terms from the Romans. Similarly, when the Roman Empire drew the Hellenic world into its orbit, no Roman emperor dreamed of investing himself with a Greek name. Instead, the Greeks called themselves 'Romans' – a designation still applied to them in Greek folksongs.

It was just the other way round with the Hittites, and we have to face the fact that the Indo-European settlers possess no known name of their own because they adopted the appellation 'Hattili' from the original inhabitants of their new home.

In spite of various scholarly attempts at correction, we continue to apply the name 'Hittites' to people who did not speak Hittite at all. For want of a better term, the legendary autochthons who were the true Hittites have been christened 'proto-Hattians', rather in the sense of Old Hittites. Because the layman may at first sight be confused by this conflict between scientific findings and the tendency of names to stick, let us recapitulate:

1. Since 1922, scholars have taken their cue from Forrer in distinguishing between Hittites and proto-Hattians.

2. 'Hittites' in the narrower sense is the name applied to those who belonged to the Indo-European language family. They were the people who, between 1700 and 1200 BC, built an empire that extended from Anatolia, via Syria, to the borders of the Egyptian sphere of influence.

3. 'Proto-Hattians' is what we call the Anatolian population from whom the Indo-European settlers adopted the name Hittites.

But who were the proto-Hattians?

What subject race succeeded in imposing its name on those who had subdued it? What sort of people furnished their Indo-European conquerors with titles, royal and divine, for a period of centuries?

There was no answer to this question. Present indications are that proto-Hattian, the language of the original inhabitants, was neither Indo-Germanic nor Semitic nor Caucasian. We appear to be dealing with an autochthonous Anatolian people, since their language bears no relation to that of their neighbours. Until recently, mystery surrounded their way of life and the location of their cultural relics. A few excavations of sites antedating the arrival of the 'Hittites' did at least suggest that the proto-Hattians had an independent and relatively advanced culture of their own. As the Hittitologist Kurt Bittel observed in 1945: 'The most that has probably been established to date is that the culture of the Anatolian highlands had its roots in settlements of the late fourth millennium from which, by a process of development whose details are still obscure, it attained its peak during the third millennium.'

The transition from the fourth to the third millennium BC represents the upper limit of the historical period. Beyond it, conventional dates lose their meaning because chronology is expressed in terms of successive epochs named after their characteristic materials: Iron Age, Bronze Age, Neolithic or New Stone Age, Palaeolithic or Old Stone Age. Of these, the Early Bronze and Neolithic Ages are already prehistoric.

Nobody had yet discovered any link with these early periods in 1945, when Bittel made the following statement in his *Grundzüge der Vor- und Frühgeschichte Kleinasiens*: 'Wherever, in large and long-inhabited settlements, we have dug down to the virgin soil, it is apparent that the earliest settlers chose to take up residence on sites that were wholly uninhabited in the Mesolithic (Middle Stone) Age, let alone earlier.'

Then, just before nightfall on a chill November day in 1958, the thirty-three-year-old British archaeologist James Mellaart inspected a large mound overgrown with grass and ruin-weed in a remote part of the Konya Plain. It contained fire-blackened walls of sun-dried brick, broken bones, potsherds and obsidian tools and weapons.

Air-dried bricks are made of mud mixed with straw, and tend to disintegrate after a few spring rains. Not only had these bricks survived, but, as Mellaart soon discovered, they were thousands of years older than the oldest Egyptian pyramid. Mellaart had not unearthed a lonely megalithic grave whose blocks of stone would still be there thousands of years hence, when the human species might itself have become extinct. North of the Taurus Mountains on a highland plateau in southern Anatolia, he had discovered a mud-brick town from the Stone Age. Excavation showed it to be the world's earliest-known town apart from Jericho. Over 8000 years old, its mud bricks were adorned with patterns, scenes and paintings from which, as from a picture-book, we can still recapture the desires, fears and experiences of its Stone Age inhabitants, down to and including the eruption of a volcano whose awe-inspiring rain of stones they depicted on their walls and whose extinct cone can be seen to this day.

Earlier accounts of the Hittites and their empire had to be content with the assertion that a proto-Hattian population 'existed' prior to the arrival of Indo-European settlers. Today, before the story of the Hittites is unfolded, it can and must be prefaced by a return to the Stone Age – a journey to the beginnings of what we now call 'history'.

IV A ROUND TRIP TO THE STONE AGE

Stone Age town

Early archaeologists were understandably preoccupied with locating historic and illustrious cities such as Babylon, Troy or Mycenae, and some of their number, like Schliemann, were treasure-hunters rather than scholars.

But the less they concentrated on well-known names as time went by, the greater their chances of gleaning information about our past in unknown and seemingly unimportant places. Concomitantly, the more refined their methods became, the more accurately they could evaluate their finds and the further they could venture into prehistoric times for which no written evidence existed.

It is in the nature of things that many such discoveries must be left to chance. Although dolmens stand out clearly against the landscape, for example, Stone Age settlements cannot normally be detected except with the aid of special techniques such as aerial photography.

On the other hand, archaeologists know of numerous places where they could not only dig but be certain of finding something if enough time and money were available. Travellers in the Near East are often struck by the sight of mounds rising from an otherwise featureless landscape like miniature table-mountains. Many of these *tilal* (hills) are simply the remains of settlements and towns which grew upwards in the course of the millennia, layer by layer, until they formed small eminences. Consequently, many famous archaeological names like El Amarna are compounded with the word 'tell' or its equivalent in the language of the area.

In view of this, it was hardly surprising that James Mellaart should have taken an interest in one such hill in 1952. As a scholar of the British Institute of Archaeology at Ankara, he had decided to undertake a survey of the Konya Plain between the Taurus Mountains and the southern salt steppe of the Anatolian Plateau. It was an area which in Roman times formed part of the province of Asia, where St Paul preached the gospel. 'And it came to pass in Iconium, that they went both together into the synagogue of the Jews . . .' (*Acts* xiv, 1). The place called Iconium by the Romans was, in fact, modern Konya, one of the oldest cities in Turkey and formerly the capital of the Seljuks whom Emperor Frederick I defeated in May 1190, during the Third Crusade.

After a preliminary survey, Mellaart was prevented by illness from conducting a closer inspection of the anonymous hill, which stood nearly 3000 ft up and about 30 miles south-east of Konya in the midst of a deserted and steppe-like but fertile tract of alluvial land. Six years passed before he revisited the place, never having explored it further because he had been excavating other Stone Age sites in the interim.

Strictly speaking, it was a double hill bisected by a river which emanated from the Taurus Mountains and drained into the salt steppe not far beyond. Because everything has to be called something, the hill was known simply as Çatal Hüyük after a fork in the road at its northern extremity. Readers ignorant of Turkish will not be surprised to learn that 'hüyük' means precisely the same as 'tell', or 'hill'.

Originally trained as an Egyptologist, Mellaart launched his first dig at Çatal Hüyük in 1961 and developed it in the two succeeding years. It soon became clear that he had found a Stone Age settlement, but the real surprise consisted in his discovery of a full-scale town when most authorities currently assumed that the Konya Plain had been altogether uninhabited during the Neolithic period.

Even on its own, the larger of the two hills at Çatal Hüyük boasts an inhabited area of 32 acres, being almost 500 yards long and some 275 yards wide. It is the largest site of its kind so far discovered in Asia Minor.

Although only about one-thirtieth of the site could be excavated in the three seasons spanning 1961–3, the finds made there were so numerous that a halt had to be called for the sorting and preparation of material.

Mellaart took advantage of this breathing-space to condense his progress reports in the journal *Anatolian Studies* into a book which he published under the unassuming title *Çatal Hüyük. A Neolithic Town in Anatolia* (London and New York, 1967). Unsensational as this makes it sound, the exploration of Çatal Hüyük was to revolutionize our existing knowledge of the Stone Age.

I shall not describe Mellaart's excavations in detail or adhere to their chronological order. The interested reader should consult Mellaart's own account, which is agreeably free from the absurd footnote-itis and complexity that afflicts so much specialized literature in German. For my part, I propose to pick out individual aspects which illuminate the way of life, abilities, knowledge and emotions of men and women who walked the earth 9000 years ago and whose heirs we indirectly are.

We shall meet a number of superlatives dating from a period more than thirty-five centuries prior to the emergence of the advanced civilizations that flourished beside the Euphrates and Tigris. Çatal Hüyük may well be the oldest urban centre so far discovered and is, apart from Jericho, the largest Stone Age town known to us; it has yielded the world's earliest-known mural painting and landscape painting; finally, it has also yielded what are probably the oldest pieces of woven cloth and the earliest intramural altars.

Like all towns, Çatal Hüyük grew upwards over the centuries as its ground-level was raised by demolition and levelling, refuse and ash. We can still observe this phenomenon in long-inhabited cities such as Rome, Athens or Jerusalem, where historic sites dating from the year dot lie several feet below modern street-level.

Çatal Hüyük grew in this manner to a height of more than 54 ft above the present level of the plain, but sampling cuts have shown that it is necessary to dig down 60 ft or more in order to reach the lowest inhabited level, beneath which lies virgin soil. To put it more graphically, this is equivalent to the height of a six-storeyed house. (At Jericho, by comparison, virgin soil is reached after only 45 ft.)

However, Çatal Hüyük was not rebuilt over its full extent each time, stratum by stratum, so it would be wrong to picture the site as a kind of layer-cake. The town tapered downwards at the periphery, where its buildings rose in terraces. (Since the 'town centre' remains unexcavated, nothing can yet be said about its architecture.)

If Mellaart wanted to find out how the separate levels were disposed, he could not simply cut a trench through the hill as archaeologists often do in order to gain a general impression. This would undoubtedly have destroyed too many ground-plans in the various layers, so he had to uncover each level horizontally before penetrating the next. Although extremely laborious and time-consuming, this is a very rewarding procedure because it alone enables one to draw a proper town-plan of each building-level.

Mellaart identified ten levels in all, the top or most recent level being referred to as I and the lowest or oldest as X. Levels beneath X are excluded because they have yet to be dated.

However, even Level X dates back to 6500 BC – not a hypothetical figure but one that has been confirmed by the radiocarbon method.

The oldest material from Jericho datable by the radiocarbon method is somewhat more recent, but stratigraphic findings based on inter-level relationships permit one to conclude that Jericho, too, goes back to the eighth or even ninth millennium BC. It will therefore depend on Çatal Hüyük's unexplored 12 ft whether or not this 'Hittite' town can claim the world record for antiquity.

According to Mellaart, the following dates may be assigned to the various levels (radiocarbon dates in italic; all computations based on a half-life of 5730; doubtful dates in parentheses):

	O		
	I		
ca. 5720			
	II	5797±79	
ca. 5750			
	III		
		5807±94	
ca. 5790			
	IV	(6329±99)	
ca. 5830			
	V	5920±94	
ca. 5880			
	VIA	5781±96	destruction
		5800±93	
		5815±92	beginning
		5850±94	
ca. 5950			
	VIB	5908±93	
		5986±94	beginning
ca. 6050/6070			
	VII	6200±97(?)	
ca. 6200			
	VIII		
ca. 6280			
	IX	6486±102	
ca. 6380(?)			
	X	6385±101	
ca. 6500			
	Pre-X floor levels (not yet dated)		

We may therefore take it that Çatal Hüyük was already inhabited *ca.* 6500 and remained so until about 5720. Habitation was abruptly discontinued thereafter and subsequently resumed on the smaller neighbouring hill.

Nothing is known about this sudden hiatus, but signs of burning in the upper levels make it likely that one of the many fires whose traces have been found at Çatal Hüyük contributed to the abandonment of the original site.

From the archaeologist's point of view, this abrupt discontinuance is a great stroke of good fortune. Any later occupation would have destroyed a great deal, at least in the upper levels. As it is, the remains of a town inhabited for almost a thousand years lie there almost undisturbed. We cannot, for all that, be certain that it was really deserted by its last inhabitants *ca.* 5700 BC because 7000 years of rain may long ago have washed more recent layers away.

We owe the preservation of what has survived to a second stroke of good fortune. As the British archaeologist Sir Leonard Woolley somewhat wryly remarked, members of his profession would really prefer it if every ancient capital lay buried beneath the ashes from a conveniently sited volcano. In default of a volcanic eruption, the best thing that can happen to a city – from the archaeologist's angle – is that it should be sacked and burnt to the ground.

To continue in the same vein, we can be grateful to fire for doing what two volcanoes in the neighbourhood of Çatal Hüyük failed to achieve. Its mud-brick walls were so petrified and preserved by sundry conflagrations that bones, pigments and relics of Stone Age cloth and leather have survived to this day – indeed, we can even tell what colours the town's Stone Age inhabitants favoured when taking the air.

Before summarizing the results of Mellaart's excavations, I should like to look more closely at a term which has been used several times in the last few pages: the radiocarbon or C-14 method of dating. In addition to this modern archaeological aid, I shall describe a few of the other techniques that help archaeologists to make deductions worthy of a master detective.

Modern archaeological methods

One of the main problems besetting the archaeologist is how to date finds and levels as accurately as possible. The more recent the period, the more close-knit the network of dates and cross-references and the greater the scope for classifying a discovery with precision or rectifying previous miscalculations. Coins or potsherds, for instance, can assist the chronological classification of a new site if it is known when the coins were struck or the particular types of earthenware manufactured. Inscriptions, too, are a useful aid to dating.

Because the historical date-framework only goes back to about 3000 BC, it used to be impossible to quote earlier dates except in relative terms. In other words, one find could be said to postdate or antedate another but neither could be definitely attributed to a particular decade or century. Consequently, estimates of the age of a find tended to differ very widely, sometimes by as much as several hundred years. It was not until the late 1940s that the development of the atomic bomb enabled relics of the 'prehistoric' period to be accurately – that is to say, absolutely – dated.

Credit for the discovery of this so-called radiocarbon method belongs to the American chemist Willard F. Libby, a member of the team that built the first atomic bomb and subsequently a professor at Berkeley, Chicago and Los Angeles. It was Libby who, at the end of the 1940s, evolved a technique whereby the age of organic substances such as wood or bone could be ascertained with remarkable accuracy. He was awarded the Nobel Prize for Chemistry in 1960.

Libby's method is based on the recognition that all organic substances apart from normal carbon atoms contain a special carbon variant which occurs in a ratio of one to one million.

Whereas normal carbon has the mass number 12 and is not radio-active, this 'deviant' carbon isotope has the mass number 14 and is. They are thus defined, using the chemical symbol for carbon, as ^{12}C and ^{14}C or C-12 and C-14.

The radioactive C-14 isotope is not constant but decays over a determinate though very prolonged period. A living organism offsets this loss by continuously, through its metabolism of this carbon isotope, reintroducing C-14 formed from nitrogen by the effect of cosmic radiation. If the organism dies, the supply of C-14 ceases. Furthermore, if the dead organic object is buried, continuing bombardment with radiation from the atmosphere can no longer reach or affect its C-14 content.

Since it has been estimated that half the C-14 isotopes present in organic matter decay within a fixed period – the so-called 'half-life' – the amount of C-14 relative to total carbon content will indicate how long the process of decay has lasted, or, to put it another way, how long the organic substance has been dead.

We thus have a broadly reliable method of ascertaining the age of organic substances whereby the antiquity of objects and fossil remains can be determined up to 50,000 years in the past. The method cannot be applied to older material because all its C-14 isotopes have decayed.

This C-14 or radiocarbon dating method has proved an in-estimable boon to archaeologists since its discovery. It was the first objective method which enabled a framework of absolute dates to be constructed without recourse to conjectures advanced by individual experts. Numerous estimated dates could thus be confirmed by radiocarbon dating, whereas others had to be drastically revised. It was, for example, a great surprise to learn from radiocarbon measurements that the Olmec culture of Mexico was considerably older than many authorities had ventured to assume. The result was that links could be established with the mysterious glyphs of the Maya and with their calendar, which, though consistent in itself, had hitherto hovered in a chronological void unrelated to any fixed date.

It cannot be too strongly emphasized that this only happened about 12,000 years ago – in terms of human evolution, a mere micro-second. Coming, as it did, after a quasi-interminable 'run-up' lasting hundreds of thousands of years, the great leap forward occurred with such relative speed that it seems revolutionary although, like any other revolution, it must already have manifested its rudiments, origins and impulsions on a smaller scale. Revolutions happen overnight, but their preconditions come into being long before.

Some prehistorians reject the term Neolithic Revolution while accepting the process itself. Their reservations stem less from scientific disagreement than from a conflict of ideologies. Gordon Childe employed Marxist terminology and took his cue from Marx in basing his interpretation of human development on production relations. Although this approach was widely rejected on ideological grounds during the 1950s, it is now recognized that Marx's philosophy of history can provide a perfectly reasonable explanation of at least some phases and processes.

Whatever our personal attitude, a familiarity with the concept and nature of the Neolithic Revolution is essential because some of the archaeological research into past ages is being conducted in parts of the world where Marxist ideology holds sway and where, in consequence, this interpretation is taken for granted (e.g. in the case of Lepenski Vir, a Danubian Stone Age settlement in the Iron Gorge, one of the world's most interesting archaeological sites after Çatal Hüyük).

Irrespective of the theories espoused in either camp, the term Neolithic Revolution has gained widespread acceptance over the years because it fits the facts.

All that remains to be asked is why this radical change in man's way of life occurred when it did, not before or after. There seems to be no obvious reason why our forefathers should not have captured a few inoffensive sheep at a far earlier stage, thereby discovering that the natural tendency of a flock to multiply would save them the trouble of hunting deer and wild bulls. Besides, anyone who has read a book on dogs will know that the dog has been man's best friend 'from time immemorial'.

Here, however, it should be remembered that certain extraneous factors have to coincide with certain spiritual and intellectual developments in order to produce the 'Eureka!' on which any discovery or invention is based. There must also be a compulsion to exploit what has been discovered.

Until the advent of the Neolithic Revolution, no such incentive existed. For as long as the low population-density allowed, our ancestors roamed at will and reaped where they had not sown. This was the age of the so-called hunter-gatherer, a period when man found it more convenient to move to wherever berries or seeds could best be picked or harvested at a particular season of the year. In warm regions where nature provided sufficient food in the immediate vicinity, nomads sometimes settled down. The only difference between them and farmers was that they did not sow, only harvested.

This early form of settled life paved the way for agriculture. Tuberous roots were the first and easiest crops to grow. Because these can normally be sown and harvested throughout the year in a warm climate, they too provided a source of food which required minimal effort and no storage facilities.

The growing of cereals came later. This called for reasoning power of a substantially higher order because it presupposed the ability to store food and husband it. Even in a bad year, the community could not afford to use its entire stock of grain but had to conserve some as seed-corn. In modern parlance, it had to abstain from current consumption. But there was another factor involved too: cereals were not suitable for immediate use, like roots that could be boiled or baked, but required preparation with the aid of tools – in this case, some form of pestle and mortar. Thus, the cultivation of cereal crops presupposed a certain level of technical development.

Purely in theory, though not perhaps always in practice, one can trace the development of early agriculture into an intensive process aided by fertilization, irrigation and ploughing. Only when all these were combined did man become a true 'farmer' whose husbandry and skills rendered him more or less independent of the quest for food.

So the essential feature of the Neolithic Revolution consists, when all is said and done, in man's development from a gatherer into a producer. But this transition could only occur if soil and climate afforded the necessary scope.

This was another bone of scholarly contention. Having begun by concentrating largely on the 'fertile crescent' between the Euphrates, Tigris and Jordan, where a number of ancient cultures were unearthed, archaeologists opined that agriculture as well as civilization hailed from that area. If only because of the excavations at Çatal Hüyük, this theory had to be revised. The discovery of Lepenski Vir, a settlement which began to develop quite independently *ca.* 5700 BC (just after the abandonment of Çatal Hüyük), inspired talk of a 'fertile crescent' in the Danube area, although Lepenski Vir betrayed influences – associations would be a more cautious description – pointing to the east. Jericho and the Natufian culture (now also on Israeli territory) seem loosely connected with the Danubian settlement.

It has recently been postulated, therefore, that the Neolithic Revolution occurred in several places at once and then spread west and north-west. This northwards advance was associated with the gradual return of warmth after the last Ice Age. Although a temperate climate had prevailed in Central Europe for some time, albeit interrupted by a cold spell between 9000 and 8000 BC, it may in general be assumed that cultural development started in climatically favoured regions and then spread gradually to areas where living conditions were harder. We shall now see what life at Çatal Hüyük was like in the wake of this Neolithic Revolution.

Life in the Stone Age

After periods of almost imperceptible development, history seems to take an abrupt leap forwards. Two thousand years after the end of the last Ice Age, with its entirely different living conditions, and only shortly after the Neolithic Revolution had wrought upheavals in social structure, Çatal Hüyük presents us with the phenomenon of a 'finished' town that was already building on established traditions.

The 'Hittites' of the Stone Age – some of them positive giants 5 ft 10 ins tall but averaging 5 ft 7 ins for men and 5 ft 2 ins for women – were already living in what might be called standard one-room apartments. Depending on the size of the main room, these could have varying numbers of secondary store-chambers. Most of the living-rooms covered an area of 270–290 square feet – e.g. measured 19 ft × 14 ft – and were larger than many a 'living-room' in a modern house. There were larger dwellings of up to 520 square feet, also smaller ones, depending on size of family, of as little as 120.

Each room was kitchen, living-room and bedroom combined, and each followed a set pattern which never varied from one level or one family to the next. A single interior lay-out may thus be taken to apply to the whole town.

One-third of the available space was devoted to the kitchen. This contained a rectangular open hearth slightly raised and provided with a kerb, also an oven partly let into the wall to conserve heat but lacking a flue of its own. Beside the oven was a deep but low recess, evidently used for storing fuel. The roof above the hearth and oven was pierced by a smoke vent which also served as an entrance, there being no other access to the interior.

Outside the kitchen area, raised platforms ran along two walls in the shape of an L. Often provided with rounded kerbs, these were used for sitting, working and sleeping. They were the proto-type of the Turkish divan and, like the latter, covered with mats and furs. Towards the kitchen end, the platform was built up into a bench, but the rectangle formed by the convergence of the two platforms had its own special kerbing.

Depending on size of family, the unoccupied walls were pierced by a number of cave-like apertures leading to the unlit subsidiary rooms used for storing provisions. Opposite the main bed in the living-room itself, a series of small windows let into the wall just below the eaves gave on to the roof of the house immediately below. Lighting would have been a considerable problem but for the fact that Çatal Hüyük was terraced.

So much for the 'fixtures and fittings' available to an urban family at the end of the Stone Age. If Mellaart had found no more than this, the tally of Stone Age settlements already discovered – some as far north as the Hebrides – would at least have been swelled by one. But at Çatal Hüyük paintings had survived on the walls and each living-room contained altars. One should not, therefore, imagine that the general appearance of a Çatal Hüyük dwelling was as bleak and colourless as our diagrammatic view suggests. Each room was a combination of living-room and shrine, and this may explain why the interior lay-out was so strictly preserved for 800 years: altars required a permanent position and everything else had to conform.

More will be said about the paintings and altars at a later stage. I should first like to show how, on the basis of reconstructed religious traditions, it is still possible to distinguish between the man's sleeping-place and the woman's.

The woman always slept on the larger platform next to the kitchen, whereas the man occupied the far smaller corner platform and the rest of the 'beds' were allotted to children.

If we estimate how many people could have slept in such a living-room, bearing in mind their physical stature, we find to our surprise that no dwelling was intended for more than eight persons, in other words, for a family with more than six children.

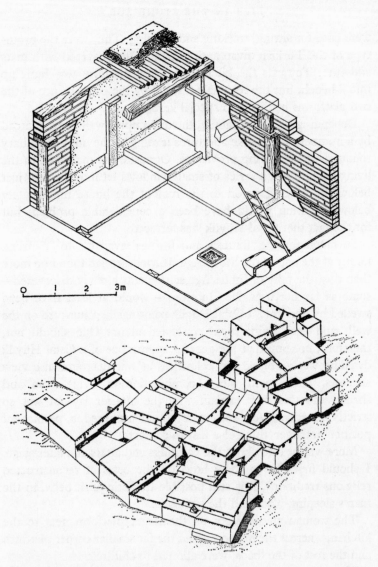

Above: diagrammatic view of a typical living-room at Çatal Hüyük, showing timber-framed walls, platforms, bench, hearth, oven and ladder.

Below: Çatal Hüyük was a terraced town without any streets. Roof and ladder provided the sole means of access to its houses. (Schematic reconstruction of a section of Level VI, *ca.*5800 BC.)

According to Mellaart, most families were even smaller.

This conflicts with earlier theories on the subject of large families in prehistoric times, especially as broods of a dozen or more were far from rare in nineteenth-century Europe. What can account for this?

The graves at Çatal Hüyük suggest one possibility because most people died at forty or under. Even then, however, families could easily have numbered upwards of ten children. Infant mortality must undoubtedly have been high, yet the graves have not yielded as many children's remains as this expectation would warrant.

Even assuming that older children were quick to start families of their own and make room for their growing brothers and sisters, we soon find our calculations going awry. If these are based on the assumption of one birth annually, older children of marriageable age would inevitably have been overhauled by later arrivals.

In that case, did the people of the Stone Age practise birth-control? The plain fact that no dwelling in Çatal Hüyük could accommodate more than six children would seem to make this likely.

Or did Mellaart get his sums wrong? Were more children crowded into the beds than he thought possible? Was the infant mortality rate so high that no family ever had more than six children living at the same time?

We can verify this too, even after 8000 years. In so doing, we shall also learn why we can distinguish with such certainty between the male's bed and the female's. Macabre as it may sound to modern ears, every Çatal Hüyük family buried its dead beneath the beds in the living-room – by sexes. Male remains were always interred beneath one platform – logically, the man's sleeping-place – and women's and children's remains beneath the other, where the mistress of the house slept. This is why we also know how big a family was. The living and the dead continued to share the same quarters, the former sleeping above the latter.

At this point, anyone disposed to regard the 'Hittites' of Çatal Hüyük as 'people like you and me' experiences a sudden jolt. We can picture and reconstruct the way in which the people of those days invented tools – we can even, by a stretch of the imagination, transport ourselves back into the primitive environment of the time – but we find it hard to fathom a world of ideas in which human habitations simultaneously functioned as shrines and cemeteries. What could have impelled these people to live with their dead?

Having come up against our first unexpected barrier, we shall leave this question in abeyance. An answer may emerge later on.

To revert to urban life in the Stone Age: even if many outstanding problems remain unsolved because only part of Çatal Hüyük has so far been excavated – for instance, no sewers, sanitary installations or wells have yet come to light – the development of trade, commerce, art and religion can be traced with some precision.

What did the inhabitants of Çatal Hüyük eat? Once again, anybody who conceives of them as the primitive cave-men of the old-fashioned child's encyclopedia, gnawing half-raw haunches of venison round blazing fires, is in for a disappointment. By Level VI, or *ca.* 6000 BC, no less than fourteen different food-plants were cultivated. The principal field crops were emmer, einkorn, naked six-row barley and bread-wheat. There were field peas and purple peas, lentils, two species of vetch, Shepherd's Purse and the salt-loving *Erysimum sisymbrioides*, which yielded vegetable fat. The presence of several other salt-loving plants proves that, being an offshoot of the saline central Anatolian steppe, the Konya Plain was itself highly saline as long ago as 6000 BC. Almonds, acorns and pistachios, apples, juniper and hackberry (*Celtis australis*) were introduced from the highlands – probably from the Taurus Mountains south of Çatal Hüyük. Hackberry occurs in the earliest levels and was apparently used for making wine. In addition to wine, the inhabitants undoubtedly made beer, of which, so we are informed by sacred texts of much later date, large quantities were sacrificed to the gods.

One mural painting, believed by Mellaart to represent insects circling flowers, suggests that honey was another familiar commodity, but the people of Çatal Hüyük may also have obtained a sweetening agent from tree-bark as the nomads of southern Anatolia do to this day. All these foodstuffs, together with the berries, eggs and meat dishes found as grave-gifts, combined to produce quite a varied menu.

The remains of domesticated cattle and dogs have been found in the very lowest levels at Çatal Hüyük, but it is uncertain whether sheep had been domesticated by this time. Definitely identified among the game animals in which the Konya Plain then abounded are red deer, wild boar, wolf, fox, gazelle, wild ass and leopard. Tortoises were also eaten for variety's sake, and their remains have been found in the household refuse of those days.

We know from a mural painting – a hunting scene of ca. 5700 BC – that dogs were already kept for sport and companionship. In addition to deer, the painting shows a canine which at first glance resembles a dachshund.

Having satisfied our curiosity about food and accommodation, let us turn to clothing. What did the people of this Stone Age period wear?

When Çatal Hüyük was burnt to the ground soon after 6000 BC (Level VI), the heat was so intense that it carbonized clothing worn by the bodies interred in the mud of the sleeping-platforms. Charred scraps of cloth were preserved beneath the skulls and larger bones. They are sizeable and finely woven fragments, and it takes a mental effort to grasp that they are among the earliest textile relics known to man: scraps of cloth with fringes and strings, cloth which even in those days had been crudely repaired and darned. Inside one 8000-year-old skull, Mellaart found a large fragment of plain tabby weave with a fine piece of twined heading cord. The threads were thin and fine and spun from sheep's wool or the fleece of the angora goat – we do not know for sure, but the material is certainly not linen because flax was not yet cultivated.

None of the houses so far excavated at Çatal Hüyük has yielded weavers' spindles or the stone loom-weights used to keep threads taut while weaving, so we may assume the existence of a special weavers' quarter which has yet to be located. It is also probable that Çatal Hüyük's small textile industry had developed and applied the technique of dyeing cloth, if not on a grand scale at least more efficiently than the individual family group.

Indirect evidence of dyeing comes from some stone beads whose holes still bear traces of red pigment although there is no element of red in their chemical composition. This proves that threads and fabrics could be dyed at least one colour – a handsome hue which recurs in mural paintings of women and female deities wearing robes adorned with bright red patterns. Even today, some of the commonest wild plants in the neighbourhood of Çatal Hüyük are madder, woad and weld, which respectively yield a deep red, a rich blue and a strong yellow.

It is actually possible to distinguish various types of weaving. In addition to the simple under-and-over method, shawl- and fishnet-like weaves were used. Cloth tapes were also found, and a young woman buried in a shrine in Level VIA wore a skirt composed of strings whose ends – still in the Stone Age, be it remembered – were weighted with small copper cylinders. This was a startling discovery, and not only from the aspect of costume, because the conventional distinction between the Stone and Bronze Ages suggests that metalwork should not have been produced in the Neolithic period.

We can even infer a knowledge of the cloth-printing technique from mural paintings and extant stamp-seals, which enabled coloured designs to be impressed on fabric.

The skins and furs of various animals were also worn, of course. Men, in particular, wore leopardskin aprons, though these may have been reserved for religious functions.

No footwear has been found, but this may be fortuitous because people would hardly have gone around barefoot during the cold season. Thanks to the discovery of a knife-sheath in a grave, we know that leather was tanned, worked and sewn. And this brings us to the range of wares and products manufactured by the inhabitants of Çatal Hüyük. The great conflagration in Level VI preserved some Stone Age 'industrial goods' which are not only unique of their kind but have radically revised our previous conception of Stone Age culture.

'Far too often,' Mellaart writes, 'the archaeologist is forced to evaluate a culture from a few broken pots, and tools and weapons of stone and bone, which may conceivably present a false or incomplete picture. At Çatal Hüyük it is clear that the crafts of the weaver and woodworker were much more highly esteemed than those of the potter or the bone-carver, and one may well wonder whether these two crafts have not been generally under-rated or at least inadequately represented among the achievements of the Neolithic period.'

Apart from clothing fabrics, the inhabitants of Çatal Hüyük manufactured mats and rugs which are almost more interesting, from the aspect of cultural history, than the ancient scraps of cloth mentioned above. Their rush carpets, partly reconstructed from impressions in mud floors but partly preserved in the original, were usually woven in a pattern of quadruple warp and weft from fine strands of rush or marsh grass barely a millimetre thick. It was even possible in some cases to identify the pattern, which ran diagonally to the outer edge. In fact, the patterns are identical with those which are still, more than 8000 years later, used in the Konya Plain and southern Anatolia – evidence of the tenacity with which designs, once evolved, are handed down, and of the links that still unite us with the cultures of the past.

We find a similar loyalty to tradition where rugs are concerned. Although these Stone Age carpets have not survived, Mellaart thinks he knows what they looked like – indeed, he goes so far as to print colour plates of them.

The rooms at Çatal Hüyük were not adorned with figures and scenes alone. Large areas of wall bore coloured patterns which, according to Mellaart, deputized for tapestries because they were exact copies of the rugs on the floor. One is immediately struck by their resemblance to the Anatolian kilims (thin woven rugs) still produced in the area to this day.

In contrast to the knotted carpet, the kilim is woven. The essential feature of the kilim technique is that weft yarns do not run the full width of the rug but only as far as the coloured pattern requires. Where two yarns of different colour meet, the ends are returned far enough to enable them to be secured. Kilim rugs can thus be recognized by the characteristic slits bordering each motif, and it is just these slits that can so clearly be discerned on the painted wall-mats at Çatal Hüyük, likewise a rectilinearity of design engendered by the weaving technique itself.

Empires have crumbled in the meantime and the Bronze and Iron Ages have been succeeded by an age of technology in which man has flown to the moon, yet the purchaser of a kilim rug in a Baghdad, London or New York shop could turn the clock back 8000 years and acquire the same item from an ancient 'Hittite' in Çatal Hüyük – a strange amalgam of tradition and progress, antiquity and modernity.

Twentieth-century bowls, spoons and boxes differ just as little in design from the wooden examples found at Çatal Hüyük. Contrary to general belief, woodwork was a well-established craft in the Stone Age. As we already know from our discussion of the town's architectural history, all joists and posts, whether of juniper or hard oak, were squared. The appropriate tools – polished greenstone adzes and chisels – have been found in great quantities.

Although fragments of pottery came to light in the earliest levels, household utensils were originally made of wood. Mellaart unearthed wooden plates, vessels and bowls, great wooden meat dishes more than two feet long – even an 8000-year-old egg-cup, thin-walled and perfectly fashioned from fir-wood with a finish as clean as if it had been produced on a modern lathe. Rectangular or oval boxes with well-fitting lids were a particular speciality. Though carbonized, these have survived intact.

Even in the most recent levels, pottery never became emancipated from these wooden exemplars. In Level II (*ca.* 5700 BC), for instance, many clay vessels imitate the rectangular shape of wooden boxes or have wooden feet, a fact which prompts Mellaart to assume that the potter's role at Çatal Hüyük was subordinate to that of the woodworker.

'Generally,' says Mellaart, 'the importance of ceramic production in the Neolithic has probably been greatly overrated. It was a technological advance like any other and was no doubt useful for cooking, but it was easily breakable, hard to transport, in these early phases not so easy to fire well and aesthetically not very attractive.' It was not until the firing technique improved that well-fashioned and often lavishly decorated pottery utensils came into general use.

Human and animal figures were modelled in clay from the very first. Fired clay was also used, at least from Level VI (*ca.* 6000 BC) onwards, for the manufacture of beads, pendants and seals.

What about the typical Stone Age products that gave their name to this vast epoch in human history – the stone hammers, chisels and axes? Çatal Hüyük has yielded many such tools, but they seem quite banal in comparison with the other finds made there.

What is surprising is the high quality and finish of these and many other products. There are mirrors of obsidian, a hard and vitreous volcanic rock, so smoothly polished that not the smallest scratch can be detected on their surface. There are ornamental stone beads so finely drilled that a modern steel pin cannot penetrate them. We really do seem to have underrated the manual skills of our so-called Stone Age ancestors and overrated the changes introduced by later and better-known civilizations.

Although the Babylonians, Sumerians, Phoenicians, Egyptians and Cretans were once seen as having burst into full cultural flower from nothing – straight from the proverbial 'mists of time', as it were – it is now accepted that they were preceded by peoples who can be shown to have possessed a whole range of skills not previously attributed to them.

Another equally surprising fact is that the inhabitants of Çatal

Hüyük lived in an environment containing materials not found in the Konya Plain. One of the essential preconditions of their skilled craftsmanship was an extensive network of commercial links. Even the oak and juniper used for building purposes did not grow in the plain but had to be imported from the mountains. Fir-wood undoubtedly came from the Taurus, alabaster from the Kayseri district, marble from western Anatolia. Every single stone used in the manufacture of tools had to be brought from far away, notably the flint which was fashioned into blades. The provenance of the rock-crystals, jasper and apatite remains obscure, but trading links with the peoples of the Mediterranean are evidenced by the remains of marine molluscs.

However, most of the blades and weapons at Çatal Hüyük were made of obsidian, which, though not exactly on its doorstep, could be obtained a few days' march away on the edge of the Konya Plain. Here stood several volcanoes, some of them still active: Mekke Dağ, Karaca Dağ, the twin-peaked cone of Hasan Dağ and, far away to the north-east, Erciyas Dağ.

These fire-breathing mountains were the source of the obsidian. It is, however, improbable that craftsmen could have polished this glassy volcanic rock to mirrorlike smoothness after only a few generations' experience. We can only surmise that the inhabitants of Çatal Hüyük possessed a tradition of craftsmanship far older than at first supposed. After all, the little copper cylinders on the hem of the woman's skirt prove that they already knew – long before the advent of the Bronze Age – how to smelt metal.

It could naturally be argued that this copper was not smelted by the people of Çatal Hüyük but acquired by them from some unknown source (not that this would explain away the use of copper in the Stone Age). Here too, the evidence enables us to be more precise, for Çatal Hüyük yielded slag from which copper had been extracted. In other words, its inhabitants smelted metal several thousand years – repeat, several thousand – before the beginning of the Bronze Age proper. Both copper and lead have been found at levels definitely attributable to the Neolithic period.

Does this mean that the beginning of the Bronze Age should really be dated in the Stone Age?

The use of copper has no immediate bearing on that of bronze because the latter is a copper-tin alloy possessing qualities quite different from those of its constituent metals. Although iron, too, was known and smelted long before the start of the so-called Iron Age, we do not date the Iron Age any earlier on that account.

As long as a new metal remained so scarce that people used it as jewellery and only occasionally for tool-making, it did not lend its name to the period in question. Its rarity stemmed from a dependence on random discoveries of ore and an inability to extract the metal on a large scale.

Only exploitation by means of systematic mining could transform an ornamental metal into a functional one. Only the wide diffusion of a material and its use in the manufacture of ordinary hand-tools justifies us in applying its name to a whole epoch. We should also remember that, in early times, the interval between a discovery and its exploitation was greater than in our own day.

Having so far employed the term 'Stone Age' for simplicity's sake, I take this opportunity of differentiating a little.

It was the curator of the Danish National Museum in Copenhagen, Christian Thomsen (d. 1865), who classified prehistory as we were broadly taught to do at school. He broke it down into a Stone Age, a Bronze Age and an Iron Age. Today, this tripartite system is far from adequate.

The Stone Age was later subdivided into an Old Stone (Palaeolithic) and a New Stone (Neolithic) Age, but archaeologists did not stop there. The Palaeolithic period was itself subdivided into an earlier and a more recent phase, the Lower and Upper Palaeolithic Ages, and the Palaeolithic and Neolithic periods were further separated by a Middle Stone (Mesolithic) Age. Finally, discoveries of copper at the close of the Neolithic Age entailed yet another differentation: the Copper-Stone or Chalcolithic Age.

On the basis of this scale I should, instead of referring generally to the 'Stone Age', have used the term Chalcolithic because metals were employed in addition to the stone artefacts found at Çatal Hüyük and elsewhere. But I could just as well have talked of the Wood-Stone or Ceramic-Stone Age because the discoveries made at Çatal Hüyük have rendered the term Chalcolithic imperfectly applicable. The old chronological divisions were named after what had survived, not what was in common use. Stone and metal being more durable than wood, textiles or leather – except in cases where these perishable materials have been conveniently preserved by fire – by no means every term adopted took its name from the predominant material.

It is probable that all these designations will one day have to be revised in accordance with newly established criteria. For the moment, we can only be on our guard against an excessive reliance on data provided by encyclopedias and specialized literature. Each work gives a different set of figures, and the figures that most often agree may not necessarily be the most correct. Precise demarcation is rendered impossible by a multiplicity of viewpoints, especially as dates that hold good for Northern Europe differ from those that apply to Asia Minor or China in accordance with the speed at which an innovation spread and the availability of trade routes. *The* Stone Age and *the* Bronze Age did not exist as such. There was merely a general use of stone, wood or various metals for tools and household utensils in certain areas and at certain (not necessarily contemporaneous) periods.

Art or magic?

Whether we call a period the Stone, Neolithic or Chalcolithic Age, we are always tempted to conceive of the ancient world as a more primitive version of our own.

This projection of the present into the past works quite well in the case of articles that have a clearly discernible function or are still in similar use today. Tools like axes or ploughs have remained fundamentally unchanged for thousands of years, except as to material. Whether of flint or iron, arrow-heads are immediately recognizable because they looked much the same in the Middle Ages as they did in the Stone Age.

If we were transported back in time to a house at Çatal Hüyük, we should not have to dispense with pots, cups, jugs, plates, egg-cups or carpets: much of what we now possess in a refined form existed in prototype. The difference between now and then consists merely in that cultural 'increment' (e.g. glazed windows, better heating facilities and new sources of illumination) which we term progress.

This idea of progress, and with it the ability to draw inferences about the past from the present, loses its relevance precisely at the point where objects retain the same appearance but undergo a change of function.

For instance, we adorn a wall with pictures because we like them or find them 'beautiful'. The stag at bay that hangs above many a modern sofa recurs at Çatal Hüyük or in the far older cave paintings of southern France. The crucial difference is that Stone Age paintings were not merely decorative. Despite their resemblance to modern works of art, they possessed an entirely different function. This is exemplified by the Stone Age cave paintings mentioned above, for what point could there have been in 'decorating' a gloomy cavern with pictures of animals even at points which the glow from a log fire could barely illuminate? Similarly, Çatal Hüyük prompts us to wonder what sort of macabre and morbid impulse could have driven our ancestors to adorn their walls with huge pictures of vultures picking at headless corpses.

But the question itself has been wrongly phrased. As Walter Torbrügge says in his art book *Europäische Vorzeit*, 'Prehistoric art should be judged by criteria that arise from the reason for its creation. Aesthetic effects seem rarely to have been intended, though the intention can never be ruled out.'

Here, as in the death-cult, we meet a barrier that cannot be surmounted simply by drawing comparisons between now and then. This is no continuing development from the primitive to the refined, as with tools, nor is it a question of artistic trends from the abstract to the representational or vice versa. It is something fundamentally different.

Basing our approach on the effect that prehistoric paintings have on us, we have grown accustomed to classifying them as 'art', the simplest common denominator of 'art' being that it embraces anything beyond the immediate necessities of life and the function of a particular article. The function of an earthenware cooking-pot does not require that it be incised or painted with lines, patterns and figures. But this non-essentiality is what endows art with a scope that transcends the purely functional use of an object.

If, on the other hand, we approach this question by asking *why* the people of the Stone Age painted their pictures and fashioned their clay statuettes, the key-word becomes not art but religion.

Religion should not be taken to mean tenets, dogmas or the sort of divine faith associated with Christianity. We are here dealing with early forms of religion which are still entirely rooted in magic and myth. This being so, they can be more readily comprehended by psychological means than through what may, in the broadest sense, be termed theology.

Because art and religion are the two main threads linking prehistoric Anatolia with the empire of the Hittites who called themselves the Nation of a Thousand Gods, we must make an apparent digression into religious psychology before reverting to 'art'. As we shall see later, this will also equip us to overcome the psychological and emotional block created in our minds by Çatal Hüyük's bizarre death-cult.

The tremendum and the fascinosum

Few scholarly works devoted to special problems ever achieve a second or third edition. Most publishers are happy to sell a few hundred copies. The religious historian Rudolf Otto expected a similar fate to befall his 200-page book, *Das Heilige – Über das Irrationale in der Idee des Göttlichen und sein Verhältnis zum Rationalen* (Sanctity – On the Irrational Element in the Idea of Divinity and its Relationship to the Rational), when it came out in 1917, in the middle of World War I. He was wrong. The book with the ponderous title became a modest best-seller and has so far run to 30 editions. A new impression was published in 1971, 54 years after its first appearance.

Otto traced the origins of religion back to two emotional experiences. The first was that of terror, or the dread of something awesome and overpowering, to which he gave the Latin designation *tremendum* (from *tremere*, meaning to quake or tremble). One familiar illustration of how a god can be engendered by man's experience of a terrifying and (formerly) inexplicable natural phenomenon may be seen in the mythical personage who gave his name to the German *Donnerstag* (Thursday). Being unable to account for thunderstorms, the ancient Germans converted the natural phenomenon which filled them with such dread into a force more potent than man – a force conceived of as a god who drove through the sky in a chariot and struck sparks from the clouds by smiting them with a hammer. This weather-god Donar (Thor) was the supreme Germanic deity and corresponded to the Greeks' thunderbolt-hurling Zeus, who also clearly originated as a personification of fear. The names differ but their origins are similar. To quote Otto: 'Religion is born not of natural fear nor of a putative "cosmic dread". For terror is not natural or common fear; it is itself a first self-arousal and sense of the mysterious – albeit initially in the crude form of the "uncanny" – whether it be fear of ghosts, panic fear, or experience of the superhuman element in Nature.'

The second primeval experience is of wonder, awe and amazement, which also have the power to inspire terror. This awe aroused by the 'wonder-ful', which can lead to reverence and become spellbinding, Otto calls the *fascinosum* or fascinating, and he stresses from the outset that the *tremendum* and *fascinosum* are positive and negative aspects of that same sense of 'absolute dependence' which Friedrich Schleiermacher had earlier called the hall-mark of religion. Otto therefore follows him in talking of the 'harmony of contrasts' and dual nature of these two experiences, which he summarizes in the term 'numinous'.

This *numinosum*, or 'divine quality', was sensed by early man in all that surrounded him: punitive and intimidating when earthquake struck or tempest raged, beneficent when Nature revived in springtime, when the sun rose or rains and floods dispensed their life-sustaining moisture (e.g. in the Nile Valley). These phenomena did not occur automatically, in accordance with fixed laws or sequences, but were occasioned by divine beings. Thus, all things housed deities of their own. Every watercourse had its river-god, every mountain its mountain-god, every tree its wood-nymph.

The belief that all objects are in some mysterious way endowed with life is termed animism, from *anima*, the Latin word for soul. To the animist, natural processes are 'animate', in other words, brought about by some immanent being.

Related to the *tremendum* and *fascinosum*, though not discussed by Otto, are another two basic experiences which have likewise conduced to the emergence of religions.

One of these basic experiences – akin to the *tremendum* – is death. Two contrasting forms of religion have arisen from man's experience of its inexorable finality and his quest for a life hereafter. One embraces the doctrine of reincarnation, which enables human beings to be reborn as many times as they need to attain the perfection required for entry into nirvana, or personal extinction.

Other religions cite the fact of death in postulating the immortality of the soul. Death is not the end of all things; instead, the soul can live on in another world, the realm of the dead. The dead are not really dead (which is why the living provide them with food for their journey and sacrifice to them thereafter); they simply inhabit another world.

Yet another variant developed from the idea of a kingdom of the dead. Based on the concept of justice, this type of religion held that, if a man had done his best on earth, his soul went to the abode of the god or gods; if he had failed to observe the divine commandments, he was punished. Thus, earthly life became a testing-ground for the real life that ensued after death.

The fourth basic religion-engendering experience, this time related to the *fascinosum*, is the ecstasy of sexuality, often regarded as divine because it enables man to create life like a god.

In contrast to most of modern humanity, people of earlier times considered large families a real asset. Only a large community was strong enough to repel its enemies, and numerous children were a guarantee of family and communal survival. The ability of men and beasts to reproduce their kind was vitally important, hence the so-called fertility-cults for which sexuality assumed divine significance. These four basic experiences do not, however, constitute a religion in themselves. The emotions of fear, awe and love are merely a prerequisite. For a religion to be born, some other crucial factor is needed.

We have already said that the world was thought of as animate and inhabited by spirits, in other words, that certain beings were deemed responsible for every natural or inexplicable phenomenon. But if someone was responsible, that someone could be asked for favours: the fertility-god for children, the harvest-god for rain, the thunder-god for immunity from lightning.

To propitiate the deities, men began presenting them with gifts – sacrifices designed to influence them and induce a benevolent attitude. It is precisely at the point where human beings seek to influence the powers on which they feel dependent by means of prayer, sacrifice and 'good' behaviour of a specific kind, that religion begins. No one likes to feel at the mercy of the unknown, everyone craves an ability to control his fate and steer it aright.

In addition to sacrifice, however, there was another means of nudging one's personal destiny in the required direction. If a man was as strong as the unseen powers he could *impose* his will instead of praying and imploring. This defiant human reaction formed the basis of man's belief in magic – in an ability to enforce his desires by means of spells and incantations.

We smile at this today. We construe invocations of the devil, even if they do occur in Goethe's *Faust*, as fairy-tales or parables. We shrug our shoulders at primitive people's fear of the 'evil eye'. We stand amazed at their belief in word-magic, the basis of all curses, and have lost our awareness that the Biblical account of Creation is founded on just such a belief in the power of words: 'And God said, Let there be light: and there was light.'

We cannot understand why Rumpelstiltskin only retained his magical powers for as long as nobody knew his name, but this too is magic: the acquisition of power over persons or things through a knowledge of their names. A knowledge of certain words and formulas is the very basis of sorcery – one reason, perhaps, why Jehovah forbade the Jews to take his name 'in vain'.

Although we dismiss such magic as superstition, our ancestors believed in the existence of these powers. They were a way and means of imposing, or trying to impose, their will on fellow-men and invisible beings. If they failed, it merely meant that the formula had been incorrectly recited or that the ritual itself contained some error. One reason why religious ceremonies display such prodigious powers of survival may be that they still contain a remnant of the magic which, for example, enables a priest to summon up the physical presence of Christ during transubstantiation with the words 'This is my body, this is my blood . . .'

If Christianity brings the Stone Age closer in this way, our knowledge of the present can also contribute to a better understanding of magic. Terms may change but facts endure. We have no need to mobilize any 'unseen powers' to grasp what magic is. Anyone who has witnessed the power of one word from a doctor to induce hypnotic paralysis – anyone who has seen or experienced how autogenous training, a form of self-hypnosis, can by means of simple verbal formulas render parts of the body absolutely insensitive to pain or impose behavioural tabus which the subject can violate only by suppressing his fears, if at all – will have a greater sense than others of the powers which, although we no longer refer to them as such, were once termed magical.

I cite this only as an aid to the imagination of those who adopt a positive attitude towards this phenomenon. People would hardly have attributed so cogent an effect to the spoken curse or blessing and would soon have abandoned magic, conjuration and prayer if their efficacy had not been recognized on some plane or other, be it only in the imagination. Assuming, however, that conjuration, curse and blessing elicited a real psychical response from the person affected, and thus produced an effect, the error of magic should probably be seen in its attribution of results to 'the gods', because this equated them with the random effects of an oracle.

We do not have to go back to the Stone Age to observe magical associations of this type. Even today, devout members of the Greek and Russian Orthodox Churches regard their icons as 'windows of heaven', not just paintings of saints. It is the saint himself who appears in the picture. As at Communion, a transubstantiation and conjuration occurs the moment the painter paints his picture: instead of merely portraying a saint, the picture itself becomes sanctified because the saint *himself* looks out of it.

Having reconstructed this process in its logical sequence, at least theoretically, we must suppress any inclination to reflect further on the Stone Age people who live on within us and revert to the subject of their art.

We have, however, built a bridge to a new understanding of the dictum that prehistoric art should be judged solely by criteria that stem from the motive for its creation, not by those of aesthetics. The next chapter will make it plain that early painting was rooted in magic.

Pictures as magic

Looking at a portrait photograph today, we say: Yes, that's so-and-so. We know quite well that it isn't really the person in question, just a likeness. Our magic-minded ancestors drew no such distinction. Just as the princess gained power over Rumpelstiltskin by discovering his name, so they gained power over things that could be drawn or painted. Even in modern Hebrew, the word for 'thing' or 'object' is related to the word for 'say' or 'speak'. It is therefore typically West European to quarrel over whether one says 'This is my body' or 'This symbolizes my body': all Hebrew says – construe it in magical terms or not – is 'This my body.'

With this 'it is' or 'let it happen', man was simply doing what could also be done by the gods whose power he feared. If God, as the Biblical myth of Creation tells us, fashioned man out of clay 'in his image' and thus made him his creature, man too could fashion and dominate 'creatures' of his own by reproducing and naming them.

This magical affinity between object and likeness, between being and representing, underlies all the divine effigies of early times and is thus the origin of 'art' as a whole. That which we now term Stone Age art was conjuration, nothing more. If a man drew or painted the likeness of an animal, he had it – magically speaking – in his grasp: a pictorial hunting scene 'attracted' a successful outcome to the chase itself.

At Çatal Hüyük, as in Stone Age cave drawings, we consequently find numerous scenes that anticipate the hunters' personal desire for victory over large and dangerous beasts such as the bull or stag.

One of the most recent paintings, which dates 'only' from 5800 BC, came to light in Level IIIA. Over five feet long and nearly

8000 years old, this hunting scene had been painstakingly restored after each of four new coats of plaster.

It depicts five or six men of varying stature armed with bows, slings or clubs. The figure kneeling on the bottom-most stag may also be using a lasso. Some of the hunters are clearly naked, whereas others wear leopardskin 'kilts' that stream away horizontally from the body. The herd of red deer consists of three stags, two hinds and two calves. One stag has already been thrown to the ground by two men and is just being dispatched. All in all, it is an extremely animated scene and one that also supplies information about our ancestors' weapons and hunting techniques.

Differences in size are symbolic of the figures' relative importance. Medieval paintings, like children's drawings of our own day, exaggerate the stature of important persons. We can therefore state with certainty that the large figure on the left of the picture is the leader of the hunting party.

But this unperspective treatment of size also permits inferences to be drawn about the impression of 'size' made on contemporary man by creatures such as the bull. A cult-room in the same level, IIIA, contains a painting over nineteen feet in extent and covering three walls. It is dominated by a bull over six feet long, surrounded by a swarm of diminutive hunters. The stags on the neighbouring wall are of similar proportions.

Examining a carefully copied and restored section of this reconstructed line-drawing – it includes the group of figures between the bull and stags in the corner of the room – we notice that, if only in the case of this particular group, we are looking not at a hunting scene but at a hunting dance of indisputably magical significance. The figures face in different directions, skipping, leaping and standing. Mellaart thinks that the dance was intended to guarantee the successful kill depicted further along the same wall to the right.

The dance evidently followed a ritual pattern of some kind, because closer scrutiny reveals a division into three superimposed rows, the three figures in the middle row being larger, i.e. more important, than the rest. Although nearly all the figures wear leopardskins, two in the middle row are further distinguished by being painted white or red-and-white instead of red all over.

But these two figures are distinguished from the rest by yet another characteristic: they are headless. The heads have not simply flaked off – they were never inserted in the first place.

Although magical hunting pictures have been found at other Stone Age sites, headless figures that move with seeming normality among the living remain unique to Çatal Hüyük. We often find them portrayed there, but especially in Levels VII and VIII (*ca.* 6200 BC), which also yielded the strange vulture-paintings referred to earlier. The latter make it quite apparent that these early paintings were concerned with the expression of religious ideas and had no decorative or aesthetic purpose.

They are terrifying pictures if we consider that the birds (probably Griffon vultures like those still found in the Konya Plain) were depicted life-size, with a wing span of about five feet. Judging by their size relative to the human figures beside them, it is the vultures that dominate the scene, not only visually but thematically. They are picking at helpless, headless figures. In one of the earliest vulture-paintings from Level VIII, a man can be seen trying to ward off the birds with a sling.

It is hardly to be supposed that these pictures represent real-life incidents in which men were attacked by vultures. No bird of prey, let alone a vulture, attacks human beings without good cause. Moreover, the heads are not merely severed – they are missing altogether. Headlessness can have nothing to do with decapitation, therefore, but must denote something else.

Here, the ornithologist comes to our aid. Vultures are carrion-eating birds. If the pictures show them picking at human beings, the latter must already be dead. Headlessness therefore betokens that a person is dead or doomed to die.

Perhaps we can now hazard a better interpretation of the magical hunting-dance as well. The two headless figures are dead leaders: men who have died while hunting or may – so the painter anticipates – lose their lives on some future expedition and thus continue to move about like the living.

But why the vultures? All their victims are painted in attitudes typical of skeletons found in the graves beneath the mud beds. This suggests that the vultures may have had some connection with burial rites.

We were repelled from the outset by the notion that putrescent corpses were interred beneath the living-room beds. We can now deduce from these pictures that they were not. The solution lies in a combination of two facts: the dead were buried intramurally, but only as skeletons. The paintings tell us what happened beforehand: corpses were evidently exposed in special places so that the vultures could do their work. If a picture found in Level VI has been correctly interpreted, special 'mortuaries' built of reeds and other light materials were used for the purpose. At all events, the decomposing skulls discernible below the gabled reed-and-matting roof make this interpretation a likely one.

Peculiar though the practice of excarnation or flesh-stripping may seem to us, it has been far from rare. The 'towers of silence' associated with the Parsees, who fled from Persia to India during the seventh and eighth centuries AD, are nothing more nor less than places of excarnation above which vultures wheel on 'wings of death', as visitors to Bombay can observe to this day.

What is more surprising is that this type of twofold burial should be verifiable so early on, because it enables us to draw quite philosophical conclusions about the way in which people saw themselves 8000 years ago and where they located the seat of their innermost being – their self and soul.

As so often happens, language is revealing here because it preserves age-old concepts in words that are seemingly new. The modern Hebrew term for (national or personal) autonomy and independence, for example, is related to the Hebrew for the essence of man, his real individuality. This word, which corresponds most nearly to our 'soul' is in turn derived from the word *ezem*, meaning simply 'bone'. A Hebrew-speaker who wants to refer to his very own self, therefore, still says 'azmi' – my bones. This is a manifestation of the ancient idea that the essential and most durable constituent of the human being is his bones, because flesh is perishable.

Only this world of ideas can help us to construe Biblical dicta such as 'the Word was made flesh' and 'fleshly lusts' less superficially than we learnt to do in Bible class. 'And the Word was made flesh' is not just an archaic way of saying that a god became man; it also implies that this god exposed himself to the perishable and insubstantial.

If the people of Çatal Hüyük really exposed their dead until the perishable flesh had disappeared, then buried the bones alone, perhaps we can now overcome our initial repugnance at the idea of intramural burial. What they laid to rest beneath their beds was the 'imperishable' part of the body, not a rotting corpse.

So, even then, people associated their death-cult with the idea of immortality and may well have possessed a more differentiated religion than we were previously justified in assuming. What tallies with this is that levels of roughly the same age at Jericho have yielded human skulls decorated to resemble living faces with the aid of paint and shell-filled eye-sockets.

Another mural painting at Çatal Hüyük likewise enables us to infer the existence of a special death-ritual. Vultures were normally depicted with anatomical precision, but one wall-painting shows them with ordinary feet instead of talons. Mellaart not unnaturally concludes that it does not portray real vultures but human beings disguised as vultures and performing something that is evidently a funerary rite. If this interpretation is correct, it would provide a transitional link with the fetish dances of primitive tribes.

It is even possible to deduce when the remains were buried. Mellaart was struck by the fact that skeletons in the same layers exhibited varying degrees of excarnation, in other words, had not all been exposed to the vultures for the same length of time. Since the houses regularly had their plasterwork and paint renewed in the spring, it is reasonable to assume that the inhabitants of Çatal Hüyük took the opportunity to bury all those who had died during the preceding year before applying a fresh coat of plaster.

If the inferences drawn from their wall-paintings are essentially correct, we have already learnt a great deal about the motives, attitudes and behaviour of these Stone Age people.

But that is not all. Just as art and magic originally went together, so there is a relationship between art and the death-cult from which further associations can be deduced.

I shall discuss these in a later chapter, but first I should like to single out one of the many extant wall-paintings. It is unique in its way, being the earliest-known landscape painting in the world, and may also be one of the few Stone Age pictures whose religio-magical associations are not immediately demonstrable.

Found in Level VII, the picture dates from about 6200 BC. Mellaart describes it as follows:

In the foreground is shown a town with rectangular houses of varying sizes with internal structures reminiscent of Çatal Hüyük houses clearly indicated ... The rows of houses rise in terraces up to the top of the mound ... Beyond the town and much smaller as if far away, rises a double peaked mountain covered with dots and from its base parallel lines extend. More lines erupt from its higher peak and more dots are grouped beyond its right slope and in horizontal rows above its peak, interspersed with horizontal and vertical lines. A clearer picture of a volcano in eruption could hardly have been painted: the fire coming out of the top, lava streams from vents at its base, clouds of smoke and glowing ash hanging over its peak and raining down on and beyond the slopes of the volcano are all combined in this painting.

Comparing Mellaart's description with the original, we cannot fail to marvel at his powers of imagination and interpretation. Few of us would have identified the checkered pattern as Çatal Hüyük, and even fewer would have associated the rest of the picture with a mountain spewing fire.

anyone standing on the site of Çatal Hüyük, but only there,
....art's interpretation becomes promptly and startlingly in-
....gible. It is not hard to find a local point of reference: within
sight of Çatal Hüyük at the eastern end of the Konya Plain rises
the only twin-peaked volcano in central Anatolia, the 10,700 ft-high
Hasan Dağ, which did not become extinct until the second
millennium BC.

The inhabitants of Çatal Hüyük would undoubtedly have
witnessed a volcanic eruption, a sight that must have filled
them with terror. It says much for the level of Stone Age civilization that people of the Chalcolithic period had the ability to
record such an event pictorially. To this extent, the Çatal Hüyük
landscape is comparable with a documentary photograph of our
own day.

But here, too, features can be detected which take us into the
realm of magic. To quote Mellaart again:

Moreover, these volcanoes and Hasan Dağ especially, were the
source of much raw material, in particular that of obsidian, for
Çatal Hüyük, a source from which the site probably derived
much of its wealth. It may be surmised that it was not only for
its great cutting power, its transparency, reflective power and
its jet black appearance that this material was so highly prized.
Its volcanic and thus chthonic origin would have linked it to
the underworld, the place of the dead, and it was a true gift of
mother earth, and therefore imbued with magical potency.

These considerations may help in explaining why an artist
late in the seventh millennium BC recorded the wonder and
awe of a volcanic eruption against the foreground of the town
of Çatal Hüyük on the wall of one of its shrines.

This first-ever landscape painting in human history may,
after all, be a cult-picture based on experience of the *tremendum*
and *fascinosum*. Even if we reject Mellaart's interpretation, we
shall see that, roughly 4000 years later, Hittite kings were to
name themselves after sacred mountains.

Death-cult and after-life

There is a religious background to the fact that we owe a substantial part of our knowledge of man's early history to graves and grave-goods alone. This poses the question whether towns like Çatal Hüyük should be thought of as abodes of the living, cities of the dead, or a combination of both.

It seems that, from the first, human beings have differed from animals in regarding death as something more than an end to life. Even 40,000 years ago, Neanderthal Man buried his dead with grave-gifts. These sacrifices confirm that human beings already associated religious ideas with death. We are naturally ignorant of the nature of their ideas about an after-life. The familiar imagery of a kingdom of the dead inhabited by the shades of the living only occurs in later mythologies of the historical period, though these must certainly have derived from very ancient sources. The predominant idea was of an 'underworld' which subsequently developed, in Christian thinking, into a subterranean hell.

Burial practices have themselves changed over the millennia in accordance with prevailing attitudes towards the dead.

In the Natufian, a Stone Age culture in the Carmel area, as at Çatal Hüyük and the somewhat later settlement of Lepenski Vir, but also in Cyprus and other places, the dead were buried in their homes. Secondary burial was customary, in other words, excarnation preceded the interment of bare bones. Frequently, as numerous items of evidence attest, burial did not include the entire skeleton but was confined to isolated parts, e.g. the skull. Of equal antiquity is the practice of burying a child's skeleton beneath the threshold of a new house, probably as a form of sacrifice.

The interment of the dead in a living-area presupposes that

they were not conceived of as hostile and remained part of the family even after death. In 1907, J. Zehetmaier rather primly summarized this practice in his book *Leichenverbrennung und Leichenbestattung im alten Hellas* (The Cremation and Burial of the Dead in Ancient Greece) as follows:

Here too, in accordance with age-old Indo-Germanic custom, the dead man was laid to rest in the earth within the human habitation. Having been so close to his own in life, the late lamented had to abide with them in death, sharing the family's joys and sorrows, food and drink. In life he had reposed nightly in a crouching position beneath the roof of the simple circular hut; in death he was enabled to assume the same position for his eternal slumber beneath the domestic hearth.

This favourable attitude towards the dead must one day have become tinged with emotions of fear or hostility. It was feared that the dead might return and wreak revenge of some kind. People therefore began to cover them with heavy slabs of stone or bury them in rock-graves – a Stone Age custom faintly echoed by the tombstones in our modern cemeteries.

The practice of burying the dead in dwellings persisted, but that of living with them ceased. Lepenski Vir exemplifies this. 'Once a dead person had been interred in a domestic shrine, the house in question was no longer used as an abode of the living,' writes the archaeologist Dragoslav Srejovic. He even surmises that the occupants began to deceive their dead by building normal dwellings but reserving them entirely for burial purposes and living elsewhere themselves.

Srejovic concludes: 'So recent investigations of the archaeological material at Lepenski Vir give grounds for assuming that these buildings were cult-shrines, not genuine houses.'

At that stage, therefore, a distinction was drawn between habitations for the living and abodes of the dead, who were conceived of as occupying them for ever.

The results of this change were twofold. The separation of the dead from the living for fear of their magical influence after death

Entrance to the sanctuary of Yazilikaya near Hattusa. It consists of two natural recesses in the rock with numerous divine figures carved on their walls (*ca*.1350-1250 B.C.)

Procession of twelve deities in the sanctuary of Yazilikaya. 3 ft. 6 ins. high, this relief shows gods in warrior guise equipped with sickle-swords and the typically Hittite pointed helmet of the Weather-god (ca.1350-1250 BC.)

Above: clay vessel in the shape of a twin-headed duck, found at Hattusa in company with numerous other small sculptures, seals and stamp-seals (height 9 ins., 15th century BC.)
Below: divine figures like those carved into the rock face at Yazilikaya have also been found at Gavurkale, near Ankara.

gave rise to the earliest form of cemetery, whose modern counterpart is justified mainly by considerations of hygiene. Outwardly, these necropolises were modelled on the settlements of the living, so archaeologists do not always find it easy to tell them apart and identify their discoveries beyond doubt. The numerous 'priests' dwellings' and cult-rooms found at Çatal Hüyük will present us with a similar problem later on.

On the other hand, the living were at pains to guarantee their dead as permanent an earthly abode as possible. Since those who inhabited the realm of the dead did not die a second time, it became necessary to build houses for eternity, as it were – in other words, cult-shrines which would endure from generation to generation. This is why the finds made at prehistoric sites consist almost exclusively of graves and burial installations: it is they, and not the abodes of the living, that have survived the millennia.

To quote a few familiar examples . . .

We should know far less about the civilization of ancient Egypt but for the survival of tombs such as the Pyramids, that is to say, buildings erected 'for eternity' and not for occupation by the living. Nor was it for the sake of the living that our European ancestors laboriously assembled random boulders into houses of stone: their efforts were expended on behalf of the dead who were laid to rest within these megalithic graves. Again, only ruined walls remain of Mycenae, Agamemnon's palace, but the one inner chamber still complete down to the last cornerstone is the so-called Treasury of Atreus – a tomb. Finally, if the geologist H. G. Wunderlich is right – and there is some evidence to support his theory – the palace at Knossos, too, was a city of the dead and not of the living.

It is impossible to go into detail in a limited and, of necessity, highly simplified survey. My only concern is to illustrate the close links between death-cult and civilization, tombs and architecture, solidly constructed buildings and the concept of eternity, with sufficient clarity for our present purpose. Having so far encountered nothing but intramural or extramural burial, we are suddenly confronted at the end of the Stone Age by a quite novel and revolutionary form of body-disposal: cremation.

After all that has been said about the relationship of the living to the dead, the disposal of bodies by fire must have meant a break with tradition and the traditional world of ideas.

If the intention hitherto had been to preserve and retain at least the 'essence' of a human being, his bones, or even to keep the entire body 'alive' by embalming it as the ancient Egyptians learnt to do, the cremation of a corpse must have betokened the contrary: a radical and drastic break with the dead and their total destruction, effected by burning the 'soul' inherent in their very bones.

It could be surmised that the people of the time regarded this as a means of freeing themselves from the magical and malevolent influences of the dead whom they had now come to fear. It might equally be conjectured that a more spiritual conception of life after death had prompted the idea of discarding the earthly body altogether – though this would probably be a back-projection of today's ideas into the past.

There is much evidence to suggest, however, that this change in burial customs was expressive of quite another attitude, and that this, in turn, was based on external conditions.

We have tacitly assumed until now that the dead were always buried in a dwelling or sham dwelling. In the case of a nomadic or pastoral tribe, however, this assumption lapses. Why should nomadic tribes have built permanent abodes for the dead when they had none themselves? Why sever their ties with the dead by burying them and moving on? For nomads, cremation and the retention of ashes was the sole means of taking the dead on their travels. Their wish to preserve clan unity with the dead was the same, therefore. All that had changed was their attitude towards the 'soul'.

What does this imply? Among Semitic peoples, bones were regarded as the enduring part of a human being. Ideas of this nature were resistant to change, even in an increasingly settled community, so cremation might indicate that supremacy had passed to another race from another cultural domain where different attitudes prevailed.

In fact, the transition in Anatolia from inhumation to cremation coincides precisely with the period at which we can detect an influx of new and undoubtedly non-Semitic tribes. Near Hattusa, the future Hittite capital, inhumation and cremation were practised side by side.

As far as we can tell from the discoveries made so far, cremation took some time to become established. It did not attain major importance in Hungary until the Bronze Age. The Late Bronze Age produced a widespread Urnfield culture which linked a group of interrelated European cultures from early in the second millennium BC. Having become diffused in Eastern Central Europe from the thirteenth century BC onwards, the practice of urn-burial spread westwards and northwards. There is evidence of urn-burial and its characteristic pottery west of the Rhine by the eleventh century, and by 750 BC it had reached southern France. Cremation also took root in the Mediterranean area between the eleventh and ninth centuries, and was customary among the Greeks and Romans by the beginning of the Iron Age.

Cremation was not superseded by inhumation until the advent of Christianity, which itself derived from the Semitic culture-province.

So types of association with the dead help us to make inferences about changing cultures and cultural areas, though the idea that the dead enjoy some form of after-life is common to them all. Even in the case of urn-burials, people continued to present the dead with funerary gifts.

This was not necessarily linked with a belief in resurrection in the Christian sense. The concept of resurrection was alien to Judaism, for example, even though it was being debated and championed by individuals at the time of Jesus.

We should therefore beware of applying our own criteria to the burial customs of prehistoric man and his relationship with the dead. What matters is to grasp the close links that have always existed between death-cult, culture and religion. That is why we find birth and death equally represented in the cult-rooms of Çatal Hüyük.

Gods of the Stone Age

The close relationship of magic and 'art' is not discernible in Çatal Hüyük's wall-paintings alone, even though their uniqueness cannot be too often stressed. When Mellaart began to excavate the town, he soon unearthed figures of baked clay, soapstone or carved stalactite like those familiar to him from other prehistoric sites. They were exuberant female figures of the type which art historians somewhat ironically call 'Venus of . . .' after the places where they are found. Actually, the term Venus is misleading because the intention was to convey fertility rather than feminine pulchritude.

The statuettes were not portraits, still less Stone Age pin-ups, but had a magical function. By exaggerating parts of the body like breasts, hips and genitals, people hoped in some magical way to induce fertility. A woman who looked at such a figure would believe herself fecund in consequence. Underlying this was the idea of magical participation: because a fertility-symbol not only *displayed* what it represented but, like an icon, actually *was* it, the beholder believed in the possibility of its transmission to his or her person. The same idea persists to this day, as when superstitious people advise a pregnant woman not to look at certain objects in case the 'shock' is transmitted to her unborn child.

Like an amulet, however, this type of magic effigy works independently of the beholder. Mellaart found one statuette of a parturient woman in a grain bin, where its obvious function was to increase the harvest by means of sympathetic magic (the beneficent counterpart of anathema or bewitchment).

We do not know if such statuettes were already regarded as independent deities with names of their own, or whether they merely symbolized their characteristic effects. If they were only intended to stress and symbolize fertility, one statuette would have been interchangeable with another.

What is certain is that these fertility-symbols evolved, as time went by, into various deities with clearly differentiated functions. In Greece, for example, the effigy of the fecund woman developed into the goddess Ge or Gaea, who survives in our own parlance as 'Mother Earth' because the earth in its fertility brings forth all that mankind requires for life. Where the idea of feminine youth and beauty was uppermost, she became Aphrodite or Venus. Where emphasis was laid on fertility in general and the fertility of grain in particular, the mother-goddess or corn-mother became known as Demeter (Latin: Ceres).

There was also a need to unite the concepts of motherhood and maidenhood in the twin figures of the 'two mistresses'. Greek texts found at Knossos tell of this 'Great Goddess' or 'Cybele', and an ivory sculpture of her was unearthed at Mycenae. But a similar idea seems already to have existed at Çatal Hüyük, which yielded the strange figure of a goddess with two heads and two pairs of breasts but only one pair of arms. It is probably fair to assume, therefore, that this figure represents a precursor of the Cybele of later times.

Interestingly enough, these statuettes exemplify yet another development, namely the transition from patriarchy to matriarchy. And this proves, among other things, that religious ideas are additionally dependent on social and economic conditions.

Up to Level IV, or as late as *ca.* 5900 BC, male effigies are found alongside female, though in far fewer numbers: eight gods as opposed to 33 representations of female deities. The figures found after this period are exclusively female, in other words, mother-goddesses.

Rather belatedly, this change reflects a transformation whose acquaintance we have already made: the Neolithic Revolution during which men ceased to be nomads and hunters and became settled farmers. In the hunters' societies of the Palaeolithic and Mesolithic periods, a community's survival and prosperity depended on the courage and stamina of the men who had to hunt their quarry. Consequently, man was the symbol of survival. As soon as our ancestors began to domesticate animals and sow grain, woman's social importance increased while that of man, now a mere tiller of the soil and feller of wood, declined. There was an obvious analogy between seed-time and harvest, conception and childbirth. Fertility in women corresponded to the fertility of beasts and soil.

Cult-figures, too, are expressive of this change. Anatolian Stone Age sites slightly younger than Çatal Hüyük, e.g. Hacilar, have yielded no male statuettes at all: matriarchy had established itself and led to the supremacy of female deities.

Greek mythology taught that it was no god but the primeval mother-goddess Gaea who sprang from Chaos and, without the aid of a male partner, gave birth to Uranus, Orea and Pontus (sky, mountain, sea), whereas the Bible is based on a patriarchal conception of the world and speaks of a male god creating man before woman.

Male deities not only recurred at a later stage but regained their dominant status. This derived from the next sociological change, which rendered the pantheon an even closer reflection of conditions on earth. The rule of the strongest having been superseded by the permanent rule of a king who controlled the destinies of an entire community, it was only logical that gods and goddesses should be assigned a supreme ruler of their own, be it Zeus, Wotan or Marduk.

At Çatal Hüyük this development had yet to take place. Discounting the female deities that occur not only as sculptures between 1·2 and 7·8 ins high but as large plaster bas-reliefs representing pregnant or parturient figures, one's dominant impression is of quite another cult: the bull-cult.

Although not peculiar to Çatal Hüyük, this bull-cult is probably the earliest example of a cult which survived longer (at least 7000 years) and became more widely diffused (from India to Northern Europe) than any other form of religious worship. The Zeus who abducted Europa in the guise of a bull, the Golden Calf of the Bible, the worship of the (horned) sacred cows of India, the horned helmets of the ancient Germans – all these are manifestations of a cult as familiar to Egypt as to Minoan Crete, whose bull-man ruled the Labyrinth of Knossos.

The bull-cult also formed a link between proto-Hattian Anatolia and the Hittite Empire, so we shall meet it again in due course.

Where Stone Age Çatal Hüyük is concerned, the comparatively recent level termed IIIA yielded a picture of a large bull more than six feet high. It bears a stylistic resemblance to other Stone Age paintings of the hunting-magic type, but the portrayal of a bull or stag did not yet constitute an act of worship.

Different standards apply to the numerous bull-symbols found at Çatal Hüyük, of which only a few examples can be mentioned here. Two forms of bull-symbolism can be distinguished. In most cases the entire head of a bull was modelled in clay and adorned with real horns. Heads of this type were frequently embedded in the wall in superimposed rows, rather like sportsmen's trophies. Some of the heads were painted with geometrical patterns, others had coloured hand-prints over their muzzles.

The second form of representation dispensed entirely with a portrayal of the beast and became abstract. In such cases, horns were let into pillars. These were sometimes extended to form a bench stuck with as many as seven pairs of horns.

That these were not mere collections of hunting trophies representing so-and-so-many beasts killed becomes apparent from other cult-rooms where bulls' heads form only a proportion of the appurtenances. In a cult-room in Level VII, for example, we find a huge vulture-painting in company with pictures of bulls and human skulls. Although their relationship defies our comprehension, they belong to the same religious context in just the same way as do the crucifix, host and eternal flame whose juxtaposition in a Roman Catholic church would appear arbitrary and unintelligible to a non-Christian. We can only say that the bull-cult may also be related to the death-cult.

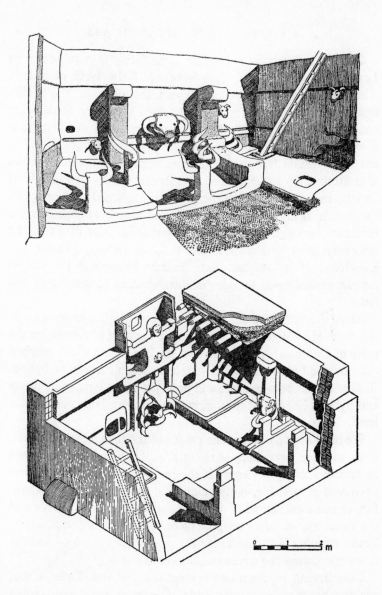

Çatal Hüyük's numerous shrines were dedicated to the bull-cult. There are many examples of modelled bulls' heads and benches set with real pairs of horns.

The female figure in relief (*below*) represents a woman giving birth to a bull. (Shrines from Level VI, *ca*.5800 BC.)

Simpler to interpret is another scene found in a cult-room in Level VIA: a symbolic representation of the birth of a bull. The mother-cow is nowhere to be seen. Instead, there is a human figure with arms and legs spread wide. We know from other bas-reliefs at Çatal Hüyük that this pose represents the attitude of a woman in childbirth. We can also deduce that the figure is not only female but pregnant from numerous other examples characterized by spherical and protuberant bellies. A bull's head appears immediately below the parturient figure. In other words, the woman is giving birth to a bull – an idea so strange that the juxtaposition might be dismissed as fortuitous were it not for the discovery of several such scenes at Çatal Hüyük, likewise our knowledge of folk-myths that illustrate how naturally ancient peoples looked upon the idea of interbreeding between man and beast.

Zeus, the father of the gods, had considerable experience in this field. He visited Leda, daughter of the king of Aetolia, in the guise of a swan, with the result that she laid an egg which hatched out into the beauteous Helen who later became queen of Sparta. Similar unions between man and beast produced strange monsters and hybrids like the Minotaur, with his human body and taurine head.

We need not take it that the people of the time knew no better. Even in those days sheep gave birth to sheep and human beings to human beings, not eggs. If the impossible was none the less portrayed as possible, it was clearly in order to convey a significance transcending what the eye beheld. To revert to Leda and the swan: the essential purpose of the story was not to illustrate Zeus's cunning but to advertise Helen's divine ancestry – and the more miraculous the circumstances the better.

Like dreams, myths translate ideas into pictures. Dreams, too, enable what is patently impossible to be experienced and – when converted into images – seen, an additional factor being that the dreamer often feels his experiences to be real.

We know from dream-analysis that these images are only

manifestations of some underlying idea. Moreover, the imagery of dreams often utilizes the same symbols as a myth and gives utterance to a pictorial language that not only construes 'left' as the contrary of 'right' but simultaneously, in a figurative sense, betokens 'un-right', or wrong. Freud consequently distinguishes between the dream-façade and the dream-idea that lies behind it.

This casts doubt on our ability to grasp the true significance of the bull-cult if we confine ourselves to describing what we see. There is a chance that it expresses something other than the idea we embrace when associating the bull with potency and assuming that its cult was a fertility-cult. We shall consider this subject in greater detail after acquainting ourselves with the bull-cult of the Hittites proper.

Still within the context of religious cults, however, we must tackle yet another controversial subject which illustrates that many archaeological inferences are based on personal interpretation, nothing more.

When Mellaart proceeded to compare the number of excavated dwellings with the number of shrines, he was disconcerted by the ratio that emerged.

Forty-eight houses were demonstrably cult-buildings which had not been used for residential purposes, and another fifteen probably belonged in the same category. As against this total of 63 cult-buildings, Mellaart found only 103 dwellings. This would mean that Çatal Hüyük had rather more than one 'temple' to every two dwellings, as Mellaart somewhat tentatively points out.

Even if we compare the number of positively identified shrines with that of dwellings and putative cult-buildings combined, the ratio of 48 to 118 is singular enough. Are we really to assume that the people of Çatal Hüyük built what was, by their standards, a large town of which only half was used for residential purposes? Or was this concentration of cult-buildings merely a sign that Mellaart, as he eventually came to believe, had stumbled on the priests' quarter of the town?

On the other hand, if the ratio of 103 dwellings to 63 cult-buildings was really correct, had Çatal Hüyük ever been intended for habitation? Was it, after all, a necropolis like Lepenski Vir?

Again, perhaps we are simply mistaken about the cult-buildings and see temples where none exist. After all, the fact that some Roman Catholic and Orthodox believers keep a crucifix and other devotional aids in one corner of their living-room would not prompt an initiate to conclude that the entire premises were consecrated and divorced from everyday life.

The problem is that all the houses at Çatal Hüyük were built and appointed along the same lines. Even the rooms believed by Mellaart to be places of worship differ in no respect from the living-rooms. The cult-rooms, too, have mud beds arranged cornerwise, a hearth and ladder on the south side, and doors leading to storage chambers. Like the cult-rooms, the living-rooms were adorned with wall-paintings and, though more rarely, bulls' horns. The fireplace was used in cult-rooms and living-rooms alike. Remains of grain, egg-shells and children's toys came to light in cult-rooms, none of which was equipped for sacrifice. There were no altars or tables for the bleeding of animal sacrifices like those found at other early sites, e.g. Beycesultan, nor were there any pits for sacrificial blood or bones. Finally, how could sacrificial beasts have been transported across the roofs at all, given Çatal Hüyük's architectural peculiarities?

All this seems to conflict with the idea of special cult-rooms. Evidence in favour can only be inferred from additional fixtures and fittings. For instance, the wall-paintings in the putative cult-rooms display unusually careful workmanship. We also find plaster reliefs and bulls' horns let into the benches in such a way that they substantially encroach on the available space. Not only do the putative places of worship contain more cult-statues than other rooms, but it seems typical of them that votive figures were embedded in the walls and human skulls stood on pillars or lay beneath paintings of bulls. 'All these features do not occur in normal houses,' writes Mellaart, 'and the combination of several of them leaves one in little doubt that the building in which they are found was used as a cult room or shrine.'

He sees an additional pointer in the fact that of eleven so-called 'red-ochre burials' (in which the bones were painted red for religious reasons), six were found in buildings definitely identified as cult-rooms and three in very badly damaged buildings whose fragmentary reliefs suggested that they had served a similar purpose. On the other hand, not a single red-ochre burial was found in any of the straightforward dwellings.

Conclusions could also be drawn from a variety of grave-gifts. Obsidian mirrors associated with female burials were found mainly in cult-rooms, for instance, and male grave-gifts of polished bone belt-fasteners exclusively in 'shrines'.

Unless we are prepared to assume that the appointment of rooms and quality of grave-goods accorded with the social status and wealth of the individual, there really are indications that the cult-rooms were, if nothing else, 'special' rooms. But why, in that case, were the dead buried in dwellings as well as shrines?

Oswald Spengler postulated in his *Decline of the West* that the palace of Knossos had been a necropolis inhabited only by those who were connected with the death-cult. In 1972 the geologist H. G. Wunderlich revived this theory and strove to reinforce it with some extremely plausible arguments.

The Danubian Stone Age settlement of Lepenski Vir was clearly a necropolis too, not a residential town.

If this assumption is correct, the striking concentration of cult-rooms and shrines at Çatal Hüyük would seem to suggest that we are confronted by yet another Stone Age necropolis.

Another solution was recently advanced by two experts from Berlin. Ernst Heinrich, who for years directed the German excavations at Uruk-Warka and is now back in Syria as head of the Deutsche Orientgesellschaft's team there, and Ursula Seidl, a staff member of the Deutsches Archäologisches Institut, have theorized that the cult-rooms or shrines at Çatal Hüyük used to be isolated 'residential nuclei'. Ordinary houses were then constructed around these ancestral homes until they merged to form a town. Out of respect for them, and because ancestor-worship had been practised there longest of all, the inhabitants of Çatal Hüyük gradually developed these ancestral homes into clan cult-centres which ultimately became temples and cult-centres for the entire community.

Plausible as the idea of clan shrines is – and it would certainly account for their number – one remains unconvinced by the theory that separate architectural nuclei could coalesce until they formed an urban centre as orderly and well-defined as Çatal Hüyük. One also wonders how ordinary dwellings could have merged in this way if the shrines already stood cheek by jowl. If the latter were really so jammed together, Çatal Hüyük would have become uninhabitable.

But the people of the Stone Age may not have shared our conception of the word 'shrine'. In a world where every tree, every stream and stone was thought of as animate, the distinction between sacred and profane may not have existed. Just as the dead were buried in dwellings, so the living may have dwelt in shrines. Çatal Hüyük was still a long way removed from the notion of a holy-of-holies inaccessible to all but a select few.

We have obviously reached another block: we know that Çatal Hüyük had a death-cult and that its people worshipped fertility-goddesses and the bull, but we do not know how this came about.

Even if Çatal Hüyük was inhabited by the dead, not the living, this is no reason to dismiss all that has been said about life in the Stone Age. Since necropolises were always modelled on the abodes of the living in order to deceive the dead, it does not ultimately matter whether we are describing a necropolis or a residential town: all the discoveries made there – whether paintings or shrines, tools or grave-goods – are products of the living.

We should not, therefore, be disheartened by conflicts between archaeological findings and learned theories. Much has been established beyond doubt, and it is amazing to reflect how much we already know about a mud-brick town built more than 8000 years ago in the Stone Age. Çatal Hüyük has supplied us with more information about contemporary life than many a grandiose edifice of the historical period.

The stone trail

In about 5600 BC, after existing for more than a thousand years, Çatal Hüyük was suddenly abandoned. We do not know why. The Stone Age town may have been devastated by fire. On the other hand, its lack of streets and agglomeration of graves and shrines may have rendered it too antiquated and inconvenient.

But Çatal Hüyük did not die yet. It acquired a new lease of life on the hill across the river. Seven hundred years later this town, known to avoid confusion as Çatal Hüyük West, was likewise abandoned. So far, no conclusive signs of violence or deliberate destruction have been found.

With that, the history of the town came to an end. Oblivion shrouded the site for almost 7000 years, from *ca.* 4900 BC to our own day, when it yielded up its relics of a time long past.

But Çatal Hüyük is not the only archaeological site in the Anatolian Plateau to have provided information about life in the outgoing Stone Age, or Chalcolithic period.

Thanks to an almost unbroken series of chronologically connected or overlapping finds, archaeologists have been able to span the great gap between Çatal Hüyük's extinction and the Indo-European settlement of Anatolia, which gave birth to the Hittite Empire.

Dozens of sites scattered across Anatolia from Troy to Ararat enable us to trace the diffusion and development of that which Çatal Hüyük represents in embryonic form.

I shall naturally refrain from listing these excavations in full. A detailed list would be of interest to the archaeologist alone, so our own will confine itself to those sites that exemplify the transition from the Chalcolithic to the Bronze Age. Anyone in search of a comprehensive survey should consult U. B. Alkim's volume *Anatolia I* in the *Archaeologica Mundi* series, which forms the basis of what follows.

Chronological Table of Prehistory and Early History (after Alkim)

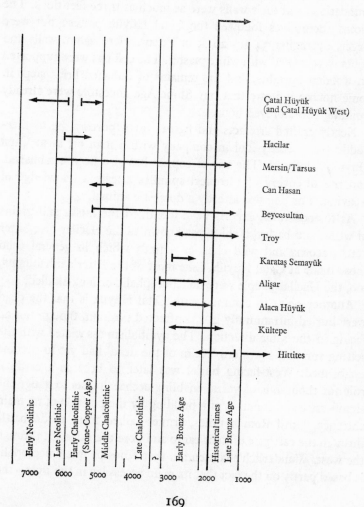

Çatal Hüyük
(and Çatal Hüyük West)

Hacilar

Mersin/Tarsus

Can Hasan

Beycesultan

Troy

Karataş Semayük

Alişar

Alaca Hüyük

Kültepe

Hittites

Early Neolithic

Late Neolithic

Early Chalcolithic
(Stone-Copper Age)

Middle Chalcolithic

Late Chalcolithic

Early Bronze Age

Historical times

Late Bronze Age

7000   6000   5000   4000   3000   2000   1000

Contemporaneous with Çatal Hüyük West but nearly 150 miles away, Hacilar (*ca.* 5700–5000 BC) is almost a repetition of what we already know. This confirms that Çatal Hüyük was no exception but a 'typical Stone Age town'.

Fifteen miles south-west of Burdur at the western end of Lake Burdur in the Anatolian Plateau, Hacilar had the same mud-brick houses standing wall to wall, though these buildings had stone foundations and their walls were as much as three feet thick. The rooms themselves followed the Çatal Hüyük pattern but were larger, averaging 34 ft×20 ft in extent. Here again, walls and floors were coated with white plaster. The ceilings were supported on wooden uprights, and the remains of unbaked brick steps in some houses indicate that our Stone Age ancestors were already building two-storeyed houses.

Neatly crafted artefacts and figures often portray the mother-goddess or fertility-idol in company with a man or, as at Çatal Hüyük, a leopard. The use of copper has also been established, and the discovery of biconical spindles attests a knowledge of weaving. The dog was already a domestic animal.

As to foodstuffs, experts have identified the husks and grains of wheat and barley, a chick-pea known as the Hacilar pea, bitter vetch, acorns and wild cherries – finds which in general echo those made at Çatal Hüyük. Like most of the latter's inhabitants, too, the Hacilar people were dolichocephalic or long-skulled.

Another point in common with Çatal Hüyük is that the dead were buried intramurally in a contracted position, though not all facing in the same direction. The symbolism associated with the setting sun and a western 'realm of the dead' had yet to become established. West-facing burial was later to become a cardinal rule for thousands of years, enabling archaeologists to gauge the significance and function of a building by the position of its main entrance. Until Roman times, armies sallied forth to do battle through the east gate of their camp and bore their dead in through the west. Wunderlich's contention that Knossos was a necropolis is based partly on the fact that its main access lay in the west – the entrance of the dead.

In about 5000 BC Hacilar was burnt, devastated and abandoned, probably as a result of invasion. It was not excavated until 1957–60, once again by James Mellaart.

The excavation of ancient Mersin (known as Yümük Tepe and fifteen miles west of the modern town of Mersin) and the neighbouring site of Tarsus had been started 20 years earlier. Eighty feet high and more than 30 building-levels deep, the hill failed to yield any architectural relics of the earliest period. However, potsherds and articles of earthenware did betray definite links with Stone Age Çatal Hüyük and Can Hasan although Mersin and Tarsus were situated south of the Cilician Gates beside the Mediterranean. It was also possible to demonstrate connections with the north Syrian cultures of Ras Shamra and Byblos – yet another sign that commercial ties existed between Anatolia and the Mediterranean area. Mersin acquired its first perimeter wall in the middle of the fifth millennium but was abandoned as a major site ca. 3200 BC and not reinhabited on a large scale until the Middle Bronze Age, or ca. 2000.

Finds made at Tarsus become more interesting during the latter part of the Bronze Age, when the city, which was fortified ca. 2500 BC, served as the capital of a local kingdom.

Tarsus (Turkish: Gözlükule), the birthplace of St Paul, enables us to trace the three phases of the Early Bronze Age with such precision that an exact chronology can be deduced. Of great assistance in this respect were some imported pieces from an Egyptian tomb of the 4th Dynasty found in company with Cilician earthenware vessels. Other phases could be dated by means of finds from Mesopotamia and Cyprus or small bottles of characteristic design from Syria. Cilicia was thus in contact with northern Mesopotamia, Syria and – directly or indirectly – Egypt, a fact increasingly reflected by commercial links encompassing the whole of Anatolia.

Can Hasan, inhabited ca. 5000–4500 BC and situated just over 40 miles south-east of Çatal Hüyük as the crow flies, has also yielded ceramics indicative of connections not only with Syria but with Çatal Hüyük West and Mersin as well. Its architecture likewise echoes that of Çatal Hüyük. The rectangular houses follow exactly the same mode of construction, and many of them had two storeys. As at Çatal Hüyük, the walls were timber-framed and adorned with geometrical patterns. Can Hasan derives special importance from the very early pieces of worked copper found there.

Little more advanced than Çatal Hüyük, the above settlements display most affinities with the east Mediterranean area. Beycesultan, which was inhabited from *ca.* 4800 BC onwards and is therefore in the same chronological bracket, exhibits some quite different features attributable mainly to its geographical position.

Beycesultan is situated in western Turkey near the source of the Büyük Menderes (Maeander), some 35 miles south-west of Afyonkarahisar. The excavations carried out there are of the greatest interest because they disclose surprising links with the Greek world, including Crete.

Beycesultan's Late Chalcolithic pottery is characterized by geometrical patterns and parallel lines drawn in white on a black ground. These are found not only at Mersin and Can Hasan but at Poliochni on the island of Lemnos, and their contemporaneity suggests a dating of fifth-fourth millennium BC. However, finds matching the Late Chalcolithic pottery of Beycesultan have also come to light on the Cycladean islands of Samos and Cos and in Thrace and Macedonia.

Little is known about Beycesultan's architecture because the excavations do not cover a wide enough area, but the walls were also of mud brick braced and supported with balks of timber.

Particular importance attaches to the metal artefacts unearthed in the Chalcolithic levels, the most valuable finds being various copper tools, a silver ring, and the oldest metal dagger so far discovered in Anatolia. Two burins and three needles attest the quality of Beycesultan's metalwork.

In the Early Bronze Age, or *ca.* 3000 BC, Beycesultan introduced some characteristic developments of the Çatal Hüyük culture. In place of numerous clan shrines, communal cult-rooms seem to have been established for the celebration of local religious rites – premises which some archaeologists have identified as temple complexes.

The interior of these sacred chambers was furnished with an altar and two terracotta slabs situated at fixed intervals. Sunk in the ground behind each of these slabs were recesses designed to hold sacrificial drinking-vessels and receive libations of wine. In front of them, pairs of horns had been erected. Remains of matting beyond the raised altar-slabs suggested that the chamber could be partitioned into a profane area and an inner sanctum. Although the bull-cult is an obvious reminder of Çatal Hüyük, the latter betrays no signs of this definite trend towards the establishment of shrines in the formal sense. The crucial point, however, is that Beycesultan has obvious affinities with Crete, where the bull-cult clearly existed at this period, complete with bulls' horns and double-axes. Together with some flat violin-shaped stone idols, likewise typical of Crete, this seems to prove that Anatolia exerted an influence on Cretan culture. For instance, the ground-plan of the palace at Beycesultan is reminiscent of the Minoan palace of Mallia in Crete.

Professor Bahadir Alkim of Istanbul University believes that Beycesultan was a staging-post between the Aegean world and Asia Minor proper, especially as the existence of links with Troy and the Balkan area can also be demonstrated.

Another link with Cretan culture was found during the excavation of Karataş Semayük, some four miles east of Elmali-Antalya in Lycia. Not far from this settlement, which was particularly densely inhabited during the Early Bronze Age, archaeologists found a necropolis in which the dead were buried in a contracted position in pithoi, or large storage-jars, often as many as six skeletons to a single vessel. Scratched on these large urns were shapes such as swastikas, goats and shrubs, but also a motif reminiscent of a pagoda-like ideogram on the Cretan Phaistos Disk.

According to Alkim, this find is just as corroborative of 'the theory of the Phaistos Disk's Anatolian provenance' as the examples already mentioned, including the Anatolian timber-framing which is also found in Knossos.

Sir Arthur Evans, the excavator of Knossos, did in fact state, as early as 1921, that the Neolithic culture of Crete must have had its roots in Anatolia. He also held that the bull-cult, too, implied a link with Asia Minor and added that the name of the Taurus Mountains itself pointed in that direction. (The Greek word *tauros*, Latin *taurus*, means 'bull'.)

In addition to links with other cultures, however, a process of internal development can be observed. To quote only two of the 25 or more archaeological sites in central and eastern Anatolia, Alişar and Kara Hüyük betray definite signs of such a transition.

Alişar, situated about half-way between Kayseri and Boğazköy in the bend of the Halys, was inhabited from *ca.* 3200 BC, in the Early Bronze Age, until the Hittite period. Enclosed by a perimeter wall, Alişar presents the excavator with a typical example of the fortified towns of the Early Bronze Age. Trojan influences are evident, as are contacts with northern Syria – or, at least, a so-called 'Syrian bottle' was found, though this had been made in a native workshop. The idols of baked clay or stone either conform to the Cretan violin shape or resemble flat round disks. One new feature is that the dead were buried in a variety of ways, some in pithoi and others in cist-graves or in the ground inside the town.

We find the same lack of uniformity at Kara Hüyük, which lies about five miles south of Konya and was inhabited *ca.* 2800–1800 BC. The dead were still buried inside the town, but sometimes in cist-graves and sometimes head-downwards in pithoi. Different traditions seem to be competing here. This was a transitional period whose effects can also be discerned in the field of craftsmanship. At Alişar, hand-modelled and wheel-made ceramics are found side by side.

Quite suddenly, in the period 2300–2100 BC, this gradual 2000-year process of development assumed a fixed and characteristic shape which heralded yet another cultural phase.

One example of this can be found in the excavations at Alaca Hüyük, just over 20 miles in a straight line north-east of Boğazköy.

Inhabited from 3000 to *ca.* 1200 BC, Alaca Hüyük used *ca.* 2300 to be the centre of a rich and powerful kingdom whose gold and silver relics put Schliemann's 'Treasury of Priam' in the shade.

In thirteen royal graves excavated there between 1935 and 1948, the Turkish archaeologists R. O. Arik and Hamit Koşay discovered skilfully fashioned articles of gold, silver and electron (a gold-and-silver alloy), also bronze and terrestrial iron. Dating from 2300–2100 BC, they provided evidence of a quite new stage in cultural development. After a period of stereotyped repetition and reciprocal influence, and despite the retention of traditional motifs, an individual style seems to have evolved.

The first objects to be found, 20 ft down in shaft-graves, were some peculiar 'standards' composed of ornate lattice-work or, in many cases, portraying bulls and stags. The bull was evidently the symbol of the male deity (the later Hittite Weather-god) and the stag that of the 'Great Goddess' whom we rediscover among the Hittites as the 'Sun-goddess of Arinna'.

We now sense that, in addition to their magical significance, these cult-symbols aimed at aesthetic effect, and that the gold diadems and brooches had a purely ornamental function. Moreover, human and animal figures are equipped with strongly emphasized sexual organs like those found in figures from other sites, whereas none of the Çatal Hüyük cult-effigies – not even the fertility-idols – display any at all.

Artistic development and a changed attitude towards sexuality apart, Alaca Hüyük differs from earlier sites in a third respect: the dead were buried outside the town as well as inside. The thirteen royal graves were situated outside the residential quarters. What is more, all the dead were lying in a contracted position on their right side, heads pointing westwards in the direction of death and the setting sun.

Shaft-graves like those at Alaca Hüyük, similar both in size and mode of construction, had been found by Schliemann at Mycenae, though there the dead were no longer buried in a contracted position. Apart from this further link with the Cretan-Mycenaean cultural area, however, there is a pointer in the opposite direction: Caucasian royal graves, too, bear a striking resemblance to those of Alaca Hüyük and Mycenae. Nearly 100 miles north-east of Boğazköy, Horoztepe yielded cult-standards of a somewhat later date but similar to the Alaca Hüyük finds, the only difference being that they were more closely related to Caucasian examples than to Anatolian. How we should interpret this affinity to the Caucasian culture-area remains an open question. It is possible that ties of kinship existed between the inhabitants of Anatolia and the Caucasus: after all, some authorities hold that the Indo-European Hittites, too, were migrants from that area.

Had Caucasian tribes really migrated to Anatolia before the Hittites? We do not know, just as we have no precise idea when the Indo-European Hittites themselves arrived, but it has recently been conjectured that they were already living in Anatolia at this period. This would have given them several centuries in which to assimilate the existing Anatolian culture and adapt themselves to its ways before founding an empire.

One example of this process is Kültepe, the last link in the chain that extends from Stone Age Çatal Hüyük to the Hittites.

Kültepe or 'ash-hill', lies about eleven miles north of Kayseri in the eastern part of central Anatolia. A distinction must be drawn between Kültepe Hüyük (the residential and administrative district of the local prince) and the bazaar of Kültepe in the plain north-west of it, where Assyrian merchants once settled with some of the indigenous inhabitants. The Assyrian word for bazaar being *karum*, the place is also known as Kültepe Karum, or, to use the town's original name, Karum Kanesh.

Friedrich Hrozný carried out a brief preliminary excavation

here in 1925, and his work has been continued from 1948 onwards by the Turkish Historical Society.

We now enter the so-called 'historical' period because Kültepe is the source of Anatolia's earliest-known written records, kept in a script which the Anatolians had not invented but adopted from the said Assyrian merchants.

Regular visitors to Anatolia from *ca.* 2500 BC onwards, these merchants founded trading settlements over the years (the conventional term 'colony' is misleading in this context). We know the names of ten such commercial centres in Anatolia, though eight of them have yet to be located. Bazaars of this type have only been identified at Boğazköy and Kültepe, of which the latter appears to have been a commercial headquarters.

The cuneiform tablets found at Kültepe are straightforward business records – receipts, contracts and promissory notes typified by the following extract: 'Two sacks one-and-a-half pitchers, half of wheat, half of barley, and three-and-two-thirds shekels of corn silver are owed to Addad by Hasuman, Tarhula and Subunahsu. The wheat and barley they will restore next harvest-time, the silver they shall pay next seed-time. Habuala and his wife Burka are sureties.'

The 'Kültepe tablets' (also called the 'Cappadocian tablets' because they became known by that name as long ago as 1881) also deal occasionally with marriage and divorce settlements and hereditary rights, but seldom with historical events. They do, however, teach us a great deal about commerce in the Early Bronze Age.

Although Kanesh/Kültepe and Assur were separated by over 600 miles of steppe and mountain passes, commercial activity was brisk. The establishment of regular trade routes plied by donkey-trains enabled Anatolia to export precious stones, livestock, copper, silver and gold in exchange for imports of luxury articles and the alloys required for bronze manufacture.

Gold and silver served as currency, their ratio of value being 1:8. Copper of good quality fetched up to 1/70th of its weight in silver, poor copper as little as 1/200th. One metal – 'amutum' – was 40 times as valuable as silver. It must have been iron, a substance of supreme rarity more than fifteen generations before the Iron Age.

The Assyrian merchants made a good living. Profits of 100 per cent or more were standard, and money was often lent at more than the customary rate of interest (30 per cent). Local rulers shared in these business dealings. They levied taxes and had first option on all imported goods. In return, they had to guarantee the security of the trade routes.

Kültepe in the second millennium BC also reveals that the Assyrians introduced certain Mesopotamian and north Syrian features which merged and mingled with the indigenous culture.

The Indo-Europeans who migrated to Anatolia at about this period or earlier had only to adopt all these cultural assets, which ranged from ceramics of considerable variety and perfection to cylinder-seals and a Stone Age pantheon that had developed under Mesopotamian influence. We thus rediscover at Kültepe proto-types of certain Hittite gods, e.g. the Weather-god driving a chariot drawn by a bull, the tutelary god of the fields, star symbols, and the Mother-goddess.

Some time after the year 2000, Kültepe was devastated by fire. Deposits of soil over six feet deep indicate that a long while elapsed before Kültepe was reinhabited. According to its excavators, the site remained deserted for over 50 years.

The new settlement of 1800–1700 BC abruptly introduces us to a new culture containing elements alien to Anatolian art – small lead figures, for instance, and the moulds in which they were cast.

But the crucial discovery was made at Kültepe Hüyük, identi-fied as the 'palace of the king of Kanesh'. On the floor of a room in another palace near by, archaeologists found a bronze spearhead bearing the following cuneiform inscription in Akkadian: 'Palace of Anitta, the king.'

Anitta, king of Kussara, was already known from other texts. These represented him as the ruler of a city-state, but Anitta was more than that: apart from being the author of the earliest-known

Hittite text, he was the Hittites' first monarch and probably the son of the man who had destroyed and burnt Kültepe 50 years earlier.

The new rulers of Anatolia had made their entrance. No thunderclap heralded the dawn of the Hittite Empire: it came into being quite unobtrusively – almost imperceptibly. What had begun was no absolute novelty but a new thing born of an old.

'The so-called "Hittite" culture of the second millennium BC represents not an end-product but a beginning,' writes Jean Marcadé, Professor of Archaeology at Bordeaux University. 'It should not be construed as a brilliant heritage adopted by Anatolia from Indo-European tribes that did not reach Asia Minor until a late stage. It may prove to have derived from the regional cultures which had arisen in this country long before, and which, enriched by alien influences but stimulated more by reciprocal contacts, had given the spirit of Anatolia its characteristic impress.'

Only now, after our long round trip to the Stone Age, can the story of the Hittites be told – a story requiring as much research after thousands of years of oblivion as the impressive Neolithic town to which most of the foregoing section has been devoted.

V THE ASCENT

A curse on Hattusa

No one can say when the Indo-European tribes we call Hittites migrated to Asia Minor. We only know that, once there, they began *ca.* 1750 BC to subdue their neighbours and seize the reins of power.

One thing is certain: they did not suddenly and unexpectedly burst into Anatolia from elsewhere. No cohorts of savage horsemen ranged the countryside, no armies tramped through towns and villages, pillaging and setting them ablaze, no barbarians swooped on native cultures and destroyed them, raping the womenfolk and killing the men. None of the stereotyped ideas about invasion by hordes of land-hungry tribesmen apply in this case.

The settlement process cannot, of course, have been entirely peaceful. The proto-Hattians would not have surrendered their land and possessions voluntarily – who would? – but the steady and almost uninterrupted development of the indigenous population makes it likely that Anatolia underwent gradual settlement rather than conquest.

Archaeological discoveries confirm this impression. At Karum Kanesh, Hittite ceramics were unearthed in a level dating from the year 2000, and the 'Kültepe tablets' found there already allude as a matter of course to personal names of Indo-European origin. This implies that Indo-European tribes must have settled in Anatolia at least 250–300 years prior to the founding of the Hittite Empire.

They did not come as rulers: they became such after absorbing the advanced culture of Anatolia for generations, after modifying it and fusing it with their own characteristics to such an extent that they ended by calling themselves after their Hattian subjects and adopting their gods as well.

By 1800 BC the Indo-European settlers, who may best be conceived of as nomads, had borrowed and learnt so much from the proto-Hattians that they began to assert their military strength and establish strongholds of their own. They were aided in this by ceaseless feuds between the proto-Hattian princes, who were for ever invading their neighbours' domains in quest of plunder and power.

This is exemplified by a letter from Prince Anumhirbi of Mama to Prince Warsama of Kanesh in which he complains bitterly that 'the Man of Taisama' has invaded his territory, destroyed twelve towns and driven off cattle and sheep. The Man of Taisama being the 'dog' (vassal) of Prince Warsama, Anumhirbi chides him as follows: 'You wrote to me thus: The [Man] of Taisama is my slave, I shall pacify him . . . Since the [Man] of Taisama is a [dog], why does he act thus [high-handedly] against other rulers? The [Man] of Sibuha [is] my [dog]; does he, pray, act [high-handedly] against other rulers? Is the Prince of Taisama to become the third prince among us?' (The words in square brackets, both here and in the quotations that follow, are translator's amplifications designed to aid the reader's comprehension of texts notable for their extremely compressed style.)

The fact that the Hittites behaved just like the Man of Taisama is apparent from the earliest of their historical accounts, a text composed by the King Anitta whose bronze spearhead was found at Kanesh/Kültepe.

Like all texts of this period, it opens with the author's name, lineage and title followed by a request that it be read aloud to the unlettered.

'Anitta, son of Pithana, King of Kussara. Speak: It was pleasing to the Weather-god of Heaven. And, since it was pleasing to the Weather-god, the King of Nesa fell captive to the King of Kussara. The King of Kussara came down out of the town with a great host and took the town of Nesa by storm during the night. He seized the King of Nesa but did no harm to any of the inhabitants of Nesa, treating [them] like mothers [and] fathers.'

Anitta goes on to enumerate a whole series of battles and

conquests, after all of which he carries off vanquished rulers and effigies of the gods. 'But thereafter I, Anitta, the Great King, brought the god Siusumi of Zalpuwa back to Nesa. And Huzziya, the [present] King of Zalpuwa, I brought alive to Nesa.'

One of these campaigns presented a favourable opportunity to capture Hattusa, the town from which the Hatti took their name and which was later to become the Hittite capital.

'And famine gnawed at the city of Hattusa, so I let it be. But, when it was grievously afflicted with famine, the god Siusumi delivered it over to the god Halmasuitta, and I took it by storm in the night.'

Although he had treated the inhabitants of Nesa like 'mothers and fathers', he destroyed and cursed Hattusa for some undisclosed reason.

'But in its place I sowed weeds. Whosoever becomes king after me and peoples Hattusa once more, let him be smitten by the Weather-god of Heaven!'

It is one of the enigmas of Hittite history that, having been threatened with all manner of divine penalties, Hattusa should have been not only rebuilt about a century later but adopted as the Hittite capital. Perhaps its favourable strategic position tipped the scales. The citadel of Hattusa stood on a rocky mountain, and the town was one of the few places in the Anatolian hinterland with an abundant all-year-round supply of water.

Be that as it may, Anitta sacked Hattusa and conveyed the spoils of war to Nesa, which he enlarged and made his capital. 'And in Nesa I built the city. Behind the city I erected the house of the Weather-god of Heaven and the temple of the god Siusumi. The house of the god Halmasuitta, the house of the Weather-god, my Lord, and the house of Siusumi did I build.'

To show what far-off lands he had visited, King Anitta built something else: a small zoo containing 'two lions, seventy wild boar, three reed-hogs', and many bears, leopards and wild sheep.

Then he embarked on another campaign. 'But the following year I made war on the Prince of Salatiwara. Just as he was marching to battle, the ruler of Burushanda came to pay me homage, and he brought me a throne and sceptre of iron as a gift of allegiance.' Anitta goes on: 'But when I marched to Nesa, I took the ruler of Burushanda with me' – a polite way of saying that Burushanda remained Anitta's captive even after he had voluntarily submitted and brought him precious gifts of iron. If nothing else, this minor episode shows that Anitta had acquired sufficient power in the course of his campaigns for other princes to place themselves under his 'protection'.

Of course, all these campaigns were waged on a diminutive scale. Anitta's army consisted, as he proudly reports, of 1400 warriors and 40 chariots, but they were enough to make him the most powerful ruler in Anatolia. He and his father Pithana are therefore regarded as the founders of the Hittite royal line.

We are as ignorant of their dates as we are of the precise location of Nesa, but the inscribed spearhead found at Kültepe Hüyük, which was destroyed *ca.* 1750 BC, proves that they lived earlier than that.

We meet no further references to a Hittite king for 80 or perhaps 100 years after Anitta's conquests, and then only to another semi-legendary figure.

We do not even know the exact name of this monarch. Cuneiform texts allude to him mainly as Tabarna but often as Labarna.

Tabarna (*ca.* 1680–50) was the true founder of the Hittite royal dynasty, because the list of kings from his day until the end of the Hittite Empire is virtually complete.

It was Tabarna, too, who rebuilt the devastated city of Hattusa and made it his royal seat. Perhaps he knew nothing of the curse that hung over it, or perhaps he simply ignored it on the grounds that even gods were amenable to negotiation. At all events, he styled himself Great King and King of Hattusa and even changed his name to Hattusili, after the new capital.

To avoid confusion with subsequent kings of that name, specialized literature continues to call him Tabarna or Labarna. However, the avoidance of one confusion has automatically bred another, because Tabarna's successors adopted his name as a royal title – much as the personal name Caesar became dissociated from its original bearer and was used to convey rulership in general.

So far, I have tacitly assumed that this Tabarna was a descendant of the Hittite kings Pithana and Anitta, although no direct evidence can be adduced to span the two- or three-generation gap. However, there are two clues which make such a connection likely. One is supplied by Tabarna himself, who often assumed the cognomen 'Man of Kussara' – and Kussara was the royal seat of Pithana.

This does not, of course, prove that Tabarna was in direct line of descent from Pithana and Anitta, but the assumption is reinforced by our second clue: Anitta's royal seat continued to hold some significance for the Hittites later on, because all their sacred texts were couched in 'Nesan' and there is general agreement that this language hailed from the town of Nesa. This would put a second ligature over two place-names linking Tabarna with Pithana and Anitta. Had Tabarna merely been a foreign conqueror who had seized the city of Kussara, the Hittites would never have composed their sacred texts in the language of Anitta's royal seat.

A document written four or five generations later, the so-called Telepinu decree, tells us that Tabarna followed in the footsteps of his predecessors and extended his sphere of influence by conducting campaigns based on Hattusa, also that he installed his sons as governors of newly conquered territories. The decree puts it thus:

'Labarna was Great King in former times. Then were his sons, his brothers and his kinsmen, the people of his clan and his soldiers, united. And the country was small. But wheresoever he marched to battle, there held he the land subdued with a strong arm. He ravaged the land [ever and again]; he made it powerless . . . But, when he returned from battle, each of his sons went to some land . . . The great cities were delivered [into their hand].'

Campaigns, conquests, tidings of victory – in essence, this is all that can be said about the first three Hittite monarchs and their reigns. They remain vague and shadowy figures, half legendary and half historical. But with Hattusili, Tabarna's successor, the picture changes: Hittite history becomes identified with the career of a distinct and well-defined individual.

Hattusili's testament

The king who succeeded Tabarna of Hattusa *ca.* 1650 BC was a man who likewise called himself 'Hattusili' or 'Man of Hattusa', though he continued to bear the title Tabarna in token of his kingship.

So Tabarna Hattusili I assumed power in about 1650. It would be tedious and depressing to enumerate the series of campaigns with which the mighty of those days were preoccupied. Although many of these accounts derive a certain charm from their pious embellishments and formal language, it is distasteful when a ruler's success consists purely in his military triumphs and when chroniclers convey the impression that this is only right and proper.

Of course, no discussion of the Hittites' history can avoid references to their military campaigns and conquests. Wars are a constituent of history, but we should not be misled: formative developments in literature, art and civilization are no less important to a people, if not more significant, than its rulers' political ambitions, which all too often stifle what is human and humane.

Even in the case of Hattusili I, however, we shall see that the Hittite chroniclers did not confine themselves to recording feats of arms. We must none the less start with the account of yet another campaign. Once again, our information about Hattusili comes from the stilted and stereotyped phraseology of the Telepinu decree:

'Thereafter did Hattusili reign as king. Then were his sons, his brothers, his kinsmen, the people of his clan and his soldiers, united. But wheresoever he marched to battle, there held he the land subdued with a strong arm.'

This is, almost word for word, the same formula as that used by the Telepinu decree to describe the earlier deeds of Tabarna. And so it goes on:

'He ravaged the land ever and again; he made it powerless. But, when he returned from battle, each of his sons went to some land. The great cities were delivered into their hand.'

Then comes a sentence that disrupts the rigid pattern of these victorious tidings:

'But afterwards, when the servants of the princes turned faithless, they began to devour their houses, conspire against their masters and spill their blood.'

For a long time, these few sentences represented the sum total of our knowledge about the reign of Hattusili I. Then, exactly 50 years after Winckler's excavation of Hattusa/Boğazköy in 1907, the royal citadel at Hattusa yielded a bilingual text in Hittite and Akkadian in which Hattusili personally recounts his victories and defeats with almost pedantic precision.

We learn that the Hittite dominions in the Anatolian Plateau were now so well secured that Hattusili could afford to leave Anatolia, cross the Taurus Mountains for the first time, and push southwards.

This time the object was to reinforce the young king's prestige, not his authority. An obscure people speaking an alien tongue, the Hittites suddenly debouched on to the contemporary world stage, captured a string of cities in northern Syria and advanced as far as Alalah on the lower reaches of the Orontes, the river beside which they were later, at the zenith of their power, to put an Egyptian Pharaoh to flight.

Northern Syria and Mesopotamia were at that time the main centres of political and economic power in the Near East. Until now, conquering armies had always set off northwards over the Taurus. This time it was the Hittites who had advanced from the opposite direction – for them, a marvellous opportunity to plunder the wealth of northern Syria. Rather ingenuously, Hattusili mentions that he filled his house 'with treasures'.

Inevitably, however, the subject tribes at home in Anatolia

seized their chance and defected. Only Hattusa kept faith: 'The Great King Tabarna, beloved of the Sun-god – it set him on its lap, took his hand and ran ahead of him [in battle].'

Hattusili took two years to restore order. He was then able to march on northern Syria once more. Proudly, he reported: 'In those days he set off. Like a lion, the Great King crossed the river Pura and overcame the city of Hassu like a lion with his paw. He heaped dust upon it and filled Hattusa with its possessions. Of silver and gold there was neither beginning [nor] end . . . and their gods [divine effigies] I brought up to the Sun-goddess of Arinna.'

If the reference to gold and silver prompts us to construe this as a mere orgy of looting, it is because we find it hard to penetrate the contemporary world of ideas. 'Treasure' was not a conqueror's sole objective. Anyone who succeeded in carrying off a city's divine images acquired power over the city itself, hence an explicit reference to Hattusili's capture of a statue of the Weather-god of Haleb (modern Aleppo), the Hittites' strongest adversary in Syria. The capture of foreign gods meant that they became of service to those who had captured them.

This is why the victors conveyed them into their own temples and installed them among their native deities. The more gods they had the better: they could sacrifice to them and secure their help. What this chronicle records, therefore, is not only the king's acquisition of gold and silver but the growth of his power and authority.

Then came the campaign which altered the position at a single stroke and expunged a 700-year-old disgrace – one that the Hittites regarded as their own although it antedated their arrival in Anatolia by centuries. Seven hundred years earlier, the almost legendary King Sargon of Akkad had crossed the Euphrates and marched westwards into Anatolia. He must have inflicted a wound that had never healed. Once more filled with pride, Hattusili wrote: 'None [of my predecessors] had ever yet crossed the Euphrates. I, the Great King Tabarna, crossed it on foot, and my soldiers crossed after me [likewise] on foot. Sargon [of Akkad] had also crossed it and defeated the soldiers of Hassu.

'But he did no [harm] to the city of Hassu, cast no fire into it nor sent up smoke to the Weather-god. But I, the Great King Tabarna, defeated the king of Hassu, cast fire [into the cities] and sent up smoke to the Sun-god of Heaven and to the Weather-god. And the king of Hassu I harnessed to a cart . . .'

Conqueror's hubris, perhaps, but the Hittites' climb to great-power status had begun. Meanwhile, struggles for power had broken out at home, as the Telepinu decree implies. This time, Hattusili was opposed not by disaffected tribes but by 'his brothers, his kinsmen, the people of his clan'. Now that prestige rather than survival was at stake, conspirators had begun plotting to seize power. While Hattusili was playing the warlord far away, more than 600 miles' march from home, his kinsmen were weighing their chances. Having returned, a dying man, from his expedition across the Euphrates, which fully merits comparison with Alexander's Indian campaign, he just found time to dictate 'The tablet of Tabarna, the Great King. [Written when] Great King Tabarna fell sick at Kussara and appointed young Mursili to royal authority.'

This political testament was intended to settle accounts with his scheming kinsmen and subject principalities. Two of his sons had previously rebelled against him and had been barred from the right of succession. He thereupon designated his sister's son Tabarna and successor to the throne, but in vain, because the murmurings against him persisted. Though disappointed, Hattusili still had enough strength to order the affairs of government as he wished.

'Great King Tabarna spoke to the men of the nobility and dignitaries:

'See, I am now become ill. And I had named the young Labarna to you, that he should set himself on the throne. And I, the King, called him my son, embraced and exalted him. He has ever been my concern. But how he, the boy, comported himself was an abomination to the eyes!'

Hattusili went on to inform his nobles that young Labarna was under the influence of his mother, 'the snake', and of his brothers and sisters. He had summoned him to his bedside to talk to him. 'But he did not receive the King's will with love – how can he cherish love for Hattusa of his own just will?'

Hattusili tried every means to win Labarna over, but 'no tear did he shed, no compassion did he show – cold he is, and heartless'. So the ailing king resolved to exclude Labarna, too, from the succession. 'So I set discord against discord. Enough of it! He is my son no longer.'

Although no further reference is made to the king's nephew, the text describes his mother's reaction. 'But then his mother bellowed like an ox: You will kill him!' The king's sole rejoinder was a mild inquiry: 'Have I, the King, done him any harm? Did I not make him a priest? I have always conferred honours upon him, mindful of his welfare.'

One senses the resignation of a man who, still in control of a kingdom as he approaches his life's end, has been as disillusioned by his nephew as he was by his sons.

'Regard my son Huzziya! I, the King, had made him lord over the city of Tapassanda. The people there . . . wrought evil with him and bore enmity towards me: Rebel against your father's head! Then I, the King, deposed Huzziya.'

But Hattusili had evidently misjudged the situation, for he goes on to relate that the inhabitants of Hattusa also rose against him for fear that the throne would pass to a 'servant' instead of a king's son. Even his own daughter sided against him. She 'caused the city of Hattusa and the court to rebel', Hattusili reports, 'and the great ones and my own court nobles opposed me in open hostility.'

The result was civil war. 'Then did brother kill brother at feud, and friend kill friend. Hatti's sons died in droves. And he who still possessed an ox, a sheep, a house, a barn, a vineyard and some ploughland, his whole property, too, was ruined in consequence of the evil times.'

There is material enough for a Greek tragedy in the king's story. His sons are dead and his country is engulfed in turmoil, dissension and poverty. Then his daughter falls into his hands – the renegade daughter who is to blame for everything. He wants to punish her severely but is overcome by compassion and only banishes her.

'Then the gods gave my daughter into my hand, she that had encompassed the death of Hatti's sons. And I, the King, demanded from her all her possessions. "Were I to leave you even so much, the sons of Hatti would call me to account with their tongues."

'Then she spake thus: "You have given me up to ruin." So I, the King, gave my daughter a small portion notwithstanding.

'Then she spake thus: "Why have you given me so little?" So I, the King, said: "Little it is. But, if I gave you cattle and ploughland in abundance, I myself would drain the land of blood." '

Hattusili brings her from Hattusa to Kussara so that she can do no more mischief.

'But now she is banished from the city. As soon as she enters my house, she will overthrow my house; but, as soon as she comes to the city of Hattusa, she will cause it to rebel a second time. A house has been allotted to her in the country; now may she eat and drink . . .'

Hattusili repudiates her: 'She has called me father no longer; no longer do I call her daughter.'

Yet she remains his child for all that. 'But you must do her no ill. *She* has done ill, *I* shall not do ill in return.'

It was after this disappointment that Hattusili nominated the aforesaid son of his sister to succeed him, only to meet with a repetition of the same experience.

'His mother is a serpent. And thus shall it be: he will ever hearken to the words of his mother, his brothers and sister. And then he will draw near, draw near, to wreak vengeance. And to the vassals, dignitaries and servants who are appointed the King's men, to them will he vow: "See, for the King's sake you shall die, man for man." But for all who are Hatti's sons it will come to this: So will he draw near, draw near, to carry off ox and sheep, to whomsoever it may belong.

'I have vanquished my foes abroad with the sword and preserved my country in peace and repose. It shall not come about that he ends by plunging my country into disorder. Rather shall he never henceforth be permitted to leave the city without more ado and go where he pleases. See, I have given my son Labarna a house; much ploughland have I given him, many cattle and sheep have I given him. Now may he eat and drink. For as long as he conducts himself well, he may henceforth come up into the city. But as soon as he causes annoyance or there is any malice or commotion, he shall not come up and must abide in his house.'

With his unworthy successor-designate under house arrest, Hattusili announces his decision to the dignitaries and nobles: 'See here, Mursili is now my son. You must acknowledge him and set him on the throne. The deity has endowed his heart, too, with many gifts. Only a lion shall the deity set in the lion's stead.'

But the Mursili whom Hattusili has named his son is still young. Hattusili therefore implores the dignitaries and nobles to help him and rear him in wisdom.

'So rear him to become a hero-king. Should you take the field with him, bring him back safe.

'You who already know my words and wisdom, rear my son in wisdom for ever more. None of my family has ever yet followed my bidding. But you are my son, Mursili – do so!'

The dying king continues to address himself to Mursili direct:

'So keep your father's words. As long as you keep them, you shall eat bread and drink water.

'When the time of manhood comes upon you, eat twice or thrice a day and tend yourself well.

'But, when old age comes upon you, drink your fill. Then may you set your father's words aside.'

These quaint and Spartan dietary precepts did not, however,

exhaust the monarch's store of good advice. We learn that, more than a thousand years before classical democracy came into being in Greece, the Hittites already possessed a democratic institution in the shape of a council of nobles which limited the rights of the sovereign and was probably akin to the ancient German *Thing* or assembly – a political organ wholly alien to the East. It was the king's last wish that this institution be preserved.

'I have given you my words, and this tablet shall ever be read to you, month by month, so that you shall ever and again impress my words and my wisdom on your heart and rule graciously over my servants and the great ones.

'Should you observe an offence in someone – that he sins before the deity or utters an impious word – always consult the community of nobles. The consequences of a blasphemy, too, must be averted for the sake of the community of nobles itself.

'Whatsoever be in your heart, my son, for ever act in accordance therewith.'

One could wish that other rulers in history had crowned their careers by writing a testament so expressive of conciliation and humanity as opposed to vengeance and vainglory.

Hattusili's testament concludes with the following words:

> 'Bathe my corpse as it behoves,
> hold me to your bosom
> and against your bosom hide me in the earth.'

Last of all, the signature: 'Tablet of Tabarna, the Great King. [Written when] Great King Tabarna fell sick at Kussara and appointed young Mursili to royal authority.'

Lion succeeds lion

With Mursili on the throne, it seemed that the deity had indeed replaced one lion with another. Hattusili's fate was repeated in his adoptive son. Although Mursili completed what Hattusili had begun, his life ended on an equally tragic note.

The crown council of dignitaries and noblemen evidently succeeded after Hattusili's death in quelling the civil strife that had been kindled by the family revolt against the late king. To quote another stiff and stilted passage from the Telepinu decree:

'When Mursili reigned as king in Hattusa, then were his sons, his brothers, his kinsmen, the people of his clan and his soldiers, united. He held the enemy land subdued with a strong arm. He rendered the land powerless.'

We know these words almost by heart because Telepinu never varied them whoever was on the throne. But the really interesting information is encapsulated in two short sentences:

'Then did he march on Haleb [Aleppo]. He destroyed Haleb and conveyed the captives and possessions of Haleb to Hattusa.'

This was even more than Hattusili achieved. Although the late king had seized the statue of Haleb's Weather-god during his conquest of Hassu and brought it back to Hattusa, Mursili was the first to take the important city itself, thus becoming the most powerful monarch in northern Syria and consolidating Hittite influence in that area. Other documents make several references to his victory over Haleb because it brought the Hittites an economic boost as well as a political and military triumph. From now on, they not only controlled the trade routes but held the trade centres as well.

However, what appears to be statesmanlike foresight may only have been an act of personal vengeance on Mursili's part, because a later document asserts that his march on Haleb was occasioned by a wish to avenge his father's death. This becomes feasible if we assume that Hattusili fell sick or was wounded during the earlier campaign – hence his summary appointment of Mursili as successor to the throne on his return. We cannot be certain that this interpretation is correct, for all its plausibility, because political logic alone could have prompted Mursili to launch another invasion of northern Syria and bring it fully under his control. Whatever the truth, the second ruler in line of descent from the semi-legendary King Tabarna had succeeded in transforming an unknown Anatolian principality into a kingdom whose sway extended to distant territories far beyond the borders of the original Hittite heartland.

This alone would justify us in regarding Mursili as a major Hittite king. However, he now embarked on something that gives the appearance of pure adventure – and undoubtedly was one, given that 'mighty deeds' are only acknowledged by posterity if all goes well.

Mursili resolved to march further east and, like Hattusili, reach the Euphrates. More than this, he followed the course of the Euphrates southwards with the intention of attacking Babylon, the hub of the contemporary world, which had attained its earliest prime under Hammurabi at a period when the Hittites were still unheard of.

It was a 500-mile march from Haleb to Babylon, or nearly twice as far as from Hattusa to Haleb. The Hittites' route led through the kingdom of the Hurrians, who could have cut off their retreat at any time. Although the fertile banks of the Euphrates guaranteed a supply of food and water for men and horses, it was an expedition devoid of all logistical support and communication with Anatolia. If the Hittites were defeated by the Babylonians, they would be wiped out.

But the gamble paid off. Telepinu records the 'mighty deed' in a single laconic sentence: 'Thereafter he marched on Babylon and destroyed it.'

It was a prodigious feat. Mursili did not, of course, 'destroy'

Babylon, but Hammurabi's dynasty was overthrown and Mursili's prestige soared. Although the Hittites never extended their empire to Mesopotamia and Babylon, the very fact that they had succeeded in capturing and ravaging the metropolis of the known world brought them a great-power reputation which could not fail to reinforce their position in northern Syria.

Encumbered with loot and prisoners, Mursili set off home – a perfect opportunity for the Hurrians to muster beside the Euphrates and rob him of both spoils and victory. 'But he vanquished the Hurrians and kept the captives and possessions of Babylon in Hattusa,' reports Telepinu. Mursili's venture had been a success from start to finish.

It can fortunately be proved that this was no fabrication to the greater glory of the Hittites because, for the first time in their history, we possess a non-Hittite account which parallels their own. A Babylonian chronicle contains the equally terse statement: 'In the time of Samsuditana the Man of Hatti marched to Akkad.' This quotation not only attests that Telepinu was correct but provides the first chronological checkpoint in Hittite history.

Samsuditana was king of Babylon, and Babylon's defeat can be dated according to the 'Middle Chronology' in 1594 BC. Quite different dates result if one uses the so-called 'Low Chronology' (see the Chronological Table in the Appendix) but correspondences can be established under either system.

At all events, Mursili concluded his march on Babylon by returning to Hattusa, where he experienced the same misfortune as Hattusili: his kinsmen had exploited his prolonged absence and risen in revolt.

'And Hantili was cup-bearer,' the Telepinu decree abruptly remarks after the passage describing the capture of Babylon. 'He had Harapsili, the sister of Mursili, to wife. Then did Zidanta [Mursili's son-in-law] approach Hantili, and they committed an outrage: they slew Mursili and committed murder.'

So a 'mighty deed' ended in assassination. Nobody chose to recall the words of entreaty in Hattusili's testament, which he had intended to be read aloud each month: 'And my words, the King's words, shall you keep. You shall eat only bread and drink wine. So shall the city of Hattusa stand upright and my country be at peace and repose. But, as soon as you fail to keep the King's words, you shall not remain alive thereafter – you are lost.'

They were words of wisdom transformed into prophecy. When the murderer ascended his victim's throne *ca.* 1590 as Hantili I, the kingdom and authority of the Hittites suffered a decline.

Although Hantili was at first able to maintain Hittite influence by conducting campaigns in northern Syria, the Hurrians pushed eastwards and drove his forces out. The vassal-city of Haleb was liberated and gained strength.

Then the Gasgans invaded the Hittite heartland from the north, compelling Hantili to build a series of fortresses and improve the defences of Hattusa itself. Later kings were also forced to take the field against the Gasgans. There could be no question of internal peace, especially as the succession remained in dispute for over 60 years and murders followed thick and fast.

Harapsili, Hantili's wife, was the first to be murdered with her sons, and the same Zidanta who had helped Hantili to assassinate Mursili proceeded to murder Hantili's son and other members of the royal family. When Hantili died without heirs as a result of this drastic pruning process, Zidanta himself claimed the throne.

The murderer had attained his objective, only to be eliminated in his turn. He was killed by his own son, Ammuna, who ascended the throne *ca.* 1550. Under Ammuna, whole provinces were lost and the kingdom irresistibly declined still further. Miraculously enough, Ammuna contrived to die a natural and unaided death, though two of his sons were killed in the furtherance of a minor dynastic adjustment. In about 1530, a certain Huzziya became King of Hatti. Tradition demanded that he too should cherish murderous intentions – this time towards a brother-in-law whom he resolved to eliminate for safety's sake. But the brother-in-law was too quick for him: he deposed Huzziya and banished him.

The series of assassinations had come to an end.

It was this same brother-in-law, Telepinu, whose logical response to the dire experiences of the past was to present the Hittites with a constitution and stable law of succession when he came to the throne *ca.* 1525, but not even he could arrest the process of external decline.

Before coming to Telepinu, however, I propose to discuss a few problems of dating which may be omitted by those more interested in the sequence of events.

Relative and absolute chronology

Unlike the fairy-tale that leads off with 'Once upon a time . . .', history begins where persons and events can be fitted into a system of reference based on facts and figures. The characteristic feature of an 'absolute chronology' of this kind is that any occurrence can be dated in relation to the present year.

Where the recent past is concerned, this presents few problems. We can often pinpoint the hour and day when something happened, not to mention the year, but the greater the lapse of time and the sparser our documentary records the harder accurate dating becomes. Although we know the day and year of Constantine the Great's death, for instance, his birth-year fluctuates by almost two decades because of discrepancies between various historical sources.

Despite these problems of detail, we refer to this system of continuous and interrelated dates as 'absolute chronology', its datum-year being immaterial provided all our calculations are geared to it.

The Greeks, for example, worked forwards from the year 776 BC (first celebration of the Olympian Games) and the Romans 'ab urbe condita' (founding of Rome in 753 BC), while Mohammedans base their system of time-reckoning on the Hegira, or flight of Mohammed from Mecca to Medina (AD 622). All these dates mark the beginning of history for their particular areas, though the Jews are the most consistent. To this day, they base their chronology on the (notional) beginning of the world, so that all dates are technically defined as 'post-Creation'. This contrasts with our Christian chronology, which recognizes an era before and after Christ's birth.

Our own system dates from AD 532, when it was introduced by the monk Dionysius Exiguus, but the chronological definition 'after the birth of Christ' first appears in documents during the eighth century and did not come into general use until the High Middle Ages.

Authors of chronological works had earlier been compelled to engage in the laborious and intricate task of converting the various Greek and Roman systems – and there were more than the two mentioned above – into the Christian. Henceforward, what was then known of the world's history could be classified in terms of a single absolute chronology.

It goes without saying that an absolute chronology is wholly dependent on the existence of records and documents which interlock or overlap one another without any temporal lacunae. If we know that one event antedates another, but not by how much, we speak of relative chronology. A typical example of relative chronology is provided by stratigraphic findings, in other words, those based on levels of excavation. An object found in one layer must be older than objects unearthed in layers properly stratified above it, but it is not always possible to tell how much older it is or what century it dates from.

But the problem of accurate dating is not necessarily a matter of age. The modern radiocarbon method enables us to pinpoint dates in the 'prehistoric' period with greater precision than many in historical periods, so called. We have a more accurate chronology for Çatal Hüyük than for many Egyptian Pharaohs.

Hittite chronology, too, remained nebulous for many years. The Hittites had no chronology of their own. They did not, like many peoples, base their calculations on a particular point in time, not did they express dates in terms of how long a king had been on the throne. If we studied them in isolation, it would be impossible to tell exactly when a particular king reigned and when the Hittites themselves existed.

We owe our relatively precise knowledge of their dates to comparative chronology, though this is useful only when one of two events can be dated with certainty. The fact that Queen Ankhesenamun wrote to King Suppiluliuma would be a relative dating (they were contemporaries) if it were impossible to specify the century in which one or other of them lived.

Because we *do* know when Ankhesenamun lived, we have a fixed point from which to gauge the approximate lifetime of a Hittite king – approximate because inadequate records do not always permit of dating to the nearest day or year, even with an absolute chronology. 'Relative chronology answers the question whether one object is older or younger than another. Absolute chronology shows us from what century, before or after Christ, that object derives' (Oscar Montelius).

But how do we know when Ankhesenamun lived? In the course of a single century's research, the earliest date in Egyptian history – that of Egypt's unification under King Menes – has plummeted from 5876 to 2900 BC, and not even the latter year has been established beyond doubt. Do we, in fact, have any firm dates at all?

If the truth be told, we possess very few really reliable dates for events in the ancient world, and many of them are widely scattered.

Egyptian chronology, for example, was partly determined by an astronomical process which takes all of 1460 astronomical years to run its course, the so-called Sothic cycle. Walther Wolf explains the implications in his book *Funde in Ägypten*:

The Egyptians began their year with the advent of the annual Nile inundation. Although very punctual, this naturally did not always occur on the same day, so they chose as their New Year's Day the heliacal rising of Sothis [Sirius], which, having for some time been invisible because it rose too late, first re-appeared in the dawn sky on 19 July [by our reckoning] in consequence of its 'heliacal rising'. The beginning of the Nile inundation more or less coincided with this day. However, because the Egyptian calendar year of 365 days was too short by a quarter of a day, the civil New Year's Day lagged behind the astronomical to the extent of one whole day in every four years. Only after 1460 astronomical or 1461 civil years – a

Sothic period, as we call it – did both New Year's Days coincide. Given that the Roman writer Censorinus testifies to such a coincidence in the year AD 139, we can, if we count back 1460 years from that date, arrive at more such coincidences.

The Egyptians, who customarily related the heliacal rising of Sothis to the civil year, made a practice of stating the day in the civil calendar on which this heliacal rising occurred in any particular year. From the displacement of the civil New Year in relation to the astronomical (one day in four years), we can thus calculate, to within four years, how many years had elapsed between the last coincidence and the Sothic date in question. Four such Sothic dates were already known. The earliest of them enabled the inauguration of the New Kingdom to be ascertained, but no aid to precise dating existed for the period prior to the New Kingdom. Then, in the temple records of El Lahun, Borchardt discovered a memorandum from the seventh year of Sesostris III which stated that the rising of Sothis had occurred on the 16th day of the 4th winter month. This information enables us to pinpoint the 7th year of Sesostris III's reign as 1872 BC. Because we also know exactly how long his four predecessors reigned, we are in a position to date the founding of the 12th Dynasty in 1991 BC. We still lack a Sothic date for the Old Kingdom and are thus dependent, when determining its chronology, on less precise calculations.

So much for Walther Wolf. Where the Sothic dates are concerned, we have an exact calendar, but much of what lies between them is just as uncertain as our dates for the Old Kingdom. The unfortunate fact is that Egyptian chronology suffers from two lacunae (*ca.* 2000 BC in the 7th–11th Dynasties and *ca.* 1600 BC during the Hyksos invasion) whose extent is variously estimated by various authorities. Historians whose estimates of these gaps are relatively short arrive at a 'Low Chronology'. Conversely, expansion of the same gaps produces a 'High Chronology' because the reigns of known rulers can be distributed over a longer period, while 'Middle Chronology' is a compromise between the other two. None of the three systems is reliable.

Further complications arise because similar dating problems have bred high and low chronologies for Mesopotamia and other culture-areas, so that even comparisons in individual periods come to nothing. The dates assigned to Hammurabi of Babylon, for instance, can vary by decades or even centuries, and the first chronologies of the Hittite kings, computed in 1922, differ from today's in respect of their starting-point by more than 200 years. Forrer dated Tabarna *ca.* 1860 on the basis of a faulty Asiatic chronology, whereas modern authorities date him *ca.* 1680, or two centuries later. Though the number of kings remains constant, we are once again confronted by differing chronologies based simply on estimated length of reign and open to correction at any time. Even the present Hittite chronology relies on notional and schematic reigns of 20 or 30 years designed to pad out the lacunae between dates that have been definitely established (see Chronological Tables at rear).

Firm dates reinforced by comparison do exist, of course, though 'firm' must be taken to allow for fluctuations corresponding to the high, middle or low chronologies of other culture-areas.

Forrer did, however, find an absolute date within the Hittite chronology too. A form of 'military communiqué' issued by Mursili II, the successor of Suppiluliuma, relates that the tenth year of the king's reign was marked by a 'sun sign' which Forrer translated as 'eclipse'. Astronomers were, in fact, able to calculate that a solar eclipse did occur during the putative reign of Mursili II – to be precise, on 13 March 1335 BC. This put Mursili II's accession in 1345 and supplied the date of Suppiluliuma's death, which is fairly widely assumed to be 1346. So far so good, but, despite the way everything fitted neatly together, other Hittitologists disputed Forrer's translation and the astronomers consulted their tables again. Sure enough, they discovered that the solar eclipse of 1335 BC would have been only partially visible in Hattusa, whereas five years earlier, in 1340, a far more impressive – i.e. total – eclipse could have been observed there. Could Mursili

II have been referring to the total eclipse of 8 January 1340? If not, why would he have omitted to mention that such an eclipse had occurred previously, in the fifth year of his reign?

If we assume that Mursili II was indeed referring to the solar eclipse of 1340 and that it really did occur in the tenth year of his reign (given that he was in Hattusa at the time and witnessed it), he must have come to power in 1350 and Suppiluliuma must have died in the same year or earlier. This would seem to dislodge Egyptian chronology as well as Hittite because it implies that Suppiluliuma predeceased Tutankhamun and could have neither received nor answered a missive from the Pharaoh's widow. The situation is not as bad as it looks, however. Depending on what chronology one accepts, the year of Tutankhamun's death can be identified with a whole range of dates: 1358, 1344 or even 1338.

The same goes for Suppiluliuma, whose reign has been dated in five different ways by six different authorities of recent vintage:

1375–35 (Riemschneider)
1380–46 (Otten and Akurgal)
1381–55 (Cornelius)
1370–30 (Werner)
1380–30 (Klengel)

The above discussion may serve to show that history need not invariably consist of dates, and that interrelationships can be more important than facts suitable for learning by rote. The true cultural milestones on the road to human advancement – the invention of writing and numerals, the emergence of drama, music and the fine arts – have never been dated and never will be.

Temporary decline

It is estimated that Telepinu ascended 'the throne of his father' – to quote a cuneiform text – in 1525. At once, we prick up our ears: given that Telepinu is further stated to be the brother-in-law of King Huzziya, he can hardly, in our parlance, have mounted the throne as Huzziya's 'son'.

Far from being a chronicler's error, this seeming anomaly stems from the difference between our world of ideas and that of the East. Mursili was not the true offspring of Hattusili, but we have already seen that the latter called him 'son' when casting him in the role of successor to the throne.

The same thing occurs in the Bible. To make it clear that a ruler's accession accords with the will of God, the so-called coronation formula (Psalm 2, 7) says: 'Thou art my Son; this day have I begotten thee . . .' – a turn of phrase so thoroughly misunderstood by Christians that they converted Jesus into the bodily son of God when all the oriental mind intended to convey was a special relationship. Even modern Hebrew expresses 'echo' by the phrase 'daughter of the voice', thereby conjuring up a vivid picture of the close relationship between sound and resonance. Again, the Hebrew-speaker can only express his or her age by the phrase 'I am a son [or daughter] of 40'.

Thus far in the list of Hittite kings, therefore, we need not dwell on the question of whether the term 'son' implies a consanguineous or purely adoptive relationship.

The new king changed all this. After a period during which succession to the throne had been determined mainly by a person's more or less fortuitous survival of indiscriminate slaughter, Telepinu regularized it by means of the decree whose historical section has been quoted in an earlier chapter and whose three golden rules make it the world's earliest constitutional law.

'The first-born prince shall become king,' it declares. 'Should there be no first-born prince, a son of the second degree shall become king. Should there be no male successor, the first daughter shall be given in marriage to a husband and he shall become king.'

This not only invested hereditary monarchy with the force of law but prevented a reigning king from choosing his own successor as Hattusili had done. The stipulation that a son-in-law could inherit the throne was attributable to Telepinu's personal circumstances: his son had died and the dynasty could only be perpetuated through the female line.

To prevent the succession from being 'readjusted' by murderous means, Telepinu decreed that the *pankus*, or council of nobles, should sit in judgement on an assassin. The murderer could be condemned to death but his family were exempt from retribution: 'To his household, his wife and his children, you may not do harm.'

The *pankus*, whose activities were limited to certain matters affecting the crown, did not correspond to a federal assembly or parliament in the modern sense even though its name signified nothing more nor less than 'all' or 'the whole'. It was more reminiscent of the Germanic popular assembly, originally formed to elect a leader.

The introduction of a hereditary monarchy was bound to diminish the importance of a body to which Hattusili had alluded a century or so earlier. The 'council of nobles' none the less remained a corrective to arbitrary despotism and, compared with the political systems in neighbouring oriental countries, a positively democratic institution.

By and large, subsequent Hittite kings adhered to Telepinu's legislation and dispensed with the absolute powers of an oriental despot. This marked them out from other dynasts of the period. Indeed, there is much to be said for the theory that this changed attitude towards monarchy was an enduring historical legacy from the Indo-European tribes of long ago.

Like their peers in neighbouring countries, the Hittite rulers proudly called themselves after deities – Telepinu is itself the name of the supreme Weather-god – and regarded their status as divinely bestowed. 'The land belongs to the Weather-god,' says an inscription. 'Heaven and earth [and] men belong to the Weather-god. He appoints the Labarna, the King, to be his regent, and gave him the whole land of Hatti. So shall the Labarna rule the whole land with his hand.' But – and this is the crucial point – the Hittite kings did not see themselves as gods. No king became divine until he died, which is why the death of a monarch is on principle rendered by the formula 'Then did he become god'.

Because the king also acted as high priest, it is hard to tell how much veneration was due to the earthly ruler and how much to the deity's representative, but court ceremonial became the regulatory institution that preserved the sovereign's life and ensured his purity as high priest.

All imaginable contingencies were allowed for by regulations framed with extreme punctilio:

'As soon as the King has alighted from his chariot and the commander of the bodyguard is standing by, the commander of the bodyguard shall bow and consign the King to the commander of the pages. But if some other dignitary has held himself in readiness and is, being the most eminent [?], standing to the fore, then shall *he* perform a bow. But if no great lord has held himself in readiness, that bodyguard shall bow who happens to be standing there, even if he then walks away from the chariot [and does not escort the King]. And, as soon as the King has alighted from his chariot, the commander of the bodyguard and his men shall bow after the King.'

There is something thoroughly hilarious about certain other regulations dealing with a human predicament whose anguish we can still savour after three and a half thousand years:

'Should one [of the bodyguard] have a full bladder, he informs another, and it [his request] is submitted to the commander of the bodyguard: "He desires to go and urinate." [If] the commander of the bodyguard says "Let him go!" and the said bodyguard is about to go and urinate, but His Majesty is just inspecting the ranks and the matter of the urination reaches the palace, so may he not on pain of death go [and urinate].'

The essential function of court ceremonial was to preserve the king's religious purity. Consequently, all who waited on him were subject to special rules of hygiene. Kitchen staff were obliged to swear a monthly oath never to give the king unclean water, and a hair found in his washing-water automatically sentenced the offending manservant to death.

'Purveyors to the court' enjoyed an honourable but perilous status. Shoemakers and leather-workers, for example, were only permitted to use hide from the royal estates. Death lay in store for them and their families if they used leather from some other source, but any such misfortune had to be reported at once: 'But if you [inadvertently] take another, tell the King and it will not count as a transgression. Then I, the King, will send it to a foreigner or give it to a servant.'

Anyone whose fear of punishment prompted him to conceal a violation of the ritual code of purity was stripped of his post: 'If anyone commits an impurity and incurs the King's wrath, and if you say as follows: "The King sees us not", the King's gods have long perceived [the transgression] and will drive you into the mountains with a reed [cane] . . .'

In addition to court ceremonial and the *pankus*, there was a third institutional restraint on the king's freedom of action: the Tawananna. This was the term for the Hittite queen, who fulfilled a special function. The Tawananna was permitted to intervene in affairs of state, administer the royal possessions and manage the royal household. Puduhepa, wife of Hattusili III, conducted an independent correspondence with foreign rulers and signed the king's letters with her own seal.

The situation became particularly difficult when the Tawananna did not happen to be the king's wife. The spouse of a reigning king could not call herself Tawananna until his predecessor's wife, the queen dowager, was dead. This often led to a secret exercise of power by the old queen, and cuneiform texts give detailed accounts of squabbles between royal mothers- and daughters-in-law.

But to wind up this 'court circular' and revert to Telepinu: the king is credited not only with issuing the decree that assured the line of succession but also with codifying the laws of the Hittites. We have no evidence of this, but the 200 extant provisions, a considerable number of them based on earlier traditions, may have been compiled and partially amended under Telepinu because current laws are often compared with their precursors.

The new legislation tended to do away with the practice of penalizing a malefactor's family, and there was a gradual replacement of the *lex talionis* by indemnities in cash or kind. Section 92 provides one such example: 'If someone steals two bee swarms [or] if he steals three bee swarms, he used formerly to be stung by the bees. Now, however, he pays six shekels of silver.'

In many cases, too, animal sacrifice was substituted for human. 'If someone sows seed a second time upon a cultivated field, a plough is set upon his neck and a team of oxen harnessed thereto. The face of the first is turned this way, the face of the other, that. The man is killed and the oxen are killed too, and he who had already sown the field takes it for his own. Such was the custom in former times. Now, a sheep is brought instead of the man and a pair of sheep instead of the oxen.'

Only offences against the deity, witchcraft and negligence in religious matters continued to be punishable with death. Telepinu's decree and the legislation attributed to him indicate that he was a ruler whose main concern was the internal good order of his country. However, his reign also witnessed the conclusion of the earliest Hittite treaty, a pact between himself and Isputahsu of Kizzuwadna.

We can deduce from extant seals that Kizzuwadna was a Cilician kingdom under Syro-Mesopotamian influence. This in turn indicates that Hittite foreign policy had lost ground because Cilicia, on the route to northern Syria and the Euphrates, had hitherto been under Hittite control. Thus, although Telepinu appears to have led an expedition to the middle reaches of the Euphrates, it is unlikely that he marched there via the Cilician Gates, the easiest route through the Taurus Mountains.

This would explain why his successors did their utmost to destroy the small but troublesome kingdom of Kizzuwadna. Subsequent treaties between the Hittite kings Hantili II and Huzziya II and the rulers of Kizzuwadna make it plain that still more territory had been relinquished.

We know as little about Telepinu's immediate successor as we do about his own demise. It looks as if the Telepinu decree was observed, at least initially, because a certain Alluwamna is listed as the husband of the king's daughter. After that, Hittite history enters an obscure phase.

If we date Telepinu's death *ca.* 1500, there follows a period lasting over a hundred years about which virtually nothing is known. Lists of later date enable us to reconstruct the names of a few kings, but it is uncertain in what order they reigned or whether they were kings at all.

The period was also a dark age because, despite a few military campaigns, the Hittites lost nearly all their external provinces and were subjected to attack in Anatolia itself by invading tribes who actually burnt down their capital, Hattusa.

Chronologically speaking, this period coincided with the Hyksos movement, which caused a similar upheaval in the history and chronology of Egypt.

There is no certainty where the Hyksos came from or what their name means. The word Hyksos is a Graecized form of the Egyptian *heka-khasut*, meaning 'rulers of foreign lands', though others render it as 'shepherds of the foreigners'. All we know is that they either invaded or gradually infiltrated Egypt from Asia. They may also have been accompanied by bands of nomadic or semi-nomadic Semitic tribesmen, or 'shepherds', who were enslaved in Egypt after the expulsion of the Hyksos and eventually left there under the leadership of Moses as 'children of Israel'. Thus the Biblical stories of Joseph (*Genesis* xxxvii *et seq.*) may possibly be a reflection of conditions that prevailed during the Hyksos period.

But why should the Hittites of distant Anatolia have been affected by the Hyksos invasion of Egypt?

One or two of the Hyksos royal names sound remarkably Hurrian. The use of the two-wheeled war-chariot forms another link between Hyksos and Hurrians, but the question remains: were they related or identical?

The Hurrians had a history of their own. Assyrian and Sumerian sources dating from the end of the third millennium BC supply our first information about this people and the land of Hurri south of the Caucasus. We also know that they came from the region of Lake Van in eastern Anatolia and are referred to as Horites by the Bible. Still later, in the ninth–seventh centuries BC, the highlands of Armenia were inhabited by a people who were related to the Hurrians and whose country bore the name Urartu (the Biblical Ararat).

The Hurrians had gradually pushed southwards from Lake Van, a fact attested by the incidence of Hurrian names from the time of Naramsin onwards. By the time Mursili marched to Babylon, it will be recalled, they were already established beside the Euphrates. Here, as Hittite influence waned, they founded the kingdom of Mitanni. It was not long before the Hurrians became so dominant that Hittite rulers bore Hurrian names. They even penetrated as far as Anatolia and took seven cities there.

To quote Idrimi, king of Mukishe: 'The land of Hatti neither mustered its forces nor marched against me. I did as I pleased.' And a letter of later date written by Pharaoh Amenophis III states: 'The land of Hatti, too, is rent asunder.'

If the Hyksos can be equated with the Hurrians, and some authorities subscribe to this theory, it would account for the chaos then prevailing throughout the area bounded by Anatolia and Egypt. Like the Hittites, the Hurrians would have attained a prime and built an empire, the difference being that the Hittites outlasted them in power and influence.

Why, on the other hand, if the Hyksos and Hurrians were identical, did the Egyptians refer to them as foreigners and not Hurrians? Why could no one say where they hailed from? Once again, language comes to our aid. The Hurrians were indeed a foreign people because their language was neither Semitic nor Indo-Germanic, even though they – or at least their ruling class – came of Indo-Aryan stock. Our knowledge of the language group to which the Hurrians actually belonged is attributable to a Hittite text.

This is the so-called Kikkuli text, the earliest-known set of written instructions on the training of horses. Although this long and extremely detailed course in the handling of light war-chariots (the text stops short at the 184th day of training) is set out in Hittite, the language is so bald and so littered with solecisms that the 'riding master' who composed it must have been a foreigner. Sure enough, the text alludes to him by name, and his name – Kikkuli – was Hurrian. Furthermore, many of the words he used did not belong to any language spoken in the immediate vicinity of Anatolia and Asia Minor. Scholars had to cast their net still wider before they identified these singular Hurrian expressions: they came from India!

This was no great gain. We know no more today than we did then, but we can surmise that, like the Hittites, these Indo-Iranians or Indo-Aryans had reached the Caucasus on their travels. It is further assumed that they learnt how to handle horses and light chariots there before moving on to northern Syria and, as 'Hyksos', disrupting the peace of Asia Minor for several centuries with their swift chariot-borne incursions.

But the Hurrians were not the Hittites' only source of trouble. The Arzawans began to establish a realm of their own and assert their authority over neighbouring states in western Anatolia, so the Hittites were compelled to fight on this front too. Gasgan tribes invaded from the north and conquered parts of the Hittite heartland. As King Arnuwanda and the Tawananna Ashmunikal complain to the Sun-goddess of Arinna:

'The temples which you [gods] possessed in these lands, them have the Gasgans overthrown. They have smashed your, the gods', statues. They have plundered silver, gold, rhyta, cups of silver, gold [and] copper, your bronze utensils [and] your vestments, and divided them among themselves.'

The same prayer goes on to protest that the Gasgans have enslaved and shared out 'musicians, singers, cooks, bakers, fieldworkers and gardeners' as well as priests, and that they have used sheep, cattle and fields for their own benefit. The seizure of vineyards is also lamented.

Such was the state of affairs in about 1400 BC. Mursili's great expedition and the conquest of Babylon lay two centuries in the past. His death had been succeeded by a period of domestic turmoil and murderous rivalry between contenders for the throne. The Hittite kingdom had been strengthened *ca.* 1500 by Telepinu's statutes and his reorganization of internal affairs, only to spend another century fighting for survival against Hurrians, Gasgans and enemies within its borders.

Yet the kingdom's second decline was only a prelude to its real ascendancy – its development into an empire worthy of comparison with Egypt.

VI THE EMPIRE

Suppiluliuma's dominions

In the second year of his reign, the Egyptian Pharaoh Tuthmosis I extolled his person and the vast extent of his territories on a memorial stele erected at the third cataract of the Nile:

'Its southern border reaches to the beginning of the earth, its northern to that river which flows in a contrary direction, which flows down towards the south. Never did the same occur through the agency of other kings. His name attains the compass of heaven, it reaches to the end of the earth. He gives sustenance in all the countries of the earth because of the greatness of the power of his majesty.'

Egypt did, in fact, attain a new zenith of territorial expansion *ca.* 1500. The area under its control extended from Nubia, 'the beginning of the world', in the south, to the Euphrates, 'the river which flows in a contrary direction', in the north. The Hyksos incursions were responsible for this concentration on the north. Having begun by adopting defensive tactics, the Egyptians decided to push the Hyksos back and recover their sphere of influence in the Near East.

The first campaign was outwardly justified by 'insurrections' in northern Syria, putative home of the Hyksos who called themselves Hurrians and were establishing the kingdom of Mitanni. This punitive expedition does not appear to have been over-successful because Tuthmosis II launched a new campaign against the kingdom of Mitanni, which the Egyptians called Naharina, or the 'two rivers', and Tuthmosis III reports that he undertook no fewer than seventeen such expeditions.

It was not until his sixth campaign that Tuthmosis III managed to strike a decisive blow: he captured the city of Kadesh on the Orontes, which then became his northern frontier.

On his seventh expedition, Tuthmosis III forced an entry into the kingdom of Mitanni by hauling boats overland across the Lebanon, probably from the Syrian port of Byblos, and sailing up the Euphrates. He defeated the Hurrians and, like his predecessors, recuperated from his martial exertions by hunting elephant beside the upper reaches of the Euphrates. An inscribed record at the temple of Karnak tells us that he and his companions dispatched 130 head.

Tuthmosis III appears to have quelled isolated revolts and disturbances on his later campaigns. Compelled to wage war against the Hittites in the north-west and the Egyptians in the south, the Hurrians had already lost power and prestige when the Hittites were still fully occupied with themselves and the Gasgans.

Fundamentally, therefore, the Hittites owed their resurgence to the conflict between the Egyptians and the Hurrians. As Hurrian power declined, so the Hittites resumed their upward climb.

It would perhaps be wrong to create the impression that political power and weakness can be measured in a pair of scales which automatically find their own level or indicate the dominance of a ruler or nation simply because the countervailing weight has decreased.

On the contrary, there are situations which slip past unexploited unless the right man chooses the right time to *do* what others only sense, think or demand. We might never have heard of the Hittites again if their throne had not passed to a man whose name occurs in the first few pages of this book: Suppiluliuma.

This monarch with the poetic name (Suppiluliuma – 'He from [the place of the] pure spring' – might be translated as 'Clearwell') came to the throne in about 1380 BC. He had previously represented his ailing father on campaigns against the Gasgans and had even, on occasion, defeated them.

As for his father, scholars are less sure of his identity now than they were a few years back. Until the 1950s, opinions were divided between Tudhaliya III and Arnuwanda. Then, in 1953, philological comparison of sources disclosed that there were evidently two kings named Suppiluliuma, both of them perverse enough to number a Tudhaliya and an Arnuwanda among their forebears and both of them fated to live in politically troubled times – except that one had reigned at the beginning of the Imperial era and the other at its close. It is still uncertain which of them had which ancestors in what order, and whether the forebears of the one have not been mistakenly attributed to both. I mention this only because obsolete lists of kings are often found in specialized works published after 1953. It is not even certain that Suppiluliuma's accession was entirely legitimate because, unlike other kings, he never mentions his mother when drawing up honorific lists of the dead. He may have been the offspring of a concubine, or again, his mother may simply have died too young – we do not know.

Like his predecessors, Suppiluliuma spent the early years of his reign fighting the Gasgans. Added together, textual allusions to these intruders suggest that he was embroiled with them for two whole decades. He felt strong enough to venture a campaign against the Hurrians shortly after his accession but was defeated by Tushratta, the king of Mitanni, who proudly sent part of his spoils as a gift to Pharaoh Amenophis III of Egypt.

Although Suppiluliuma withdrew to Anatolia, his grip on domestic affairs was such that he could begin to conclude treaties with neighbouring states. The manifest purpose of these treaties was to procure allies against the Hurrians, systematically and by diplomatic means. Thousands of years before the Austrians made it standard practice, Suppiluliuma reinforced his treaties with matrimonial ties. Wherever possible, he married off one of his relations to each treaty partner – not that this inhibited him from peppering his treaties with assertions that the other party was an uncouth barbarian who needed instruction in the meaning of decency and decorum.

One delightful instance of this blithe condescension can be found in Suppiluliuma's treaty with Prince Hukkana of Azzi-Hayasa in north-west Armenia. Having given Hukkana his sister in marriage, the king proceeds to teach him how well-bred persons should behave towards sisters-in-law from the harem of a Hittite monarch:

'Furthermore, my sister, whom I, the Sun, have given you to wife, has many sisters of varying degrees of kinship. They are now your sisters too, because your wife is their sister. But there is an important precept in the land of Hatti: no brother may have sexual intercourse with his own sister or female cousin. This is not seemly. At Hattusa, anyone who does such a thing does not remain alive; he is slain. Your country being uncivilized, it is customary there for a sister and female cousin to have intercourse with their own brother. At Hattusa, this is not permitted.'

Just in case the hapless foreign prince had failed to grasp the point, instructions of a more detailed nature follow:

'Now if you are approached by a sister, half-sister or cousin of your wife, give her to eat and drink. Eat and be merry, but do not crave to lie with her. That is not permitted. It is punishable by death, so do not attempt it on your own account. And if some other person seeks to lead you into such a course, pay him no heed and do it not. You shall be so charged under oath.'

But the treaty does not stop there. Suppiluliuma goes on to deal with ladies-in-waiting and hierodules, or female slaves of the temple:

'You must also beware of any lady of the court, whatsoever lady of the court she be, free or slave. Go not too near her, approach her not at all and speak no word to her. Nor should your serving-man or maidservant approach her. Beware of her greatly. As soon as a lady of the court approaches, leap far aside and leave her free to go her way. And beware most particularly of the following story concerning a lady of the court – for, as regards Mariya, what crime had he committed to deserve death? Did not a temple slave approach, and he become importunate? My father, the father of the Sun, chanced to be looking out of the window and seized him: "Why were you importunate with that woman?" – and he found death because of that transgression. So beware greatly of something which has cost a man his life!'

One could philosophize at length about this quaint method of concluding treaties. The existence of sisters of varying degrees of kinship implies that the Hittites kept harems and subscribed to a moral code under which ladies of the court and hierodules – a euphemism for temple prostitutes – could not have been considered disreputable.

In view of the frequent links between morality and religion, the fact that Suppiluliuma set so much store by moral observance might lead one to suppose that he was an exceptionally devout or religious man. This, however, is just what he appears not to have been. He differs from other Hittite kings in that not a single text dating from his otherwise well-documented reign bears witness to his piety. On the contrary, his casual attitude towards religious matters provides the occasion for many pious prayers composed by his son Mursili II.

Suppiluliuma was a practical man with a grasp of essentials. This is evidenced by his renewal of a pact with the kingdom of Kizzuwadna in Cilicia, which had already broken the terms of one treaty and defected to the Hurrians. The text of the new agreement puts it thus:

'I, the Sun, wrote to the Hurrians: "Send my subjects back to me." But the Hurrians answered me, the Sun, as follows: "No. These cities came earlier into the Hurri land and established themselves there. It is true that they later returned to the land of Hatti as fugitives. But in the end the ox chose its stable, and they have come into my land for good." So the Hurrians did not deliver up my subjects . . .

'Now, therefore, the people of Kizzuwadna are Hittite cattle and have chosen their stable . . . have forsaken the Hurrians and gone over to me, the Sun . . . the land of Kizzuwadna rejoices exceedingly at its deliverance.'

After this review of past history, Suppiluliuma concludes a treaty with the 'Hittite cattle' free from vengeful sentiments or a desire to inflict humiliation. On the contrary, he confers superior status on King Sunassura of Kizzuwadna. The Hurrians had called him servant; Suppiluliuma makes him a legitimate king – almost a 'brother' of the Hittite monarch – even though he remains a semi-vassal under the terms of the treaty.

Suppiluliuma achieved more with these tactics than he would have done by fire and sword. Although Kizzuwadna had to pay tribute and could not pursue a foreign policy of its own, it remained a relatively autonomous state and was better off than it had been under the Hurrians.

In this way, Suppiluliuma cleared a route to northern Syria, confident that the state of Kizzuwadna would not attack him in the rear if he launched another invasion of Hurrian Mitanni.

Before so doing he appears to have waged another war with the Arzawans of western Anatolia, because the treaty with Kizzuwadna expressly stipulates that the tributary kingdom should furnish military assistance against the Arzawans to the extent of 'one hundred chariots and a thousand men'. The war must have ended inconclusively, to judge by subsequent reports of further fighting, but Suppiluliuma plainly had little more to fear from the west. (One cannot resist mentioning that he received homage from the Prince of Mira, if only because that exalted personage rejoiced in the unprincely name of Mashuiluwas, or 'Little Mouse', more commonly used as a term of endearment.)

During the latter years of his reign, Suppiluliuma marched through the Cilician Gates and invaded northern Syria, which now belonged to the Hurrian sphere of influence. There followed a decisive struggle with the Hurrians, who had already been weakened by their earlier clash with the Egyptians.

Although this campaign cannot be reconstructed in detail, its outcome is not in doubt. King Tushratta of Mitanni was killed, the Upper Mesopotamian kingdom of Mitanni destroyed, and Syria converted into a Hittite province. A treaty from the time of Suppiluliuma gives its southern border as the Lebanon Mountains, or, to be more precise, the city of Kadesh, which had previously marked the frontier between the Hurrians and the

Egyptians and was later, after the battle of Kadesh, to become a frontier-city once more.

Suppiluliuma avoided tackling the Egyptians while he still had his hands full with the Hurrians. But by the time he came to besiege Carchemish, the last Mitannian stronghold west of the Euphrates, two of his generals were already raiding and pillaging the Egyptian territory of Amka between the Lebanon and Anti-Lebanon ranges: in other words, they had crossed the frontier at Kadesh.

The Egyptians were understandably perturbed by this. As Suppiluliuma's son Mursili observed when recording the king's 'Deeds' in later years: 'While my father was down in the land of Carchemish, he sent forth Lupakki and Tarhuntazalma into the land of Amka. They set out to attack the land of Amka and brought back prisoners, cattle and sheep to my father. But when the Egyptians heard of this assault on Amka, they were afraid.'

However much this Hittite invasion of Syria resembled its forerunners, there was more to it than the bald and laconic wording of the Hittite chronicles disclosed. The effect of Suppiluliuma's exploits on other people can, however, be gauged from his opponents' reactions, for he is the king to whom the widowed queen of Egypt, Ankhesenamun, wrote to request one of his sons as her new husband, as we saw in Chapter I.

We can now sympathize with the king's misgivings about the proposal. He was still fighting for supremacy in Syria, Carchemish had still to be taken and Syria and the erstwhile kingdom of Mitanni converted into an orderly Hittite fief, yet here were the Egyptians acknowledging his equal status by proposing to make one of his sons Pharaoh.

We can also understand the king's hesitation and the urgency of Ankhesenamun's reiterated plea: the two kingdoms were equally powerful, but the Hittites had yet to realize it.

Suppiluliuma sent an envoy to Egypt to discover if the proposal were a trap. The Egyptians had never before imported their rulers from abroad. If they now wished to make one of his sons

Pharaoh and, thus, ruler of the known world, it meant recognition, renown and respect for Suppiluliuma and his people. Being an exponent of matrimonial diplomacy himself, he was only too conscious of where such a decision could lead.

Reassured by Ankhesenamun's reply, he sent one of his five sons to Egypt in great state.

Carchemish fell after a brief siege, the kingdom of Mitanni was destroyed and Syria won for the Hittites. Then Suppiluliuma heard that his son had been murdered on the way.

One step short of fulfilment, fate had jibbed: somewhere in the desert, an assassin had changed the course of history. A Hittite's accession to the throne of the Pharaohs would have linked two worlds which clashed continually thereafter without ever attaining mutual comprehension. Even though Greece and the Christian West were substantially influenced by the culture and art of Egypt and the Near East, who knows how things would have turned out if the attitudes, experience of life and language of Indo-European tribes had wielded influence in Egypt before Rameses II restored the country to its old predominance?

It was not to be, but Suppiluliuma's grasp of practicalities impelled him to make something special out of an unexceptional situation. Instead of subjugating the occupied territories, he turned them into vassal-states. He naturally demanded slaves, gold and natural produce in accordance with the victor's undisputed prerogative, but he also pursued his old policy of conciliating the vanquished by making them 'brothers' and kinsmen.

He had long returned to Hattusa when Mattiwaza, son of the late King Tushratta of Mitanni, arrived at his court after making an adventurous escape. Suppiluliuma treated him generously.

'And I, Mattiwaza, the king's son, when I went to the Great King, had two men of Hurri and two servants who had accompanied me, the single garment I wore, and naught else. But the Great King took pity on me, and chariots plated with gold, horses, harness . . . two pitchers of silver together with cups of silver and gold . . . splendid attire – all these and jewellery, everything conceivable, did he give me.'

But this was not all, nor was it the vital point. Mattiwaza continues:

'Beside the river Marassantiya [Halys] I fell at the feet of the Sun, Suppiluliuma, Great King and hero, beloved of the Weather-god. The Great King took me by the hand and rejoiced over me, and questioned me about all things concerning the land of Mitanni. And when he had hearkened to all the affairs of the land of Mitanni, the Great King and hero spoke thus: "I shall take you as my adopted son . . . I shall cause you to sit on your father's throne." '

Needless to say, Suppiluliuma had yet another sister available. Recognizing that the time was again ripe for cementing policy with matrimony, he married her off to Mattiwaza.

But he was wary for all that. Instead of relying solely on vassals and foreign princes who, being far from Hattusa, could govern the occupied territories as they pleased, he founded a dependent kingdom in Syria and installed his son Piyasili on the throne. He chose Carchemish, the stronghold on the Euphrates, to be its capital, and banished the possibility of resistance by deporting the city's inhabitants and resettling it with Hittites and others whose loyalty was assured. The religious centre of Haleb became the second focus of Hittite power in Syria. Here Suppiluliuma installed his son Telepinu, who also exercised priestly functions.

The Hittite Empire had at last secured a firm hold on Syria. For all the disturbances and rebellions that broke out, both then and in years to come, and despite threats from the Egyptians in the south and the Assyrians along the Euphrates, the Hittites of Syria held their ground for centuries after the empire collapsed in Anatolia. These were the Hittites before whom Abraham 'bowed himself'.

With other kingdoms such as Hayasa in the north-east, Kizzu-wadna in the south and Amurru in Syria, Suppiluliuma concluded treaties designed to make them buffer-states between the Hittite Empire and Assur, Babylon and Egypt.

Having founded this great empire and taken a Babylonian

princess as his third wife, Suppiluliuma brought his 'Deeds' to a close. He died in 1346 of a plague transmitted to Anatolia by Egyptian prisoners of war.

We do not know the exact nature of this plague, but it evidently spread throughout Anatolia. Suppiluliuma's son and heir, Arnuwanda, likewise succumbed to it after a brief reign, so his youngest son Mursili became the real successor to the Hittite throne.

The Annals of Mursili

Even before 'the Sun, Mursili, Great King, king of the land of Hatti, the bold' ascended the throne, sickness and pestilence seemed to have obliterated all his father's successes.

'Before I set myself on the throne of my father,' Mursili II declared in his account of the first ten years of his reign, 'all the enemy lands round about had gone to war with me. As soon as my father became god [=died], Arnuwanda, my brother, set himself on the throne of his father. Thereafter he too fell sick.

'Now when the enemy heard that Arnuwanda, my brother, had fallen sick, then did the enemy lands go to war in earnest. But when Arnuwanda, my brother, had become god, then did those enemy lands wage war that had not done so hitherto. And the enemy lands round about spoke as follows: "His father, who was king of the land of Hatti, was a brave king and subdued the enemy lands; now he has become god. But his son, who set himself on the throne of his father, he too had formerly been a bold warrior. The one that has now set himself on his father's throne, he is small. He will not deliver the land of Hatti and its borders." '

Mursili's importance reposes in the fact that he, 'the small one', succeeded in salvaging his father's achievements. Although more sensitive than other Hittite monarchs, he actually managed to consolidate an empire which, as the youngest son, he could never have expected to inherit and seemed quite unfitted to rule.

Mursili II was not a royal visionary or philosopher, but he probably lacked the phlegmatic approach of the man of action and was destined by his experience and intelligence to see things otherwise than most. For all his political success, the king was a person at odds with himself.

The first cross he had to bear was his father's surviving wife, the Babylonian Tawananna who had taken over the management of

Hattusa in succession to Duduhepa and Henti. Mursili was eventually obliged to banish her from the city because she gave him no peace and introduced disreputable practices at court – in fact he even had to expel a prostitute from the palace.

But Mursili had to contend with problems that lay still deeper and were rooted in his childhood. A modern psychoanalyst would have no difficulty in understanding why he attributed his stammer to an extraneous event which was merely the trigger of a traumatic experience buried in the past:

'Then did a storm burst forth and the Weather-god thunder terribly from afar. And the word in my mouth became small, and the word issued somewhat haltingly from within me . . .'

Moses was also afflicted with a 'slow tongue', hence the appointment of Aaron to be his spokesman and interpreter. But Mursili's disabilities went further than stuttering and stammering: 'But as the years came and went, one after the other, the said condition began to play a part in my dreams. And the god's hand smote me during a dream, and the power of speech forsook me altogether...'

But the gods had still more punishments in store. His wife was slain by a curse, or so he believed. As for the plague that had been ravaging the country for years, he now blamed it on himself and his family.

Abruptly, the cuneiform texts assume quite another tone – one that recalls Job and the Ten Commandments and the visiting of ancestral transgressions upon children of the third and fourth generation. All at once there is talk of guilt, sin and forgiveness:

'Hattian Weather-god, my lord, and you, my gods, my lords: thus it is – one sins.

'And my father, too, sinned and transgressed the word of my lord the Hattian Weather-god, but I have not sinned. Thus it is: a father's sin redounds upon his son. Upon me, too, did my father's sin redound.

'I have now confessed it to my lord the Hattian Weather-god and to my lords the gods: thus it is – we committed it.

'And because I have now confessed my father's sin, the wrath of the Hattian Weather-god, my lord, and of the gods, my lords, shall be appeased. Look favourably upon me once more, and drive out this pestilence from the land of Hatti.'

Mursili's prayer could – with modifications – be mistaken for a passage from the Old Testament. Again and again in these 'plague'-prayers (to retain a term which has now become conventional, though 'epidemic' would be more apt), Mursili implores the gods to bring the dying to an end, for 'it is now twenty years' since the pestilence first raged.

He offers sacrifices and vicariously confesses to a guilt that is not his own. Centuries before the Old Testament took shape and more than a thousand years before Christ's birth, he rivals the Psalmist in his quest for metaphors of mercy and forgiveness:

'The bird takes refuge in his nest and the nest preserves him.

'Or, when a servant is oppressed by some matter, he makes a request of his master. And his master hearkens to him and is well disposed towards him; and that which oppressed him, he puts to rights.

'Or, when a servant is at fault in some way but confesses the offence to his master, his master may do with him as he pleases. But, because he confesses to his master, the master's spirits are appeased; and the master will not punish that servant.

'Now have I confessed to my father's offence. Thus it is: I committed it . . .'

At long last, we learn what blame Suppiluliuma incurred – or rather, we are given at least a hint that Mursili's father may not have come to the throne by wholly legitimate means:

'You gods, my lords, because you wish to avenge the blood of Tudhaliya, those who slew Tudhaliya have atoned for their blood-guilt and this blood-guilt has also laid the land of Hatti low, so the land of Hatti has already made atonement . . .' Tudhaliya was king before Suppiluliuma, and Mursili is prepared to take the blood-guilt on himself.

'Because it has now been laid on me too, I and all my family shall expiate it by restitution and atonement. And the gods, my lords, shall be appeased. Be once more well disposed towards me, you gods, my lords!'

Mursili goes on: 'Because I have done no evil and none remains of them that sinned and did evil . . . I shall make gifts of atonement to you, my lords the gods, for the country's sake, on account of the pestilence . . . Drive the torment from my heart, deliver my spirit from fear!'

This document claims our respect and veneration across the centuries because behind it, and beyond all the bargaining for favour and forgiveness, we sense that a man was earnestly debating the concepts of mercy and justice. Job did no less when he wrestled with his God.

For the first time, Mursili views history and destiny in a way that brings guilt and atonement into the everyday business of politics. The gods are propitiated not by ambition and its fulfilment but by the keeping of commandments, be they human or divine: guilt brings guilt and expiation in its train.

Although a prey to the gnawing scruples that beset a thoughtful and reflective monarch, Mursili II ruled his country like any other king. He had to wage war for at least ten years before he restored peace within the empire. He fought against the Arzawans in the south-west, against disaffected principalities in the south-east, and repeatedly against the Gasgan tribes of the north. As he relates in his Annals:

'The following year I marched to the hill-country of Asharpaya. And that Gasgan city which held the highlands of Asharpaya and had cut the road to the land of Pala, with that Gasgan city did I contend in the highlands of Asharpaya. And my mistress the Sun-goddess of Arinna, and my lord the proud Weather-god, and Mezulla and all the gods stood by me. I vanquished the Gasgan city that held the land of Asharpaya and defeated it. But the highlands of Asharpaya I laid waste. Then I returned home.'

Mursili got on well with one tribe that had played a role in his father's day. These were the Ahhiyawans in the west of Asia Minor whom Forrer identified with Homer's Achaean Greeks.

The great temple of the Weather-god at Boğazköy/Hattusa is roughly equivalent in area to a modern football field. The outlines of the temple itself can be seen beyond the foundations of the store-rooms (*ca.*1400 BC.)

The Lion Gate at Hattusa, one of the city's four entrances, is a massive memorial to the best-fortified city in the ancient world. The gate's double arches were flanked by towers and set in cyclopean walls 25 ft. thick. The lions adorned the outer arch (14th century B.C.)

This 6 ft. high relief of a warrior-god on the interior of the King's Gate at Hattusa is one of the best-preserved monuments dating from the heyday of the Hittite Empire (14th century BC.)

Top left: portrayal of King Tudhaliya IV in the sanctuary of Yazilikaya. *Top right:* ivory statuette of a mountain-god (Hattusa, 14th-13th century BC.). *Bottom left:* Hittite hieroglyphs, still partly undeciphered, and beside them a tablet inscribed in cuneiform.

The Hittites and Ahhiyawans were on friendly terms, and Ahhiyawan princes joined their Hittite peers at the court of Hattusa for instruction in the novel chariot-handling techniques of Kikkuli. It is little wonder that Hittite cuneiform texts contain Greek names such as Alaksandu of Wilusa, even if its bearer is not necessarily identical with Alexander of Ilium (Paris of Troy). Conversely, the name Mursili was adopted by the Greeks and became Myrsilios.

It would surely be worth investigating the extent to which personages and events in Greeks sagas and myths can be traced to Hittite myths and appellations. In the sixth century AD, for example, the Byzantine geographer Stephanus described in his *Ethnika* how, on their way to Troy, Paris and Helen encountered the founder of Samylia in Caria, a king named Motylos. The Hittite throne was at that time occupied by Mutalli (Muwatalli).

'It would thus be a very strange – indeed, well-nigh incredible – quirk of coincidence if the people of Ahhiya were not the Greeks who must have inhabited the area at this period,' remarks M. Riemschneider in her book *Die Welt der Hethiter*, and Friedrich Cornelius indicates that the Hittite city of Amasia, named after the Mother-goddess Ama, was the native city of the Amazons. He even discovers another etymological pointer to the Amazons, who fought against Achilles at Troy under their beautiful queen Penthesilea and furnished material for a number of dramas: Achilles fell in love with the dying Penthesilea when he defeated her. This would make it a love affair between a Greek and a Hittite, because Cornelius holds that 'Amazon' is compounded of the word 'am' (woman) and the name of her place of origin, the land of 'Azzi'.

It was not until the end of Mursili's reign that minor difficulties arose with an Ahhiyawan prince named Tawagalawas – supposedly a laborious rendering, in the Hittites' syllabic script, of the Greek name Eteocles.

It is only fair to point out that all the philological and etymological associations outlined above continue to be hotly disputed by many authorities.

Relations between the Ahhiyawans and Hittites do not play a major part in the Hittite annals, although cultural interaction must undoubtedly have been greater than existing evidence suggests. As in earlier times, the Hittites' attention was focused less on the west of Asia Minor than on Syria and Mesopotamia. It was there, in permanent confrontation with the forces of Babylon, Assur and Egypt, that the Hittite Empire had to demonstrate its strength.

In the ninth year of his reign, Mursili was obliged to lead an army against Syria because the viceroy of Carchemish, his brother Piyasili, had died there during a religious festival. A number of Syrian vassals chose this moment to defect, and matters became even graver when the Assyrians appeared on the Euphrates. Mursili defeated the insurgents, 'regulated' the situation by concluding fresh treaties, and installed a new viceroy at Carchemish.

He describes the procedure in his Annals:

'I, the Sun, marched to the land of Arawanna and assailed it. The Sun-goddess of Arinna, my mistress, and the proud Weather-god, my lord, and Mezulla and all the gods stood by me. Then I conquered the whole land of Arawanna, and the civilian prisoners whom I led back to the royal palace out of the land of Arawanna numbered 3500. As to what the officers, foot-soldiers and charioteers of Hattusa took home in the way of civilian prisoners and cattle and sheep, it was impossible to count them. And, when I had conquered the land of Arawanna, I returned to Hattusa.'

The Annals stop short at the tenth year of the king's reign, so we know little more about his remaining two decades on the throne. That Mursili II preserved his father's empire intact for 30 long years and passed it on to his son would, even in the face of such 'normal' problems as foreign rebellion and tribal raids, have been a major achievement in itself. That he contrived to ensure the empire's survival despite an epidemic which raged for two decades – and raged with such intensity that he feared there would soon be no one left to make sacrifice to the gods – was an exceptional feat on the part of a man whose greatest adversary dwelt in his own conscience.

It was always the sins of others for which Mursili and his country had to suffer. The origin of the plague had been the unexpiated murder of Tudhaliya, its immediate cause the murder of the Hittite Pharaoh-designate:

'And when my father relinquished one of his sons to them, they slew him as they were conveying him [to Egypt]. But my father was enraged, and he marched forth to the land of Egypt and assailed it. Then, too, did the Hittite Weather-god . . . ordain that my father should prevail. And he vanquished the soldiers . . . of the land of Egypt and smote them down . . . But, when they were conveying the captives to the land of Hatti, the captives brought plague into the land of Hatti. And death has prevailed within the land of Hatti since that day.'

The devout king suffered, sacrificed and atoned for the deeds of others. His son Muwatalli, a good-natured and corpulent man, led an active rather than contemplative life. He it was who avenged the humiliation of Suppiluliuma and defeated Rameses II at Kadesh, a success which finally transformed the Hittite Empire and Egypt into rivals of equal status.

A Pharaoh turns tail

It so happens that we know very little about the Hittite king who put Pharaoh Rameses II to flight.

Muwatalli (*ca.* 1315–1282 BC) may have been averse to keeping records. On the other hand, our lack of documentary evidence may be attributable to his having transferred the royal residence, gods and all, from Hattusa to Dattassa, whose site archaeologists have yet to identify. We only know that it lay further south in the direction of Syria.

There is, however, a theory that the new capital was situated in the region of Sirkeli, south of the Taurus Mountains near Adana, because that is where the first and earliest portrayal of a Hittite king – a monumental relief of Muwatalli himself – was discovered. Would he have chosen to immortalize himself at that particular spot unless his capital stood near by?

Whatever the answer, Dattassa has not been located. We may none the less assume that Muwatalli kept his official records there rather than at Hattusa. This would explain why the king was so remarkably uncommunicative: we have simply failed to discover his archives.

We do not even know why he transferred his royal seat in the first place. One theory is that he wanted to move nearer Syria so as to intervene more quickly in the event of war, another that persistent trouble with the Gasgans may have prompted him to transfer the imperial capital to a more peaceful area. After all, the heretic-king Akhenaten had not long before abandoned the traditional pharaonic capital and built himself a new one at Amarna in central Egypt.

A third possibility is that the move betokened a system of divided authority. Muwatalli reigned more in the south, whereas his brother Hattusili presided as a self-appointed viceroy at

Hakmis on the empire's northern border. The viceregal administration was unconstitutional, and Hattusili went to great lengths to represent his irregular conduct as the product of divine counsel. To all intents and purposes, however, the empire had two kings.

Hattusili even gained a measure of success. He acquired sufficient authority over the Gasgans to be able to lend his brother some Gasgan auxiliaries when Muwatalli came to grips with the Egyptians. Fraternal assistance notwithstanding, Muwatalli twice instituted legal proceedings against his brother for reasons which, although obscure, are presumed to involve conspiracy and false allegations.

And that is the full extent of our knowledge about Muwatalli. He himself has left us not a single word on the subject of his battle with Pharaoh Rameses II.

We do, however, have a detailed description of the origins and development of this conflict. Rameses ordained that a full verbal and pictorial account of it should be carved on the walls of the Ramesseum, likewise at Karnak, Luxor, Abydos and Abu Simbel.

There was nothing exceptional about its immediate cause. Yet another petty kingdom had deserted the Hittites, who mounted a punitive expedition. The only special feature was that, this time, it was Amurru which had defected to the Egyptians under Prince Bentesina – and Amurru lay plumb on the boundary between the Hittite and Egyptian spheres of influence (roughly in the area of modern Lebanon).

This presented a threat to the Hittites. The defection of Amurru not only deprived them of a buffer-state between their sphere of influence and that of a powerful rival; it diminished and weakened the territory under their political control in a vitally important area.

We do not know how Rameses II bribed the Prince of Amurru to side with Egypt – bribes and booty being the contemporary gauges of political success – but the Pharaoh promptly seized his chance and marched off in the hope of conquering the whole of Syria.

This happened in the fifth year of his incredibly long reign (66 years), so Rameses must then have been a young man aged between twenty and twenty-five.

But Muwatalli had also set out, and a clash was inevitable. After the battle, Rameses described its outcome in the following temple inscription:

'His Majesty destroyed the hordes of the Wretched One of Hatti, his mighty ones and all his brothers; likewise did all the great ones of all the foreigners who had come with him, his foot-soldiers and his charioteers, lie there on their faces. His Majesty had them hurled, one upon the other, falling before his horses, into the Orontes.'

And an Egyptian poem says of Rameses:

'When the earth became light, then did I join battle, armed for the fray like a lustful bull, and I shone against them like Montu, furnished with weapons. I thrust my way into the tumult and fought as a falcon stoops . . . I was like Re at his appearance in the morning; my rays scorched the face of my foes . . . Then did the Wretched One of Hatti send forth and revere the great name of His Majesty: "You are a ruler, the likeness of Re . . . There is dread of you in the land of Hatti, for you have broken the back of Hatti for ever." '

These written sources suggest that the battle ended in a crushing defeat for the Hittites, but it did not.

The Egyptian version of the battle of Kadesh is a masterly blend of truth and falsehood, exaggeration and understatement. Just as Rameses proclaims a victory which he demonstrably failed to win, so he ingenuously describes in the same account how the Hittites used subterfuge, skill and strategy to trick him from the outset. It is probable that only darkness saved him from total annihilation, for Muwatalli had still not committed his best troops by nightfall. Rameses owed his escape to the Hittites' failure to pursue him.

The true course of the battle was as follows.

In May 1285 BC, the fifth year of Rameses II's reign, the

The Hittites ambush Pharaoh Rameses II at the battle of Kadesh and overrun his camp with their chariots.

In another scene from this Egyptian record of events, Egyptians can be seen beating two long-haired Hittite spies captured before the battle of Kadesh.

Pharaoh and his army of 20,000 men were arrayed beside the Orontes on 'the summit of the mountain of Kadesh'. He was proceeding towards Kadesh itself (now Tell Nebi Mend, south-west of Homs), when two deserters were brought before him. 'We wish to become servants of the Pharaoh,' they declared, 'for we wish to run away from the Wretched One of Hatti. The Wretched One of Hatti tarries in the land of Haleb. He is fearful of the Pharaoh and has no desire to march south.'

Reassured, Rameses marched on to Kadesh and set up a forti-fied camp there with the intention of starving the city out. Mean-while, Muwatalli and his 12,000 Hittites, together with some 8000 foreign auxiliaries, lay in wait round Kadesh and watched Rameses fall into the trap set for him by the two sham renegades and their misinformation.

But Muwatalli's scheme was disrupted when an Egyptian patrol captured a Hittite raiding party. The two Hittites were first beaten – the temple at Luxor depicts this vividly – then brought before the Pharaoh. ' "Who are you?" Rameses asked them, and they replied: "We belong to the Wretched One of Hatti. He sent us to spy out Your Majesty's dispositions." Then His Majesty said to them: "Where is he, then, the Wretched One of Hatti? I have heard that he tarries in the land of Haleb." They replied: "See, the Wretched One of Hatti has taken up his stand, and many foreigners with him . . . See, they are arrayed for battle beyond the Old City of Kadesh." '

Rameses was thunderstruck and bitterly berated his 'great ones' for failing to reconnoitre. The vizier was instructed to set the Egyptian army in motion, but it was too late. Rameses was still sitting in council – Egyptian inscriptions give a detailed account of the whole course of events – when the Hittites advanced and surrounded the Pharaoh's camp.

So the real truth of the matter is that the Egyptian forces were caught off guard and panicked before rallying and taking up their battle stations. The odds were in the Hittites' favour. They launched a surprise attack with their swift chariots, which were manned by teams of three – two fighting-soldiers and a driver – whereas the Egyptian chariots only carried one driver and one warrior. This gave the Hittites a tactical advantage because they could whisk twice as many combat troops into action as their opponents. Unlike the belligerents of earlier times, whose chariots were mounted on solid wooden disks and trundled ponderously along like ox-carts, each army had chariots with spoked wheels that rendered them lighter and more manoeuvrable.

Casualties were high on both sides because the battle raged till evening. There can certainly be no question of an Egyptian victory, even if Rameses did conclude his account with the words: 'I swear, as true as Re loves me and my father Atum commends me: all the deeds of which My Majesty has spoken, them did I truly perform . . .' At best, the Egyptians and Hittites discontinued the engagement on equal terms.

This is apparent because, for all the Egyptian reports of victory, nothing changed. Amurru reverted to the Hittite sphere of influence and Muwatalli replaced Bentesina with a prince loyal to himself. Syria remained an undisputedly Hittite territory and Kadesh on the Orontes continued to mark the frontier.

If only morally, it was a victory for the Hittites. No longer could Egypt claim absolute supremacy: the Hittites were at least as powerful. It no longer paid to defect to the Egyptians or rely on Egyptian aid because it was the Pharaoh, and not Muwatalli, who had withdrawn after the battle of Kadesh.

The Hittite Empire was at the zenith of its glory, but sixteen years elapsed before Rameses II deigned to conclude a perpetual 'treaty of friendship' which, more than anything else, made it plain that Kadesh had won respect for the 'Wretched One' of Hatti. This is the celebrated treaty which survives in an Egyptian and a Hittite version – the one whose discovery at Boğazköy helped to identify the capital of a vanished race.

The pinnacle of power

Muwatalli did not live to negotiate the treaty that resulted from the battle of Kadesh. Having no male issue by his principal marriage, he was succeeded *ca.* 1280 by Urhi-Teshub, a concubine's son who styled himself Mursili III.

Muwatalli's brother Hattusili, who was still ruling in arbitrary state at Hakmis, his capital in the north of the country, felt that he had been unfairly bypassed. To spite Muwatalli, he had previously given refuge to the prince whose defection had led to the battle of Kadesh, Bentesina of Amurru. More than that, he had married one of his sons to Bentesina's daughter and sent another Hittite princess to become queen of Amurru.

We are not surprised to learn that Hattusili now began to encroach on the authority of his nephew Urhi-Teshub, who had returned the capital from Dattassa to its former site at Hattusa. Hattusili later claimed that Urhi-Teshub had gradually stripped him of his lands until, after seven years, he was compelled to imprison the young king 'like a pig in a sty' and exile him to Syria, whence he fled to Egypt.

In about 1275 BC, Hattusili for the second time ascended a throne that was not his by right. Being a priest as well as a general, he had doubtless suborned the priesthood with lavish donations. He had also married Puduhepa, the daughter of a respected priest from Kizzuwadna. Thus equipped, he came to the throne as Hattusili III.

It was this same Hattusili who set the seal on his late brother's success at Kadesh by concluding the Egyptian-Hittite peace treaty in 1269, the 21st year of Rameses II's reign.

If the salient clauses of this document are quoted below, it is not only because of its importance in Hittite history but because it exemplifies a form of ancient oriental contract that set the pattern for an 'agreement' whose effect on the Christian West endures to this day. We know this agreement by another name: the Old Testament, significantly referred to in former times as the Old Covenant.

The pact concluded between the God of the Old Testament and the children of Israel (v. *Joshua* xxiv *et al.*) is modelled, down to the last detail, on the secular treaties of its day. As in the treaty between the Egyptians and Hittites, so in the covenant between the Israelites and their God, a preamble defining the parties to the contract is followed by an account of what has led up to it. Then comes a definitive statement about the parties' future relationship, then the contract's detailed provisions, then a summons to the deity or deities to bear witness, and, finally, various forms of malediction and benediction. Even the insistence that covenants shall be read aloud at regular intervals is common to both Hittites and Israelites. Comparing Hittite treaties with the 'Old Covenant', the theologian Klaus Baltzer declares: 'It will always be remarkable that, in Israel, the relationship with God was conveyed and advertised in so prosaic a manner' – in other words, as was customary in the international treaties of those days.

Just as the peoples of the East concluded treaties with rulers of equal or superior status, so did the children of Israel make peace with their God. So, too, did Christians later join the same God in a 'New Covenant' which amounted in essence to a secular legal accord based on Christ's self-sacrifice and God's obligation to show mercy, this time in line with Roman ideas of justice. Although we do not now construe our relationship with the Almighty as a title enforceable at law, the effects of this contractual approach are still manifest in the doctrines and dogmas of the various Christian denominations.

The treaty between the Hittites and the Egyptians was engraved on silver tablets, no longer extant. All that remain are the clay tablets from Boğazköy, which reproduce it in cuneiform, and the temple inscriptions at Karnak and in the Ramesseum, the Pharaoh's monument at Thebes, which are written in hieroglyphs.

The cuneiform tablets from Boğazköy bear an Akkadian translation of the Egyptian version. In other words, each party sent the other a copy of the treaty's text. Comparison of the Egyptian and Hittite versions discloses that, although similar in substance, they are not exact translations.

The main difference is that the Egyptian version always gives the Pharaoh precedence over his beloved friend from Hatti, whereas the Hittites make a point of mentioning Hattusili, 'the great Prince of Hatti, the Bold', before his fellow-monarch from Egypt. Clearly, each king wished it to appear that he himself had been the instigator of the treaty.

Thus, Rameses writes:

'See, Rameses, Mai-Amana, the Great King, the King of Egypt, establishes a bond . . . that in perpetuity [shall prevent] enmity from arising between them henceforth and for ever more . . .'

Hattusili's version is as follows:

'. . . . from this day forward, see, Hattusili, Great Prince of Hatti, makes a treaty so that the bond shall endure . . . to prevent enmity from arising between them for all eternity.'

The same idea is continually reiterated in language of great solemnity. 'See, Hattusili, Great Prince of Hatti, enters into a covenant with User-mat-Re, the Elect of Re, the great ruler of Egypt, from this day forth, that goodly peace and amity arise between them for all time. He is at one with me, he is at peace with me; I am at one with him, I am at peace with him for all time.

'When Muwatalli, the Great Prince of Hatti, my brother, had passed away according to his destiny, Hattusili set himself on the throne of his father as Great Prince of Hatti. See, thus have I come together with Rameses, the Beloved of Amun, the great ruler of Egypt. We abide in peace and amity. But it is better than the peace and amity that existed on earth in former times.'

After extending peace and amity to include the kings' descendants and asseverating at considerable length that all will remain unchanged for ever more, the treaty gets down to some practical provisions:

'The Great Prince of Hatti shall never invade the land of Egypt for the purpose of stealing anything therefrom.

'User-mat-Re, the Elect of Re, the great ruler of Egypt, shall never invade the land of Hatti for the purpose of stealing anything therefrom.'

After this non-aggression pact comes a mutual guarantee of military assistance:

'But if some other enemy march against the lands of User-mat-Re, Elect of Re and great ruler of Egypt, and he send to the Great Prince of Hatti with the words: "Come together with me, as a help against him", then shall the Great Prince of Hatti come, and the Great Prince of Hatti shall slay my enemy.' The Egyptians made a similar pledge. Much of the treaty is devoted to the suppression of rebellious vassals and the extradition of fugitives.

Then, as in every treaty, coupled with threats against default, comes the solemn oath:

'Let a thousand gods from among the male and female gods of the land of Hatti, together with a thousand gods from among the male and female gods of the land of Egypt, bear witness to my words.'

Again as in every treaty, the terms are reinforced by a litany of numerous deities – in this case, more than 30 of them from a variety of cities, including 'the Goddess of the Sky, the Gods of the Oath, the Gods of the land of Kizzuwadna, Amun, Re, Setekh and the male gods and female gods, the mountains and rivers of the land of Egypt, the sky, the earth, the great sea, the winds and clouds . . .'

Thirteen years later, in the 34th year of the Pharaoh's reign, this peace treaty was sealed with a marriage. Rameses II took the Hittite princess Naptera and made her his principal wife. The Hittite Empire had attained a new peak of glory and renown.

With characteristic hauteur, the Egyptians began by taking their allies down a peg. Preserved on memorial stelae at Karnak, on the island of Elephantine near Aswan, and at Abu Simbel, the Egyptian account of the royal union opens in lofty vein:

'The Great Prince of Hatti wrote seeking to appease His Majesty, year after year. King Rameses II never lent an ear.'

By the time news reaches the Pharaoh that Hattusili has sent his eldest daughter to the Nile 'with numerous gifts', that she has crossed 'many mountains and arduous passes' and will soon 'reach His Majesty's borders', there is a change of tone:

'Joy overcame His Majesty. The Lord of the Palace was glad when he learned of this extraordinary occurrence, the like of which was quite unknown in Egypt. He sent forth an army and noblemen to receive her forthwith.

'His Majesty took counsel in his heart: How fare those whom I have sent forth, who are journeying at my behest to Syria during the days of rain and snow in winter? He made a great sacrifice to his father Seth [the deity] and bade him as follows: The sky lies in your hands, the earth beneath your feet. That which you command comes to pass. [Desist from] making rain, tempest and snow until the advent of the marvels you have sent me.

'His father Seth hearkened to all that he had said. The heavens were at peace, the summer days came. The army marched gladly home, bodies erect and hearts filled with cheer.'

Rameses continually reverts to the impression made by the Hittites on all who saw them:

'The daughter of the Great Prince of Hatti journeyed to Egypt. The army, cavalry and noblemen of His Majesty escorted her, mingled with the army, cavalry and noblemen of Hatti. There were [Hattian] soldiers, archers and cavalry – men of the land of Hatti all mingled with those of Egypt. They sat and drank together. They were united as brothers and sisters, nor did one chide the other. There was peace and friendship between them ...

'The great princes of all the lands through which they journeyed were dismayed, unbelieving and bereft of strength when they saw all the men of Hatti . . .'

The Hittite princess reached the Nile 'in the 34th year, in the third winter month'. The account continues: 'Then did His Majesty perceive that her countenance was as fair as that of a goddess. And it was a great and singular occurrence, a glorious and unprecedented marvel, the like of which had never been handed down by word of mouth. Nor did it call to mind anything in the writings of our forefathers.

'The daughter of the Great Prince of Hatti was fair before the heart of His Majesty. He loved her more, being more fair, than all else that had been bestowed on him by his father Ptah [the deity]. His Majesty caused her to be styled Queen Mat-neferu-Re [she who sees the beauty of Re], daughter of the Great Prince of Hatti, daughter of the Great Princess of Hatti. It was an unfathomable, unheard-of marvel that befell Egypt through his father Ptah . . .'

Almost a century after the death of Suppiluliuma, a Hittite king had at last become related to the Pharaohs of Egypt. Pharaoh Rameses II, Egypt's last great ruler, had remedied Ankhesenamun's failure to bring about the 'unheard-of marvel' that recalled nothing in the writings of the past – the thing which prompted Suppiluliuma to declare that he had never encountered its like: a union between the Hittites and the Egyptians.

We know nothing about Naptera's career as the Pharaoh's consort, sad to relate, even though Rameses II lived and reigned for another 30 years. This leaves the imagination free, in default of firm evidence, to discern a Hittite princess in the Ramesseum's portrait of a girl with a broad necklace containing the *nefer* symbol of beauty and perfection . . .

Now began a period of ferment and dissolution to which the Hittite Empire was also to succumb within a few decades. Our information becomes scanty and imprecise. A new era was dawning as the old one drew to a close, but the Hittite Empire under Hattusili III was still a great power whose dominions extended – in modern terms – from the Black Sea in the north to

Beirut in the south and from Izmir in the west to Aleppo in the east.

Although the boundary between Hittite and Egyptian territory was never clearly defined, there is one geographical feature that has repeatedly drawn a natural line between northern and southern spheres of interest. This age-old barrier is the Nahr el Kelb, or 'river of the dog', which flows into the Mediterranean ten miles north of Beirut.

Hugging the coast-line, the Lebanon Mountains obtrude so closely on the sea at this point that the motor-road has to negotiate a short tunnel driven through a spur of rock. This spur constituted a natural obstacle in the path of nomads and caravans moving between the Mediterranean and the mountains. Anyone who occupied it controlled the shortest and most convenient route between north and south, just outside the place of the *birot*, or springs: Beirut.

It was there, on the rock beside the River of the Dog, that all who ever held this strategic position – this meeting-place of powers and potentates – immortalized themselves. Carved reliefs, stelae and, later, bronze tablets still bear effigies and inscriptions left by Nebukadnezar of Babylon, the Assyrian king Esarhaddon and the Roman emperor Marcus Aurelius. The Third Gallic Legion is commemorated, likewise the British Second Corps who fought there in 1918.

Inscriptions in cuneiform, hieroglyphs, Latin and English are arrayed there side by side, and there, too, weathered by the sea-winds of the past 3000 years, is an effigy of Rameses II, carved at the point where his empire marched with that of the Hittites – a chunk of history in the most literal sense . . .

In the east, Hattusili did his best to safeguard Syria against the growing might of Assyria. He tried to incite Babylon against the Assyrians, using 'diplomatic' means which might better be described as inflammatory. Here he is writing to the young Babylonian king:

'I have heard that my brother is now a man and betakes himself hunting. Now say I to my brother: Go now and plunder the land of the enemy [Assyria] ... "A king who lays down all his arms and sits there [idly]!" – thus have they spoken of my brother. Let them say it of him no more! My brother, sit there no longer. March against the land of your enemy and vanquish him, for you know that you march against a land you outnumber three or four times over.'

By dint of such friendly pieces of advice to foreigners and prolonged campaigns within his borders, Hattusili III succeeded in consolidating the position of the Hittite Empire. Proudly, he wrote:

'The kings who were in accord with the land of Hatti before me, they entered into accord with me too. They showed their readiness to send me ambassadors; gifts, too, did they show themselves willing to send. They sent me gifts the like of which they had sent to none of my fathers and forefathers. Whosoever was a king compelled to pay me homage, he paid me homage. But whosoever was my enemy, him I conquered.'

When Hattusili's son Tudhaliya IV (*ca.* 1250–20 BC) ascended the throne, he inherited a large, secure and powerful empire. Although he had to conduct campaigns in the west against the Ahhiyawans, who had fallen out with the Hittites, and against the Arzawans, this was an almost normal state of affairs. What was new was that the Assyrians were raiding Hittite territory on the Euphrates, but their activities had yet to constitute a major threat.

At all events, Tudhaliya IV was the first Hittite king whose royal arms embodied a title hitherto claimed by the Assyrians alone: *Shar kissati* – 'King of the Four Quarters'.

Animated by these pretensions to world supremacy, Tudhaliya expanded Hattusa into the metropolis of an empire destined to vanish from the map only decades after his death.

VII HITTITE CULTURE

Statues and cyclopean walls

As the Hittites rose to power, so their art and architecture attained monumental proportions. Built of huge blocks of stone, many of them more than six feet long, the cyclopean walls at Hattusa transformed the Hittite capital into a fortification of unprecedented splendour. The great temple of Hattusa and its subsidiary buildings occupy an area larger than a modern football field.

I do not propose to give a comprehensive account of Hittite art such as Ekrem Akurgal presents in *The art of the Hittites*. All I shall do here is trace its major developments along the lines laid down by that standard work.

The Hittite culture boasts few genuine works of art in comparison with that of Mesopotamia, Egypt or Minoan Crete. It almost seems, too, as if the first fruits of Anatolian art were more manifold and distinctive than the products of its later development, though this impression may be attributable to a continuing absence of major finds from the Imperial era. At Hattusa, apart from small seals and pendants, there is a predominance of large-scale reliefs.

The Hattusa known to us from excavations is the royal seat of Imperial times. The city was originally built round the great temple, but it later spread to the plateau in the south and was fortified. It had a diameter of nearly three-quarters of a mile and was thus one of the great cities of antiquity.

The city precincts were enclosed by a stone wall as much as 19 ft high and 25 ft thick topped with a further wall of mud brick. Since the ground falls away steeply to the north, the wall provided extra protection in that quarter. In the south, where the ground shelves gently and the city was more vulnerable to enemy attack, the wall fulfilled a genuinely protective and defensive function. Its structural strength was consequently greater on the south slope, with the result that substantial sections have survived to this day.

To enable attackers from the south to be taken in the rear, a postern-tunnel was built at the city's southern extremity. This underground passage, which is 230 ft long, has also survived. Its corbelled architecture bears an interesting resemblance to that of other culture-areas. Passages roofed with stones butted together to form a pointed arch are also to be found in Crete, Mycenae and Peloponnesian Tiryns, and Hattusa will present us with more such affinities in due course.

The city wall was pierced at each of the cardinal points by large gateways of which only the west and east are well preserved and now constitute the two main tourist attractions of the Boğazköy/Hattusa site.

The best known is the Lion Gate on the west side of the city. This is flanked by a pair of lions carved into the huge outer gatestones where their gaping jaws can repel the forces of evil. (A similar function was undoubtedly performed by the two lions on the Lion Gate at Mycenae, though their heads have unfortunately disappeared.)

Each of the outer gateways was matched by an inner arch, so access to the city could be doubly secured. The city gates were in their turn protected by towers whose appearance can be reconstructed from small sculptures that give us some idea of what the Hittite fortifications originally looked like.

The inner gateways were also adorned with figures. The south gate, for instance, had two inward-facing sphinxes which betray Assyro-Babylonian influence and are now preserved separately in Istanbul and Berlin. They and the lions are our only examples of Hittite monumental sculpture in the round: all the other works are reliefs.

The best-preserved work of art is the warrior-god in high relief from the city side of the King's Gate in the east. This almost fully sculptural relief is one of the most elaborately executed pieces: not only are the finger-nails reproduced but the cuticles

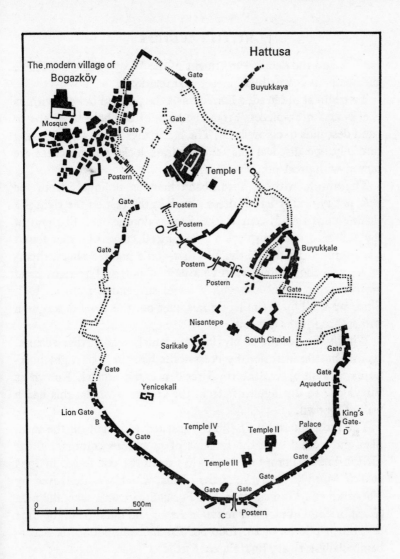

Hattusa

The modern village of
Bogazköy

Mosque

Gate ?

Postern

Gate

Buyukkaya

Gate

Temple I

Gate

A

Postern

Postern

Gate

Buyukkale

Postern

Postern

Gate

Nisantepe

South Citadel

Gate

Sarikale

Gate

Gate

Gate

Aqueduct

Yenicekali

King's
Gate.

Lion Gate

B

Gate

Temple IV

Temple II

Palace

D

Temple III

Gate

Gate

0   500m

Gate   Gate

C   Postern

Nearly three-quarters of a mile across, the Hittite capital was one of the great
cities of the ancient world. The city proper, complete with smaller temples and
gates, occupied the lower part of the walled area. The great temple stood on a
plateau of its own.

255

as well, and the detailed treatment of the Weather-god's costume and weapons is worthy of closer examination.

To begin at the head, a horn adorns the pointed helmet with its cheek- and neck-pieces. From the back of the helmet, a tape or band descends to elbow-level. The hair hangs lower still. Looking carefully, we discover that the separate locks on the chest are carved with great precision.

The apron, with an apron-band hanging obliquely from the belt, is a typical article of dress. Stuck in the belt on the right is a sickle-sword reminiscent of the Cretan double-axe. The end of the scabbard itself displays a pronounced curve like that found elsewhere in the tips of the Weather-god's pointed shoes, themselves an echo of the sweep of a pair of horns. The right hand grasps a ceremonial axe with a tassel suspended from its haft. Since we shall meet similar figures later on, this brief description will suffice for the present.

Within the perimeter of Hattusa, which was further secured against hostile intrusion by cross-walls like the watertight bulkheads of a ship, was the royal residence and citadel. Known as Büyükkale to distinguish it from the city as a whole, this had a wall of its own.

The most interesting building, situated top right on the town plan and dotted with the remains of numerous columns, is the earliest-known library in the world except the one found in 1975 at Tell Mardikh in Syria, ancient Ebla, which was destroyed by Naramsin of Akkad *ca.* 2200 BC. (For comparison's sake, the next oldest oriental library was found at Assur and dates from the time of Tiglath-pileser, or *ca.* 1000 BC. Far more important is Assurbanipal's library at Nineveh, *ca.* 650.)

This library building in the royal citadel has yielded more than 3300 complete or fragmentary clay tablets. We can deduce that these were neatly arrayed on wooden shelves from the discovery of small clay tablets listing what each shelf held, e.g. '32 tablets relating to the Festival of Purulli in the city of Nerik' or 'Tablets relating to the Deeds of Mursili'. In every case, the librarian had

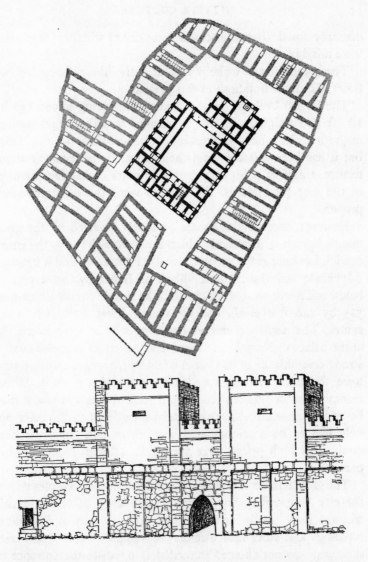

The great temple complex of Hattusa lay outside the main city walls. Enclosed by store-rooms, the temple itself displays a strange lack of symmetry. The adyton (or inner sanctum, recognizable by its altar-rectangle) stood off-centre in the courtyard of the labyrinthine building. The Hittite capital was surrounded by a wall as much as 19 ft. high and 25 ft. thick. The reconstruction (*below*) shows that its four gates were flanked by towers.

carefully noted whether a set was complete or whether some items were missing.

The column bases make it clear that the library occupied two floors, like most buildings of this period.

The largest building in the citadel, measuring about 130 by 160 ft and uniquely regular in design, was the storehouse or magazine. The other buildings cannot be identified beyond doubt, but it has been inferred from their unusually painstaking architecture, traces of paint and the use of granite, that the premises in the east (or right of the library) were the royal residence proper.

However, these buildings are positively dwarfed by the great temple known as Temple I, which is almost as large as the entire citadel. Looking at the general plan of Hattusa, we find it between Büyükkale and the modern village of Boğazköy, on a plateau below and north-west of the citadel. The temple complex measures 525 by 440 ft over-all, and the temple itself is situated in the centre. The narrow chambers enclosing it were store-rooms. As at the palace of Knossos in Crete – and the entire complex bears a strong resemblance to its Cretan counterparts – these store-rooms were found to contain huge earthenware jars (pithoi). Direct communication between temple and store-rooms was not, it may be added, an unusual feature. Sacrifices offered to the deity not only had to be accommodated somewhere but, since the king doubled as high priest, were very little different from tax payments.

The great temple of Hattusa, like several smaller temples within the city boundaries, exemplifies a peculiarity of Hittite architecture: it is totally asymmetrical, both as regards individual buildings and cities as a whole. The temple's adyton, or inner sanctum, was not situated immediately opposite the entrance in the centre of the inner court but lay off-centre and unbalanced by any companion-piece. The main entrance through the store-rooms is also off-centre. No architectural pattern can be discerned in the ground-plan of the citadel either. No one building bears any relation to another and the whole complex consists of discrete units. There are no signs of a main thoroughfare or central court-yard.

Only the four gates are symmetrically disposed, and we are led to wonder if this regularity was an oriental feature adopted by the Hittites into their own singularly chaotic architecture, which corresponded – on another plane – to the unsystematic and purely space-filling murals of the Minoan period in Crete.

Also typically Hittite are the large low windows which not only overlook the inner court, oriental-fashion, but pierce the temple's outer walls as well. This is another architectural discrepancy between the Hittites and the culture-areas penetrated by them.

Cyclopean walls, too, constructed with huge irregular or polygonal blocks of natural stone, did not occur in Anatolia prior to the Hittites' arrival. The same walls are found in the Mycenaean culture, whereas the inhabitants of Troy used medium-sized blocks of dressed stone.

Finally, the narrow store-chambers and tortuous ground-plan – developed at Knossos into the Labyrinth – have an affinity with the Indus culture of Mohenjo Daro and Harappa, as with that of Crete, but not with the ancient Orient.

The fact that the cult-room or adyton was lit by windows differentiates this temple from those of Greece, where the inner sanctum – with the individualistic exception of the temple at Bassae in the Peloponnese – was invariably a windowless chamber.

The illumination of their holy-of-holies suggests that the Hittites originally worshipped their deities in the open air. This conjecture is reinforced by the sanctuary of Yazilikaya in the immediate vicinity of Hattusa.

Yazilikaya ('inscribed rock') consists of two natural chambers each about 100 feet long. Open to the sky, these recesses were enclosed by a temple complex which attained its present form under Tudhaliya IV, when the passages in the rock had already become a shrine.

Inside the sanctuary itself, the rock face was transformed into a frieze. Forty-two deities, predominantly male, are portrayed on the west (left) wall of Chamber A alone, while the opposite wall is carved with a series of mainly female deities. The two processions meet at the far end of the small rocky cleft. Chamber A contains a total of 63 deities carved in low relief.

The rank and importance of these gods can be readily gauged from their pointed headgear. Inferior deities have only one pair of horns and one bisected oval – the symbol of divinity – on their helmets. Greater seniority is indicated by more pairs of horns and ovals, and the supreme deity or Weather-god possesses no less than five pairs. All the figures wear pointed shoes reminiscent of curved horns and all carry horn-shaped weapons.

So here, after roughly 5000 years, we re-encounter the bull-cult of Çatal Hüyük with its horn-studded benches, and it may not be unreasonable to surmise that the varying numbers of horns at Çatal were also expressive of differences in divine rank.

Closer inspection of the drawing on p. 269 brings other details to light. The god on the left, for example, is standing on a pair of mountain-tops and must therefore be a mountain deity – the Weather-god of Hattusa. The Weather-god of Heaven has considerably more horns on his head-dress and is standing on the necks of two mountain-gods. Facing him is the Sun-goddess of Arinna, mounted on a lion which is striding across more peaks, and escorting her are a younger god of inferior status and two goddesses whose divine beast is the eagle.

The minor details are of equal interest. Small symbols hover above the outstretched arms of the three deities on the left. The pretzel-like symbol, which recurs only on the Weather-god's helmet, is the ideogram for divinity. Beneath it, all three figures support varying representations of a pair of bull's horns, that of the Weather-god of Heaven being identical with the symbolic horns found at Knossos in Crete.

The dark spot above the horns carried by the Sun-goddess of Arinna represents the sun's disk, a symbol also associated with the

Egyptian goddess Hathor. Likewise related to Egyptian ideograms is the strange creature immediately behind Arinna, which
consists solely of the divinity symbol and a pair of legs. The
Egyptians, too, were acquainted with symbolic hybrids of this
kind.

Still in quest of horns, we can discern more of them on the two
bulls beyond the Weather-god of Heaven and the Sun-goddess of
Arinna. Equipped with a horn additional to the normal pair,
these are the bulls Sherri and Hurri, which draw the Weather-
god's chariot.

In other respects, our drawing discloses a routine and conventional identification of function and sex: the male deities wear an
apron and have one arm bent, the goddesses are universally dressed
in long robes and turret-shaped hats and have both arms extended.

The largest relief at Yazilikaya is the royal effigy on the east
wall of Chamber A. At 9½ ft, it is one-third taller than the
divine figures, which are only about 7 ft high. The subject is
Tudhaliya IV, who mingles with the gods but does not wear or
carry any divine attributes.

This none the less betokens a change in the assessment of royal
status. Tudhaliya IV was the first Hittite king to style himself a
god during his lifetime. This is particularly apparent in Chamber
B, which is nothing more nor less than a cult-shrine dedicated to
the monarch. Tudhaliya is again portrayed among ambulant gods,
one of whom (Sharruma) embraces him protectively to indicate his
divine support and veneration.

So Yazilikaya, too, exemplifies the close links between religion
and art, which became as monumental during the Hittite Imperial
era as it was stereotyped in form and devoid of variety. Reliefs
found in other places display an equal lack of development and
formal innovation.

The Indo-European Hittites do not appear to have had any
great talent for sculpture. Clearly, their strength reposed in the
political domain – in the manner in which they ruled other

peoples. Their impulse towards artistic creativity was far less pronounced. Most of what they left behind in the way of art and religion seems to have been borrowed from the autochthonous inhabitants of Anatolia, the proto-Hattians.

Weather-god and celestial bull

The most conspicuous and striking feature of the Hittite approach to religion was its tolerance. The Indo-European settlers whom we call Hittites did not impose their own gods on the Anatolian population, nor did they 'Hittitize' their adopted deities as the Romans Romanized the Greek pantheon (so thoroughly that divine names and functions became interchangeable). Instead, deities were taken over complete with their original appellations, many of which shared the status of their Hittite counterparts or actually replaced them. Even during Imperial times, the Indo-European rulers continued to worship indigenous Anatolian deities in the local idiom, with the result that we do not even know the Hittite names for some of them, only their original titles in, say, Luwian or Palaic.

Nor did the Hittites try to impose a hierarchical structure on their pantheon. Although most of the clay tablets found at Boğazköy deal with ritual and religious matters, it has so far proved impossible – except in a few cases – to establish any divine order of rank. On the contrary, the invocations found at the end of treaties demonstrate that equal status was accorded to principal and local deities of the most diverse functions and provenance – a broadminded attitude wholly alien to our own religion despite its allegiance to Christian charity.

The most important religious festival in the Hittite royal calendar, a spring festival, lasted for 38 days because the monarch, in his capacity as high priest, had to pay homage to his kingdom's large and varied assortment of deities and was presumably compelled to tour the country for that purpose.

It was this equal respect for a multitude of deities, and not their actual number, which entitled the Hittites to call themselves 'the People of a Thousand Gods'.

Even though the other gods were not subordinate to them, however, two supreme deities can be identified.

The Hittite 'national goddess' was the Sun-goddess of Arinna, also known as 'Queen of Hatti-Land'. She is proto-Hattian, although we only know her place of origin and her Hattian, not her Hittite, name: Wurusemu. Being fundamentally superior to the supreme Weather-god himself, she must therefore date from matriarchal times. As a Hittite prayer informs us:

Thou, O Sun-goddess of Arinna, art a respected deity.

Thy name is revered among the names.

Thy divinity is revered among the gods.

Great art thou, O Sun-goddess of Arinna.

There is no deity more revered or greater than thou.

Thou art mistress of the righteous judgement.

Over heaven and earth dost thou graciously wield royal authority.

Thou dost mark out the borders of the lands.

Thou dost hearken to complaints.

Thou, O Sun-goddess of Arinna, art a merciful deity.

Thou dost show mercy.

The blessed man is dear to thee, O Sun-goddess of Arinna.

To him dost thou, O Sun-goddess of Arinna, grant forgiveness.

Within the compass of heaven and earth art thou, O Sun-goddess of Arinna, the light.

In the lands art thou the honoured deity.

Father and mother of every land art thou.

Blessed mistress of judgement art thou.

Thou art unwearying at the seat of judgement.

Thou art honoured among the age-old and eternal gods.

For the gods dost thou, O Sun-goddess of Arinna, prepare the rites of sacrifice.

Thou dost mete out the portion of the age-old and eternal gods.

Thou dost open the doors of heaven.

And thou dost smite the gate of heaven and stride through.

But the Sun-goddess of Arinna is not, as we might have been led to expect, the consort of the Sun-god. The 'King of Heaven' and 'Lord of Hatti-Land' is the Weather-god, whom we also know solely by his archaic Hattian name Taru and the commonly used Hurrian name Teshub, not by his Hittite title. Now at last we perceive the link between this pair of deities, symbolized by their juxtaposition on the rock face at Yazilikaya: Sun and Weather unite to produce a son named Telepinu, who is responsible for the harvest.

In one text, the Weather-god says of Telepinu: 'This, my son, is diligent. He breaks the sod and ploughs. He brings water and makes the corn to grow.' If Telepinu disappears, drought and famine descend on the countryside – and it is precisely this disappearance that forms the subject of the Telepinu myth, one of the few Hittite myths to have been preserved.

Also portrayed on the rock face at Yazilikaya is another of the Weather-god's sons familiar to us from cuneiform and Hiero-glyphic Luwian texts. His name is Sharruma, but his character-istics remain obscure.

Nature-gods endowed with a less important role included the Sun-god, who also functioned as Lord of Heaven and the Under-world, and the Moon-god, who was worshipped more commonly in the south-east of Asia Minor and in northern Syria and Upper Mesopotamia. They too were of proto-Hattian origin and ante-dated the Indo-European migration.

The Hittites additionally worshipped the great Babylonian goddess Ishtar, whom they regarded as a sister of Teshub and who, thanks to an association of ideas which some might call quaint and others profound, functioned as the goddess of both love and war. She is portrayed at Yazilikaya in the guise of a Hurrian goddess named Sausga.

Despite their heterogeneous origin, all these deities – and there are many more of them – were worshipped by the Hittites on a basis of equality. They were allowed to retain their names and characteristics just like the subject peoples from whom they sprang.

The gods themselves were conceived of as immortal human beings. They toiled, suffered from hunger, were susceptible to magic, could fall sick and even die – though not, being immortal, for ever. They also kept harems and experienced the same emotions and desires as mankind: 'What is welcome to the gods and to men is in no wise different,' declares one cuneiform text, '[and] what is unwelcome is the same.'

The gods resembled human beings and were dressed like them, hence a king's ability to become divine and require worship after death because all that distinguished him from the living was his immortality in the realm of the dead. Thus the fact that Tudhaliya IV styled himself a god during his lifetime is unusual, and represents an incipient development of extraneous origin.

In the contemporary mind, gods were the masters and human beings the servants. As a result, temple regulations were largely indistinguishable from the rules governing relations between master and servant.

'Does the nature of men and gods differ?' inquires another text. 'No. Their nature is exactly similar. If a servant stands before his master, he is washed and wears clean clothes. And either he gives him [his master] something to eat, or he gives him something to drink. And he, his master, eats and drinks, and is content in spirit and well disposed towards him. But if he, the servant, is neglectful and inattentive, the relationship with him changes.'

The priests of the Hittite national religion were thus compelled to observe special rules of cleanliness in the same way as other members of the temple staff and those who came to make sacrifice. Being susceptible to hunger, the gods demanded bread and meat from the rich and a bowl of gruel, if nothing more, from the poor.

These sacrificial offerings had to be set before the gods at mealtimes. Once they had eaten, the 'left-overs' could be consumed by the priest, his wives, children and slaves – but nobody else. Even in those days, many a candidate for the priesthood may have been strengthened in his resolve by the prospect of free board and lodging.

The gods and their priests seem also to have enjoyed their glass of beer. In addition to grain, sheep and cult-objects, a royal inventory of sacrifices regularly lists casks of beer, though this beverage, together with wine, was also required to extinguish the pyre on which a dead monarch had been cremated.

Sacrifice formed a bond between gods and men. If the deity was given food and drink – if he was 'easy in spirit', i.e. replete – he would fulfil the wishes of his worshippers in accordance with the admirable Hittite precept that it is good to 'let a wrathful man drink his fill of beer' so that 'his ire departs'. Human beings were obliged to make sacrifice, but their sacrifice placed the gods, too, under an obligation. The weight attached to this mutual dependence can be gauged from the ingenuous way in which Mursili bargains with the gods in his plague-prayers: unless the pestilence ceases, there will soon be nobody left to bring them their daily sacrifice; it is thus in their own interests to end it.

The Hittite religion appears to have remained on this relatively unexalted plane. To the Hittites, religion signified exposure to the whims of natural forces which had to be propitiated – often, as in days of yore, with the aid of magic and sorcery. To that extent, their religion was not unlike the religions of neighbouring lands, whose gods differed in name alone.

The Hittite gods had yet to become dissociated from specific places and were mostly local deities who did not reside in a proper heaven of their own. Apart from the Sun-goddess of Arinna and the Weather-god Teshub, the Hittite pantheon was still a motley assortment devoid of rank or hierarchy. The concept of divine grace and protection was only gradually and tentatively making itself felt.

One interesting question is why the Hittites should have made the Weather-god their supreme deity rather than any other. Although the obvious answer – that dearth and abundance depended on climate and growth, that the weather was supremely important and its personification the most universal deity – seems logical enough, it is not borne out by the symbol or distinguishing feature of the Weather-god himself.

This, as we know from Yazilikaya, was the bull, which invariably appeared in his company. The god rode the beast, wore its horns on his helmet and was actually replaced by it in his temples, which never housed an effigy of the god himself, only a bull.

The sacrificial inventories that so often speak of beer and corn also contain regular allusions to a 'great bull of iron', a 'great bull encased in lead' or a 'great bull of silver, standing', 'a great bull' commissioned by 'my Sun' [the king].

After what has gone before, we are naturally reminded of Çatal Hüyük and the bull-cult which the Indo-European settlers took over, like so much else, from the proto-Hattians. But this brings us no closer to identifying the link between Weather-god and bull.

Unless we are prepared to assume that two cults – a bull-cult and a weather-cult – were amalgamated for no good reason, it is fair to ask why we cannot detect any inherent relationship between the god and his symbol. As with the cross of Christianity, so with the disk of the sun-cult, an emblem merely crystallizes an idea in the same way as the swastika or hammer and sickle stand for ideologies and philosophies of life in their entirety. But where lies the connection between the 'Lord of Heaven' and a bull?

In the first place, the bull-cult is not peculiar to the Hittites. It was earlier thought to have originated in the area of northern Syria and Mesopotamia, and similar borrowings from the oriental bull-cults have been found in Israel too. Thanks to the excavation of Çatal Hüyük, we now know that the bull-cult is first detectable in Anatolia. However, we are also familiar with the bull-cults of antiquity as exemplified by Crete, with the 'sacred cows' of India and their well-developed horns, and – if only from the *Asterix* books – with the horned helmets of the ancient Gauls and Germans. The bull-cult has existed for more than 7000 years, longer than any other religion and ethnically diffused across the globe from India to Europe. And because religions survive only for as long

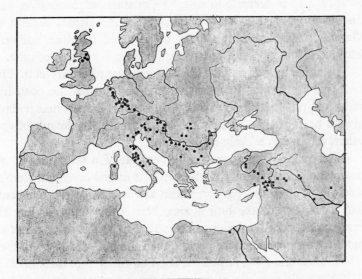

Archaeological sites that have yielded representations of deities mounted on bulls leave a 'migratory trail' of dots across the map. The route runs from the Syro-Hittite area, along the Danube, to the Lower Rhine and British Isles.

Divine encounter in the sanctuary of Yazilikaya : the Weather-god of Heaven, standing on two lesser gods, faces the Sun-goddess of Arinna, who is mounted on a lion. Bulls and horned head-gear are recurrent motifs.

as they inspire terror and awe, the qualities of *tremendum* and *fascinosum*, and then become extinct like the Greek, Roman or Germanic pantheons, it should be assumed that the bull-cult inspired fascination and veneration for a similar length of time.

The ready answer is that the bull-cult was a fertility-cult. The bull was the largest European animal and, unlike the cow, has remained untameable to this day. Moreover, human beings have always been greatly impressed by its strength. In default of any other, this seems a likely explanation.

Unfortunately, the continual repetition of a statement is no guarantee of its accuracy. India, with its sacred cows and former worship of the bull, has long been the habitat of the elephant, which far exceeds the bull in size. Nor is the bull's fertility all that some authorities seem to imagine. Any rabbit or dog, not to mention a mouse, is more prolific than the bull and cow – a fact which must also have impressed itself on Stone Age man.

It is equally possible, of course, that our ancestors attached less importance to quantity of offspring than quality of sexual organs, a bull's genitals being conspicuously larger than those of a man. This too seems plausible when we remember the phallus-cult of the ancient world, in which stalagmitic formations were worshipped as symbols of male potency, or the far from rare Greek vase-paintings in which Pan inspires terror by reason of his grotesquely exaggerated *membrum virile*.

The earliest-known bull-cult – that of Çatal Hüyük – does not, however, fit this pattern. Çatal Hüyük has not yielded a single effigy or representation of a man or beast with a sexual organ, customary though this became in cultures of later date. We can hardly suppose the people of Çatal Hüyük to have been inhibited by sheer prudishness from making representations of what they had in mind. Stone Age Anatolia produced small-scale sculptures of figures engaged in sexual intercourse, so why not effigies of a bull with a penis?

Why, again, did the Cretan bull-cult revere horned bulls' heads but never portray the bull as a male animal? Are we to believe that this was another mark of prudishness, even though there were caves in Crete devoted to the worship of the stalagmites mentioned above?

Anyone with even a passing knowledge of symbolism will long ago have objected that bulls' horns, with their symmetrical duplication, are themselves suggestive of the male sex organ. Although the horn is without doubt a symbol of potency, it need not have been invested with this symbolic significance initially or exclusively. Psychoanalysis, fairy-tales and myths all teach us about the so-called 'condensation' of various inner meanings into a single image which then becomes multisignificant.

Why, in that case, did the Hittites worship Telepinu, the god responsible for the harvest and the growth of vegetation? Telepinu was a clear expression of the fertility-concept, so why wasn't the bull *his* symbol rather than that of the 'God of Heaven'.

Many myths are nothing more than symbols that formulate in words what a picture can tell us at a glance. They are age-old reflections of an experience which people convey in word-pictures because they can express it no other way, just as the creation of the world was attributed to six days of divine toil in default of exact knowledge and scientific thinking.

No Hittite bull-myth has been preserved, unfortunately, so our quest for a meaningful relationship between bull and Weather-god would be cut short were it not for the potential assistance afforded by a myth from another culture-area. This is the Gilgamesh Epic, of which the Hittites possessed transcripts.

This Sumerian-Akkadian saga from the Babylonian domain tells of Gilgamesh (sometimes called Gishgimash), the legendary king of Uruk, whose reign is archaeologically dated *ca.* 1750–2600 BC. His greatest exploit, as the epic frequently mentions and recounts, was to seize and slay the bull 'that descended from the sky'.

According to the epic, Ishtar the goddess of love sought to destroy Gilgamesh by releasing a heavenly bull which caused a seven-year drought. Having obtained the beast from her father, the sky-god Anu, she led it 'down to earth'. The celestial bull proceeded to ravage the environs of the Euphrates:

The breath of the celestial bull caused a
pit to open;
and into it fell one hundred men of Uruk.
A pit was opened by its second breath;
and in fell two hundred men of Uruk.
A pit was opened by its third breath;
and into it now fell Enkidu.
Enkidu sprang out and seized the celestial bull
by the horn;
the celestial bull spat forth its slaver,
with the breadth of its tail it hurled its dung . . .
Enkidu hastened to seize the celestial bull,
he caught it by the tail,
Enkidu held it with both hands,
and Gilgamesh, like a skilful slaughterer,
smote the celestial bull, strong and sure,
betwixt neck and horns . . . with his sword.
When they had slain the celestial bull
and plucked forth its entrails,
they laid it down before Shamash.
They withdrew, bowing before Shamash
with much reverence;
then the two brothers sat down.

Whatever the celestial bull may have been, it had no connection with fertility. On the contrary, it inspired terror and was a hostile force whose destruction ranked as a heroic feat.

Similar happenings are related in another Sumerian-Babylonian myth, the 'Myth of the God Ninrag'. Here again it is one of Ishtar's creatures that has the ability to destroy mountains and lay the land waste. The Ninrag Myth additionally supplies some details of the creature's appearance: 'A fearful splendour was bestowed upon it as a gift by Anu in heaven', and 'its fearful splendour covered the House of Bel [the earth] like a garment'.

It rode in a chariot of lapis lazuli of 'fearsome frightfulness', and 'in consequence of the roar and rumble [of its chariot], heaven and earth quake at your passing. In consequence of the raising of your arm, a shadow reaches forth' so that the sky was 'dyed like red-hued wool'.

This could well be an account of a volcanic eruption: the earth quakes and rumbles, lapis lazuli recalls the volcanic obsidian found at Çatal Hüyük, and the sky would have become tinged with red because volcanic ash was blotting out the sun. Despite this, the whole event is described as a cosmic occurrence rather than an act by the god of the underworld, as we might have expected. A cosmic interpretation would be consistent with the repeated references to an 'arm', with the heavenly chariot and the deities involved: Ishtar the goddess of love, Anu the god of heaven, Shamash (literally 'sun') the sun-god, and – mentioned elsewhere in the myth – Anunnaki and Igigi, who are illumined by the sun-god and should doubtless be sought in the sky since they are accounted children of the god of heaven. Anunnaki, for example, is associated with the Semitic word for 'return', so that Igigi would have been 'the ever-recurring' – an apt description for a heavenly body.

Yet another variant can be found in a third Babylonian myth. The monster again originates in heaven and wreaks havoc. Again, as in the Gilgamesh Epic, there is a quest for a hero to dispose of it, but this time it is described as a serpent (Labbu): 'The cities sigh, as do the abodes of men . . . men lament . . . Who gave birth to the [mighty] serpent? Bel draws [the image of Labbu] in the sky: fifty miles its length, one mile its head . . . Who will go forth and [slay] Labbu, deliver the wide land and wield royal authority? Go forth, Tishpak, slay Labbu, deliver the wide land . . .'

So the celestial serpent and celestial bull are described in similar terms. Even the bull's natural disposition recurs in the name Labbu because it derives from the Assyrian word *lababu*, meaning 'to rage'. Labbu – softly pronounced, Lavu – is also related to the Hebrew Leviathan, 'the piercing serpent; even leviathan that crooked serpent' (*Isaiah* xxvii, 1). Further described as a 'dragon', leviathan corresponds to the Greek Typhon and to the celestial bulls, serpents and dragons that appear in numerous myths of the most varied ethnic provenance.

It is quite conceivable that the widespread role of bull and serpent in myth and religion stems from some common experience. Labbu's appearance suggests that this celestial serpent 'fifty miles long' may have been a comet. Cosmic occurrences of this kind, being universally visible but not predictable, were always regarded as bad omens because they disturbed the divine order of things. The Bible, too, associates the 'strong arm of the Lord', visible as a pillar of cloud by day and a pillar of fire by night, with the ten Egyptian plagues. This may also have been a comet which the children of Israel took to be 'the finger of the Lord'.

Unexpectedly, Hebrew brings us full circle. The Hebrew word for a ray of light is *koren*, but *koren* also means horn. A classic example of this dual interpretation occurs in Michelangelo's *Moses*. Because the Bible states that Moses had a *koren* on his head, meaning either horn or ray, Michelangelo portrayed him with horns. The fact that *koren* tended to be construed as horn, albeit at a later stage, is attributable to the Latin word for horn, the Semitic-based *cornu*, from which the name Cornelius, or 'little horn', was formed.

Because our ancestors had no explanation or term for comets, they described them according to their appearance as serpents, rays, horns or bulls. The Chinese, for example, leaned more heavily towards the serpent and dragon interpretation, whereas the horn – the bull's symbol – became central to the cult of the Mediterranean area.

Whether a comet be likened to a serpent or a bull depends on the beholder's angle of vision. If it is seen sideways on, it resembles a fiery serpent or horn. If it is approaching or receding, it looks more like a ball (the 'solid' core of the comet) trailing a pair of tails (luminous particles of gas). And, because sunlight always repels a comet's tail, a comet passing the earth presents a variable appearance readily suggestive of some struggle between cosmic forces.

Given the existence of the celestial bull or serpent concept, this may explain how the people of antiquity came to develop a bull-cult in the first place. The bull-cult would have symbolized a comet just as the goddess Ishtar symbolized love, the sun-god the sun, the moon-goddess the moon or the Lord Sabaoth of the Old Testament the 'Lord of Hosts'.

Our ancestors may well have discerned a bull's head in this awe-inspiring cosmic occurrence. True to the dictates of homoeo-pathic magico-mythical thinking, they may also have concluded that they could, like Gilgamesh, avert its dangers by killing 'the' bull or *a* bull. It is conceivable, therefore, that the bull-cult symbolized man's victory over an age-old and terrifying experience of which each new comet was a fresh reminder. This would explain why the Hittite Weather-god, like the Indian god Shiva, the Destroyer (!), stands on a bull to symbolize its subjection just like the deities of Çatal Hüyük thousands of years earlier. Four of the eight figures of male deities found at the Stone Age site were mounted on a bull, and the prototype of the Hittite Weather-god at Kültepe, which existed before the Indo-European settlers established their bull-cult, was likewise accompanied by a bull.

After all that has been said, we are entitled to wonder if the designation 'weather-god' is apt. Even though, like Zeus, he is occasionally identified as lord of the elements by the thunderbolt in his hand, the vanquisher of the celestial bull probably originated as a cosmic personage like the Sun-goddess of Arinna. The term 'weather-god' has taken root, however. Apposite or not, it defines a Stone Age deity who dominated religious thinking for thousands of years before receiving his quietus. Even the immortal gods survive only for as long as they are required by mortal men.

Myths, hymns and ordinances

Like Hittite architecture, art and religion, Hittite literature attained its high-water mark during the Imperial era – though 'literature' verges on overstatement because not even the few surviving myths are such as would merit that definition today. Most of the extant texts were committed to writing or freshly transcribed between 1400 and 1200 BC.

The majority of the cuneiform tablets that have been found relate to religious rites and precepts and give detailed instructions on how to perform certain magical acts. Even though relatively few of these precepts have been translated and published to date, the remarkable extent to which life was governed by religious ideas and rites is already apparent: roughly three-quarters of all the texts found are religious in content. They are also immensely tedious.

This is not merely because they express every idea twice over. Repetition, a stylistic aid corresponding to our own rhyme, is something they have in common with other Hittite texts and with writings from the Semitic language-area. Even the Psalms rely on a *parallelismus membrorum*, or reiteration of an idea or image in paraphrase, which invests them with serene beauty.

The really boring feature of these religious texts is the fussy precision on which the efficacy of ritual depended. Not without reason, we are reminded of modern officialese: the civil code of today was the religious precept of the Hittite era.

To quote a typical instance, the Luwian-Hittite Tunnawi ritual opens with the words:

Thus speaks Tunnawi, the old woman:
If a person, man or woman, has become unclean in some way,
or been called unclean by some other person,
or if a woman's children are for ever dying,

or her unborn children for ever falling [i.e. being miscarried],
or if the reproductive organs of some man or woman fail on
    account of forms of uncleanness,
and if that person perceives uncleanness in himself,
then shall that person, man or woman, perform the ritual of
    uncleanness as follows, it being called 'the Ritual of the
    River'...

There ensues a laboriously enumerated list of all the requisite
ritual aids, including animals such as sheep, piglets and dogs whose
sex must match that of the persons making sacrifice. The latter
must also plug their ears and dress in black. Going down to the
river at night, the old woman Tunnawi propitiates an underworld
goddess who dwells in the stream by sacrificing bread and drink.
She then takes mud from the river-bed and fashions two human
figures, twelve tongues, two oxen and two door-hinges. These
are laid out on the bank together with other objects such as wool
and eagles' wings.

Next morning, when the persons afflicted with uncleanness
appear, wool of various colours is cast over them. The old woman
displays the animals and mud figures, enunciating certain magic
formulas designed to transfer the uncleanness to these proxies.
This done, she bathes her hands in wine and begins a new invocation using warm pebbles, then bathes her hands in water and
performs a third invocation with fir-cones. Thereafter, the persons
making sacrifice are divested of the coloured strands of wool and
their limbs individually rid of uncleanness by means of a certain
verbal formula. Finally, they wash off any superficial uncleanness
by bathing in the river while the old woman scrubs one of her clay
figures to guard against fresh contamination and dispel the wrath
of the gods or spirits of the dead.

In the same way, all conceivable lapses of conduct can be
remedied with special sacrifices and acts of atonement. These
include a ritual antidote to family quarrels whose description
occupies well over a hundred lines of cuneiform.

The common feature of all these rituals is that guilt is ultimately transferred to an effigy, a live animal or even another person. We find the same disburdening procedure in the Biblical scapegoat and the self-sacrificial death of the Christian Redeemer.

A similar approach to atonement is manifest in the Hittite collections of laws. Although most of these relate to individual cases tried under the Hittite civil and penal code, the judgements make it clear that, after an early 'eye for an eye' period, offences could be redeemed with money or labour. The emphasis was on restitution rather than retaliation, a respect in which Hittite law differed markedly from other ancient oriental codes. One passage reads: 'If one person injures another and the latter falls sick, he [the guilty party] shall tend the aforesaid person. He shall give someone in his place, and [that someone] shall work in his [the injured party's] house. As soon as he is well, he [the guilty party] shall give him six shekels of silver, likewise the doctors' fees.'

Hittite chroniclers, too, showed a remarkable degree of independence compared with those of neighbouring countries. They soon stopped mythicizing their own history and, even in early Hittite times, began to compile factual and chronologically arranged accounts of their rulers' campaigns and exploits. Even Hattusili I, the first ruler to succeed the somewhat legendary Tabarna, committed his annals to writing in a recently discovered inscription. We can therefore apply the term historiography to the earliest Hittite chronicles of *ca.* 1650 BC, if not to the Anitta text which antedates them by 150 years.

Having already quoted a number of passages from the Annals of Mursili and similar texts, I need not embark on any more detailed discussion of this branch of Hittite literature.

Because the Hittites drew little distinction between profane and religious writing, prayers and hymns constitute another historical source. Like Mursili in his plague-prayers, the Hittite monarchs couched their wishes, requirements and problems in the form of petitions to the gods or represented their variously legitimate acts as divine ordinances, so that – conversely – their annals are studded with religious pronouncements and invocations.

But Hittite religious writing, too, displays a practical streak. There is an almost total absence of meditation on the ways of god and man. Isolated passages – e.g. 'Life is bound up with death and death with life. Mortal man does not live for ever: his days are numbered.' – do recall Old Testament psalms, but they are few and far between. As a rule, relations between the 'thousand gods' and their worshippers were conducted on a matter-of-fact level: expiatory rites and sacrifice, request and fulfilment – nothing more. With the possible exception of Mursili, the Hittites had no Job to ponder on divine justice, no Psalmist to praise the Almighty or wrestle with his personal destiny.

The same applies to the myths which the Indo-European settlers adopted, either from the Anatolian population or their Hurrian neighbours, and incorporated in their own body of ideas. Almost devoid of literary shape, they are simple tales which translate an idea or event into verbal imagery.

In one myth from the Anatolian area, for example, a king's claim to divine rule is not merely stated but – as befits a myth – set forth in narrative terms. The king conducts a long conversation with the proto-Hattian throne-goddess Halmasuitta in which he summons her to accompany him into the highlands, take herself off behind a mountain and not become 'his man', his relative or friend. He promises her gifts of great splendour if she will guard the mountain far from his throne, because – to quote his rather crude reasoning – 'To me, the King, have the gods, the Sun-god and Weather-god, entrusted the throne. And now I, the King, protect my land and house. Come not into my house! [Neither] shall I come into your house.'

Other myths strive to account for incomprehensible or awe-inspiring natural occurrences in the same way as Biblical stories of the Flood or the expulsion from Paradise.

One such myth tells how, once upon a time, the moon fell out of the sky and landed in the city. The Weather-god sent rain and wind after it, filling the people with fear and trembling. Next, the goddess Hapantili tried to compel the moon-god to return, but in vain. She then had to be assisted by a second goddess renowned for her wisdom and magical powers. The end of the cuneiform text is so mutilated that we do not know how this peculiar tale turns out. We only know that it was recited by a priest 'when the Weather-god thunders sorely'.

The mythical fight with the dragon Illuyanka is recorded in two very different versions. This myth bears a detailed resemblance to the Gilgamesh Epic but substitutes a serpent for the celestial bull. (Illuyanka may not be a name at all, and possibly means 'snake'.)

The older version tells how the Sun-god does battle with the serpent in the city of Kiskilussa and is vanquished by it. He laments his misfortune to the gods, and the goddess Inar prepares a great feast. She visits a mortal man in the city of Zigaratta, explains the situation and asks him to help her. The man promises to do so on condition that she sleeps with him. Inar agrees, takes him with her and hides him. Having titivated herself, she invites Illuyanka to the feast. As soon as the serpent is drunk, the man binds it and the Weather-god slays it. True to her promise, the goddess keeps the man with her but counsels him to look out of the window because he will then see his wife and children. After twenty days the man does so, becomes homesick and asks the goddess to release him.

The later version of the Illuyanka myth embodies the same elements but tends in quite another direction:

'The dragon Illuyanka vanquished the Weather-god and took his heart and eyes. The Weather-god sought to revenge himself on it. He took the daughter of a poor man to wife and begot a son with her. But, when the son was full-grown, he took the daughter of the dragon Illuyanka to wife. The Weather-god enjoined his son: When you go into the house of your wife, ask them for my heart and my eyes . . . And when he went there and asked for the heart, they gave it him. He then asked them for the eyes, and they gave him those too. He brought them to the Weather-god, his father, and thus restored the Weather-god's heart and eyes.

The Sphinx Gate at Alaca Hüyük, a Bronze Age city not far from Hattusa, the Hittite metropolis. It was the capital of a wealthy principality when the Indo-European Hittites migrated to Anatolia.

Fertility-idols of the Early Bronze Age. *Left:* bronze statuette of a mother and child from Horoztepe (2100-2000 BC.) *Right:* silver statuette with gilded head and gold jewellery, found in a grave near Ankara (*ca.*2000 BC.)

Bronze and silver cult-standards and a gold diadem from the royal graves of Alaca Hüyük (2300-2100 B.C.). In terms of craftsmanship and material, the Alaca Hüyük treasures represent a high-water mark in the Early Bronze Age art of Anatolia.

Being religious emblems, the cult-standards of Alaca Hüyük commonly incorporated horned beasts such as this twelve-point stag (the head is encased in gilded silver) flanked by two panthers and surmounted by an arch adorned with eight pairs of bulls' horns and stylized blossoms (height 9 ins., 2300-2100 B.C.)

When his [the god's] form was restored, he went to the sea to do battle. He was locked in battle with the dragon Illuyanka and about to vanquish him. But the son of the Weather-god was with the dragon Illuyanka, and he cried to his father in heaven: Slay me too, spare me not! Then the Weather-god slew the dragon Illuyanka and his son as well.'

Greek mythology was likewise influenced by this heroic legend from ancient Anatolia. In the story of the fight between Zeus and Typhon, a huge monster with a hundred dragons' heads, Zeus loses the sinews in his hands and feet, not his heart and eyes. According to the Greek myth, it was Hermes who stole them back and restored them. The fact that Typhon was not a Greek importation from the Egyptian area (the Egyptian equivalent of Typhon was Set) emerges from the geographical names employed. The Mons Cassius of the Greek legend stands on the Syrian coast, and the Corycaean grotto in which Typhon dwelt was situated beside the Cilician shores of Asia Minor – or so, at least, Apollodorus informs us in his *Bibliotheca* (first–second century AD). In pictorial representations, Typhon becomes the Greek Hydra and is related to the fire-breathing dragon of the Germanic Siegfried saga.

Something quite else is recounted in the 'Myth of the vanished god Telepinu' [the harvest-god], though only two words in it contain an allusion to the actual occurrence. These are 'fog' and 'smoke', which extinguish fire and suffocate living creatures:

'When Telepinu had departed, fog laid hold of the windows and smoke laid hold of the house. The brands were extinguished on the hearth, the gods stifled at their altars. The sheep stifled in their pen, the cattle in their stall. The ewe refused her lamb, the cow her calf. Telepinu departed . . . Weariness [?] overcame him.'

Having described the cause, the myth proceeds to illustrate what happens when the harvest-god goes his way:

'Then did barley and emmer flourish no more; then did cattle, sheep and men couple no more, and those that were with young could bring forth no longer. Plants [?] withered. Trees withered and brought forth no shoots. Pastures withered, springs ran dry. Famine arose in the land, so that men and gods perished.'

But what was the cause? One parallel might be seen in an occurrence dating from historical times: in AD 79, Vesuvius obliterated Pompeii in just the same manner, that is to say, with a rain of ash and a cloud of noxious vapour. Speculative or not, there is something to be said for the theory that this myth describes the effects of a volcanic eruption, especially as Anatolia did have active volcanoes of the sort depicted at Çatal Hüyük.

But there is another possibility, namely, that the Telepinu myth describes one specific and authentic eruption. Taken in conjunction with radiocarbon readings, finds made at Knossos and on the Mediterranean island of Thera (now Santorin) indicate that the volcano of Thera became active in 1470 BC, after a long spell of dormancy, and literally blew up. Only the rim of the former volcano remains, buried beneath 100 ft of volcanic ash and looking from the air like a Pacific atoll with a small new volcano smoking at its centre.

More finds and computations disclose that the eruption of Thera not only made itself felt for hundreds of miles around – demolishing stout ashlar walls at Knossos – but shrouded the entire Mediterranean area in a pall of ash. This would explain the proverbial 'Egyptian darkness' and the exodus of the children of Israel. It would also account for the effects mentioned in the Telepinu myth and transform the myth itself into a dim memory of a volcanic eruption which many have associated with the disappearance of legendary Atlantis.

The remainder of the story concerns the attempt to find Telepinu and appease him:

'The great Sun-god held a banquet and bade the thousand gods attend. They ate but were not filled, they drank but did not slake their thirst. Then did the Weather-god grow fearful for his son Telepinu: "My son Telepinu is not here. He flew into a rage and took with him all that was good." The gods, great and small, set off in quest of Telepinu. The Sun-god sent forth the swift eagle: "Go, search the lofty mountains, search the deep valleys! Search the watery depths!" The eagle went forth but found him not. He brought back tidings to the Weather-god: "I found him not, Telepinu, the noble god."

'The Weather-god spoke to the Mistress of the Gods: "What shall we do? We shall die of hunger!" And the Mistress of the Gods spoke to the Weather-god: "Do something, Weather-god! Go, seek Telepinu yourself!" So the Weather-god set off in quest of Telepinu. He knocked at the gate of his city, but he was not there and opened not. He broke its bolt and its lock, but to no avail. He desisted and lay down to rest. But the Mistress of the Gods sent forth the bee: "Go, seek Telepinu!" The Storm-god said to the Mistress of the Gods: "The gods, great and small, have sought and failed to find him, and shall this bee go and find him? Its wings are small, like itself. Shall they be compelled to grant that it [the bee] is greater than themselves?" The Mistress of the Gods spoke to the Weather-god: "Have done with the bee; it shall go forth and find him." The Mistress of the Gods sent forth the little bee: "Go, seek Telepinu. When you find him, sting him in the hands [and] feet. Take wax and wipe out his eyes. Cleanse him and bring him here to me." '

The bee finds Telepinu asleep in a wood and blithely stings him. At this, Telepinu flies into another rage, and various sacrifices and acts of sympathetic magic – 'as firewood is consumed, so shall the wrath, fury, sin and rancour of Telepinu be consumed' – are required to appease the god sufficiently for him to return home.

The 'Song of Ullikummi' hails from the milieu of Hurrian myth but was incorporated in Hittite traditions like the Akkadian version of the Gilgamesh Epic.

The Song of Ullikummi develops the divine 'succession myth'. Probably the earliest literary treatment of Creation and the primordial gods' struggle for supremacy, it is strikingly paralleled centuries later by the Kronos myths in Hesiod's *Theogonia*.

Before dealing with Ullikummi, the strange diorite monster which could neither hear nor speak, only grow, I shall therefore dwell briefly on this theogony, or genealogy of the gods.

The early stages are tedious. Alayu is the first to reign. Then, in the ninth year, Anu vanquishes him and throws him to the 'dark earth'. In the ninth year thereafter, Anu is vanquished by Kumarbi, who casts him down from heaven. Then the pace grows hotter. The victorious Kumarbi bites off Anu's genitals as he falls, but Anu only laughs when Kumarbi devours 'the manhood of Anu', and says: 'You exult at that which you have within you because you devour my manhood. Exult not at that which you have within you. I have placed a heavy burden therein. I have fathered three gods on you. I have got you with the mighty Weather-god, with the river Aranzah [Tigris] and the great god Tashmishu . . .' Filled with alarm, Kumarbi spits out the contents of his mouth, but two seeds remain.

'In the tenth month the earth began to groan. When the earth groaned . . . it brought into the world [two] children.' Kumarbi's two offspring were the Tigris and the god Tashmishu. The seed he expelled – though here the text becomes fragmentary – must therefore have been the Weather-god, for Kumarbi does all in his power to destroy this usurper of the kingdom of the gods.

Kumarbi's struggle with the Weather-god forms the theme of the Song of Ullikummi.

'He plots the Weather-god's destruction – Kumarbi hatches wise thoughts in his mind, strings them together like the beads of a necklace . . .'

And then he devises a solution. Too weak to fight the Weather-god himself, he begets a champion of harder material than the gods. 'He took a stick in his hand, shod his feet with the winds as with swift sandals. He departed from Urkish, his city, and betook himself to . . . where lay a great stone. The stone was three [?] miles long and . . . half a mile wide . . . His desire mounted and he slept with the stone . . . five times did he take it, he took it ten times . . .'

The dots do not denote any deliberate omissions or expurgations, merely that isolated words and whole lines are missing from the cuneiform tablets at these points. We simply do not know how the original text ran, so the narrative seems exceptionally condensed.

The gigantic stone duly bears Kumarbi a son, and Kumarbi rejoices. 'He pressed him to his heart, he fondled him. He resolved to give him a propitious name. Kumarbi said to himself: "What name [shall I give] this child . . . let him be called Ullikummi. Let him ascend into heaven and possess himself of the kingdom . . . let him smite the Weather-god, let him crush him . . ." '

Kumarbi then addresses several of the gods: 'Take this child and lead him forth with you. Bear him to the dark earth. Make haste! Place him like an arrow upon the right shoulder of Upelluri. In one day shall he grow an ell, in one month a yoke . . .'

So the gods place Ullikummi on the right shoulder of Upelluri, who is standing in water. 'And the mighty water caused him to grow. In one day he grew an ell, in one month a yoke . . .' He eventually grows out of the water and attains the height of the temples. Soon, he is as tall as the sky.

The Sun-god looks down from heaven and is dismayed by Ullikummi. 'Who is this mighty god that stands there in the sea? His body is not as that of other gods . . .'

Other gods have noticed that Ullikummi's body consists of diorite. Consulting a dictionary, we learn that diorite is a variety of greenstone, and that greenstone is an eruptive rock. We now understand the myth's imagery: what is being described here is nothing more nor less than the rapid emergence of a volcano from the sea. The myth itself invariably refers to Ullikummi as 'the stone'.

The Sun-god approaches the Weather-god, perturbed by the magnitude of the conflict ahead: 'An upheaval in heaven and famine and death on earth.'

The Weather-god inspects the great rock. 'Whereupon his arms sank down. The God of the Storm sat down on the ground. Tears ran from his eyes like streams. With tears in his eyes, the God of the Storm spoke: "Who can withstand [such a spectacle]? Who shall dare to join battle?" '

The goddess Ishtar begins by trying to enchant the monster with songs and practise her feminine wiles on him. 'Ishtar took a harp and the instrument [called] galgalturi . . . she laid [her clothes] upon the ground. She sang, [did] Ishtar. She supported herself with her elbows [?] on a rock and the stone of the sea . . . There came a great wave of the sea, and the great wave spoke to Ishtar: "For whom do you sing? For whom do you fill your mouth [with song]? The man is deaf; he hears not. He is blind; he sees not . . . So go, Ishtar, seek your brother for as long as he [Ullikummi] is not become all-powerful; for as long as his gaze is not become terrible." When Ishtar heard these words, she had done. She cast aside the harp and galgalturi . . .'

Meanwhile, Ullikummi continues to grow, 'and the height of the rock attained 9000 miles and its girth 9000 miles'. The gods arm themselves for battle: bulls are anointed and thunderbolts unleashed. Seventy gods assail Ullikummi but are defeated and fall into the sea. The Weather-god is likewise defeated: myths, too, have their fixed conventions, and victory never goes to the first comer.

Ullikummi is still standing on the shoulders of Upelluri. Ea, the god of wisdom and the watery depths, approaches him, but Upelluri – who is comparable with the Atlas of Greek mythology – has noticed nothing. 'Do you not know, O Upelluri, do you not know the tidings? Do you not know this mighty god whom Kumarbi has fashioned in order to set him against the gods, to encompass the death of the Weather-god? He has created a rival for the God of the Storm. He stands in the sea like a rock of greenstone. Do you not know him? Like a tower has he arisen; he has set himself against the heavens, against the sacred house of the gods . . . '

'Upelluri answered: "When they built heaven and earth upon

me, I knew nothing of it. When they came and sundered heaven from earth with a cleaver, I knew nothing of that either. Now my right shoulder pains me, but I know not what god it is." And when Ea heard these words, he turned Upelluri's shoulder: the rock stood on Upelluri's shoulder like an arrow.'

Ea's conversation with Upelluri gives him an idea. 'Hearken, ancient gods, you who know the words of yore. Open the ancient store-chambers of your fathers and grandfathers. Let the ancient seals of your ancestors be brought and sealed anew. Let them bring the ancient cleaver of copper with which they sundered heaven and earth. Let them cut off the feet of Ullikummi, whom Kumarbi has created so as to make of him a rival of the gods.'

Ea, the god of wisdom and the deep, does indeed turn Ulli-kummi into a cripple, whereupon the other gods regain their courage. Together, they 'began to bellow against Ullikummi like cattle. The Weather-god leapt on to his chariot . . . with thunder he descended to the sea and began to do battle with the rock . . .'

We shall never know the full truth that lurks behind a myth of this sort. We can only guess at the proper words to describe the occurrence underlying it, for myths are not fiction but experiences seen with other eyes and told in different terms.

Even when Ullikummi utters his final boast – 'In heaven shall I take possession of the kingdom . . .' – it is the Weather-god who prevails. Once again, victory goes to the god whose age-old symbol is the bull.

There is always something that eludes our comprehension, in myth as in recorded history. This is the why and wherefore – a question which each must answer for himself.

VIII FINAL OBLIVION

'. . . as if it had never been'

Although there are no records of how the Hittite Empire perished, we probably know why.

The end of the Hittite Empire was a mirror-image of its own beginnings. Then, it had been the Hittites who penetrated Asia Minor, rose to power over the centuries and ruled for 600 years. Now it was their turn to be supplanted by others.

We have no precise idea of the others' identity because their arrival coincides with a dearth of historical sources. The only people who managed to withstand this migratory influx were the Egyptians, but their references to it are not over-helpful. They called the newcomers 'foreigners' or – and this term has passed into the ancient historian's vocabulary – 'Sea People'.

Rameses III of Egypt (*ca.* 1198–66) records in an inscription in the temple of Medinet Habu that they were not a homogeneous race but an alliance of 'Philistines, Zeker, Shekelesh, Denen and Weshesh'.

This takes us little further. Of all these tribes or peoples, the only ones we can identify with any certainty are the Philistines, whom the Bible equates with the Cretans. Identification of the others is rendered more difficult because the hieroglyphs supply no vowels, with the result that some, for instance, read Shekelesh where others read Shakalsha. Unanimity reigns only in respect of the 'Denen', whom many associate with Homer's Danaoi.

With the exception of the Philistines, they could not have been true 'sea people'. This is apparent from their route, which Rameses III also records, together with a curious point of detail. In conquering Asia Minor and the Near East and advancing as far as the Nile itself, these Sea People – probably so called by the Egyptians because they came from the north, i.e. from the far side of the Mediterranean – relied on ox-carts. No seafaring race intent on conquest would have set out in ponderous vehicles requiring several oxen to pull them, least of all from an area which had long been familiar with the swift, light, horse-drawn chariots of the Hurrians and Hittites. We even have proof that these ox-carts were no colourful figment of some historian's imagination. Rameses III left a pictorial record of his struggle with the foreign invaders at Medinet Habu, and ox-carts are always in evidence.

The sequence of the Sea People's conquests is another indication that they were alien tribes who advanced overland. The Pharaoh's inscription says: 'The foreigners conspired together on their islands. All of a sudden, the countries vanished and were dispersed in battle. No country withstood their force of arms. Hatti, Kode [Kizzuwadna in the south of Asia Minor], Carchemish, Arzawa and Alashiya – all were swiftly laid waste. A camp was pitched at a place in Amurru [northern Lebanon]. They destroyed its people, and its land was as if it had never been. They drew near Egypt with fire going on before . . .'

It is therefore possible to assume that the Sea People came from the European mainland and were engaged in a large-scale migratory movement of which the 'Dorian invasion' also formed part.

How far north this movement began, we do not know. Even the Balkans are regarded as a 'transit area' by some authorities, who draw attention to Homer's emphasis on 'fair-haired' Menelaus, 'fair-haired' Odysseus and the 'blue-eyed daughter of Zeus', also to the Spartans' inheritance of a warlike disposition from the Dorians, whose name may signify the same as 'Ger-Mannen': spear-warriors.

What is certain is that, in about 1200 BC, the appearance of the known world underwent a radical change. The Minoan culture of Crete was dislodged and destroyed by a new population. The Dorians roamed southwards into Greece, which for four centuries relapsed into a dark age unillumined by historical records. The Egyptians had to repel at least two invasions by the Sea People and were afflicted with periods of weakness and confusion. The

Syrian area took on an entirely new aspect.

The Trojan War coincides with this period, as do the voyages of Odysseus and the conquest of the Promised Land by the Israelites. Some time later, an Asiatic people wandered westwards to Italy and became the Etruscans. It was a period of ethnic turmoil, of vast migrations in one direction or another.

Great nations like the Egyptians and Hittites forfeited their importance overnight or became extinct, to be replaced by new nations, kingdoms and cultures.

The cause of this ferment remains obscure. We know that migratory upheavals of this type occurred *ca.* 3000 BC in the Semitico-Arab milieu, *ca.* 2000 BC when the Indo-European tribes made their move, *ca.* 1200 BC when the Sea People invaded Asia Minor, and, last of all, in the early centuries of our own era, which witnessed a great migration by the Germanic peoples. Roughly speaking, therefore, the face of the map has changed every thousand years without our being able to advance any real explanation of the fact. Although these upheavals have been ascribed to sudden spells of cold or drought and the famines associated with them, such theories cannot be confirmed because other tribes streamed into the allegedly uninhabitable areas and settled there.

Some support for the famine theory may be seen in a clay tablet from Syrian Ugarit which had just been deposited in the kiln for firing when the city was overrun. Found there 3000 years later, this letter had originated in Hittite territory. It spoke of foreign invaders and a great famine, but we may be confusing cause and effect: perhaps the famine had been occasioned by the enemy's depradations and was a consequence of their southward swoop, not its determining factor.

We do not know, either, why the foreign invaders proved superior to the established powers despite their archaic ox-carts. As in myth, so in history, a residue of obscurity remains. We are just as ignorant of how the Hittites lost their supremacy in Anatolia after more than 500 years as we are of how they acquired

King Tudhaliya surmounted by an aedicula, or emblem of royal authority. Left and right of the king is a rendering of his name in Hittite pictograms, known as Hieroglyphic Luwian.

The Hittite Empire collapsed *ca.*1200 B.C., when Asia Minor was invaded by the Sea People. This Egyptian portrayal of the invaders shows that they travelled in ox-carts with solid, not spoked, wheels.

it in the first place.

When Tudhaliya IV concluded his treaty with Rameses II and prevailed on him to marry a Hittite princess, everything still seemed well. Two world powers had reached an accommodation and made peace. What could have disrupted such an arrangement? Probably, the fact that the Sea People's invasion had already begun, because Tudhaliya IV is the last Hittite king about whom we possess detailed information.

It is assumed that Tudhaliya was succeeded by his son Arnuwanda III, who had already won a reputation for generalship during his father's lifetime. Whether or not another Tudhaliya reigned after him is debatable. Found in 1957, a text written by the scribe Hanikkuili, who is known to have lived ca. 1200 BC, contains the words: 'When Tudhaliya, Great King, son of Arnuwanda, installed himself on the throne, the following sacrifices were made . . .' However, since Hanikkuili demonstrably copied ancient tablets as well, it is possible that this tablet was a copy of an old list of kings. A Tudhaliya-Arnuwanda succession had occurred two centuries earlier.

Thanks to a discovery made in 1953, we know that the last Hittite king was another Suppiluliuma (sometimes written Suppiluliama). A brother of Arnuwanda, he reigned ca. 1200 during a period of such turmoil and dissolution that he was obliged to make his subjects swear an oath of allegiance in order to assert his authority. The following declaration was made by a senior scribe of wooden tablets at the Hittite court: 'I shall defend the issue of my lord Suppiluliuma alone. I shall not support another man, descendant of Suppiluliuma the First, descendant of Mursili, descendant of Muwatalli and Tudhaliya.' This is only one of several such oaths of allegiance, most of them cursorily inscribed.

Externally, the Hittite government confined itself to berating renegade provinces by letter, incapable of anything more fearsome than moral condemnation. There was obviously no question of reconquering them – the rot had set in.

The Sea People, this time genuinely sea-borne, had by now reached and occupied Alashiya (Cyprus) on their way to Syria. Suppiluliuma made a last desperate attempt to recapture the island. 'I mustered . . . and swiftly reached the sea – I, Suppiluliuma the Great King. But ships from Alashiya opposed me three times in battle in the midst of the sea. I destroyed them. I seized the ships and set them ablaze in the midst of the sea. But, when I came on to dry land, the foes from Alashiya opposed me in battle.'

We do not know the sequel.

Rameses III concludes his report on the 'foreigners', or Sea People, by characterizing their attitude as follows:

'They laid hands on the countries of the whole earth. Their hearts were filled with assurance, with the belief that "Our plans will succeed." '

And succeed they did. Not only Hattusa but other cities perished in a raging inferno which left them buried beneath a layer of cinders. Over 500 years of Hittite history subsided into rubble and ashes, and the Hittite Empire was 'as if it had never been . . .'

A closed book to Herodotus

Although the Hittite Empire and its cities were engulfed by the great migration of 3200-odd years ago, the Hittites lived on.

Some of the inhabitants of Asia Minor were driven south-eastwards into Syria. Here they attached themselves to existing Hittite city-states like Carchemish or founded new principalities which were more than a mere perpetuation of the old empire on colonial territory.

Assyria, now the strongest power in the area, began by allowing these principalities their independence. Assyrian annals still referred to them as Hittite or even 'Great Hattian', and their rulers – e.g. Mutallu of Kummuchi – continued to style themselves after kings of the Imperial era. The inhabitants of these small Late Hittite or 'neo-Hittite' states were the Hittites of the Bible.

In the course of centuries, the name lost its application to the Hittites proper. In about 1000 BC, for example, the Syrian area was penetrated by Aramaic, i.e. Semitic, nomads who settled at isolated points and gained political ascendancy. These Aramaic settlers were likewise called Hittites by the Assyrians because, while retaining their own language and gods, the Aramaic tribes adopted a superficially Hittite style in the fields of art and architecture.

In many cases, this tangle of Semitic and Hittite tribes can only be unravelled by comparing scripts. The Hittites continued to use a partly undeciphered pictographic script, Hieroglyphic Luwian, whereas the Aramaic princes wrote Phoenician.

Finally, ca. 730 BC, we find King Asitawanda adorning the walls of his palace at Karatepe in northern Syria with parallel inscriptions in Hieroglyphic Luwian and Old Phoenician.

These provide the last information of truly Hittite provenance. The Hittites increasingly abandoned their own characteristics.

In art, they adopted the style of their environment, first Assyrian, later Aramaic, until they became wholly merged with other races.

The Assyrians seized one Hittite city-state after another. Carchemish fell after a rebellion in 717; Marash, in the far north of Syria, was conquered by Sargon II in 711.

Five hundred years after the downfall of the Hittite Empire there were no Hittites left – or rather, there existed no definite area or particular tribe that could properly have been termed Hittite.

The Books of the Maccabees, a historical work included in the Old Testament Apocrypha and written *ca.* 100 BC by a Palestinian Jew, allude to the Hittite Empire in their very first sentence: 'After Alexander son of Philip, the Macedonian, who came from the land of Kittim [Hatti], had defeated Darius, king of the Persians and the Medes, he succeeded him as king.'

Written more than a thousand years after the Hittite Empire collapsed, this is the last Biblical reference to its founders. In Asia Minor, the land of Kittim, other kingdoms had long since come and gone.

According to Greek tradition, it was the Indo-European Phrygians from Macedonia and the Balkans who migrated to Anatolia *ca.* 1200 BC, either in company with or as part of the Sea People. We do not know if they helped to destroy Hattusa, but this theory derives some support from the discovery of Phrygian settlements and works of art superimposed on its ruins at Boğazköy.

But although Assyrian cuneiform texts from the reign of Tiglath-pileser I (*ca.* 1100 BC) already contain allusions to the Phrygians – whom the Assyrians called 'Muski' – it was 400 years before the new settlers gained power. They are not mentioned again until *ca.* 750, when Assyrian annals make an abrupt reference to the Muski and their ruler, Mita. King Mita had joined the King of Carchemish in an alliance against the Assyrians but was defeated and compelled to pay tribute.

We know this Phrygian monarch by his Greek name. He was the

King Midas of whom Greek legend related that all he touched turned to gold. Since all his food and drink was similarly alchemized into that precious metal, Midas would have died of hunger and thirst had not Dionysus advised him to bathe in the river Pactolus. This transferred his 'golden touch' to the river, whose sands contained gold ever afterwards.

This Midas, King of the Mygdonians (Macedonians) in Phrygia, was the son of Gordius, who gave his name to the Phrygian capital, Gordium, in north-west Anatolia (now Yassi Hüyük, west of Ankara). Gordium, too, is associated with a familiar legend because it was there that Alexander the Great cut or untied the celebrated and proverbial 'Gordian knot'.

Midas himself built another city, Ankyra, and is thus credited by legend with having founded the capital of modern Turkey.

None of this has anything to do with the Hittites, and we could entirely dismiss King Midas were it not for another curious association.

Ovid gives a humorous version of the following legend in his *Metamorphoses*. One day, the forest-god Pan engaged in a musical contest with Apollo. Old King Tmolus, who was acting as judge, shrewdly awarded the prize to Apollo for his lyre-playing. King Midas, who had also been listening, preferred Pan's pipe-playing and was unwise enough to say so. This annoyed Apollo, who caused Midas to grow a pair of ass's ears. Midas hid these beneath a cap which he never removed except when having his hair dressed by a slave. Not unnaturally, the slave was threatened with every conceivable penalty, earthly and divine, if he advertised the king's ludicrous misfortune.

Finding it impossible to keep the secret to himself but afraid to give it away, he went off and dug a hole in the ground, 'and into the hole, with low, muttered words, he whispered what manner of ears he had seen on his master. Then, by casting back the earth, he buried the evidence of his voice, and, having thus filled the pit, stole silently away . . .' This preserved the secret, but only until reeds grew up over the spot in spring-time. Then, passers-by heard them whisper 'Midas has ass's ears, Midas has ass's ears . . .' – and the secret was out.

So much for a story which, like that of the gold-bearing river, was devised simply to explain what would otherwise have seemed inexplicable – in this case, the king's quaint head-gear. This 'Phrygian cap' was a red conical bonnet worn low on the forehead and curling forward at the tip, and the Greeks found it so laughable that their later works of art made it the distinguishing feature of all barbarians (foreigners), whatever their race.

Two and a half thousand years later the Phrygian cap reappeared as the *bonnet rouge* or Jacobin cap which was worn as a symbol of liberty during the French Revolution and still adorns Marianne, the allegorical figure of France, in the form of a knitted pompon-hat.

But what we call the Phrygian cap is older still. In fact, Marianne sports the head-dress of the Hittite Weather-god, which began life as a pointed tiara or turban but gradually evolved into a curving, horn-shaped cap and later acquired a pompon.

Because the Greeks themselves knew nothing about the Hittites or their gods and could not account for the Phrygians' quaint head-gear, they invented the tale of the ass's ears – fact transmuted into fiction.

By the time the Persians conquered Asia Minor in 546 and destroyed the kingdom of Phrygia, the Hittites had passed into oblivion. Their cities no longer bore Hittite names. New cultures with their own gods and their own way of life had buried the remains of Hittite civilization.

The Hittites were a closed book to the Greeks. Describing the statue of a Hittite god near Izmir on the west coast of Asia Minor in about 450 BC, Herodotus referred to it as a man 'in Egyptian dress'. He also identified Hittite hieroglyphs as 'sacred Egyptian characters'.

The Bible alone preserved a memory of this vanished race until, in our own day, archaeologists rediscovered the Hittites who styled themselves 'the Nation of a Thousand Gods'.

Appendix

List of Hittite Kings

(based on 'Middle Chronology')

	Akurgal	Klengel	
Pithana of Kussara			
Anitta of Kussara			
	ca. 1680		
Tabarna			
	ca. 1650	ca. 1650	Hattusili I
Hattusili I			
	ca. 1620		
Mursili I		ca. 1600	Mursili I
	ca. 1590	ca. 1590	Hantili
			Zidanta
		ca. 1550	Ammuna
	ca. 1525	ca. 1530	Huzziya
Telepinu			Telepinu
	ca. 1500		Hantili II
			Zidanta II
			Huzziya II
	ca. 1460		
Tudhaliya			
	1440		
Arnuwanda I			Tudhaliya
	1420		Arnuwanda (sequence
			Hattusili obscure)
Hattusili II			
	1400		
Tudhaliya III			
	1380	ca. 1380	
Suppiluliuma I			Suppiluliuma I
	1346	1346	
	1345		
		ca. 1330	Arnuwanda
Mursili II		1329	Mursili
	1315		
Muwatalli		ca. 1300	Muwatalli
	1282	ca. 1280	Mursili III
Mursili III	1275	ca. 1275	Hattusili III
Hattusili III			
	1250	ca. 1250	Tudhaliya IV
Tudhaliya IV			
	1220	ca. 1220	Arnuwanda III
Arnuwanda III			
	1190	ca. 1200	Suppiluliuma II
Suppiluliuma II			

NB. *Dates on left according to Akurgal, on right according to Klengel.*

303

Chronological tables

(based on 'Low Chronology')

MESOPOTAMIA	HITTITE EMPIRE	SYRIA-PALESTINE

		pre-3000
		    Chalcolithic
		    urban cultures

ca. 3000–2800
    Uruk period
ca. 2800–2700
    Djemdet Nasr period
ca. 2600–2350
    Early Dynastic period
    Ur I period *ca.* 2500
    Lagash: Urnashe
            Eannatum
            Entemena
            Lugalanda
            Urukagina
    Adab: Lugalannemundu
		ca. 3000
		    Transition to
		    bronze culture
		from 3000
		    Appearance of
		    Semites. Egyptian
		    and Sumerian
		    cultural influences

ca. 2350–2150
    Akkadian period
    Sargon
    Rimush
    Manishtusu
    Naramsin
    Sharkalisharri
ca. 2150–2070
    Gutian period
    Utuhengal of Uruk
    ca. 2070
ca. 2065–1955
    Ur III period
Urnammu   Gudea of
    Shulgi   Lagash
    Amarsin
    Shusin
    Ibbisin
ca. 1955–1700
    Isin-Larsa period
    Ishbierra ot Isin
	ca. 2300–2000
	    Period of the ancient
	    Anatolian royal graves
		ca. 2300
		    Akkadian campaigns
		    in N. Syria(?)
		    Palestine campaign
		    by Phiops I
		
		ca. 2000
		    Amorite invasion
		    Temporary crisis
		    of urban culture

MESOPOTAMIA	HITTITE EMPIRE	SYRIA-PALESTINE
1959–1927 Lipitishtar of Isin *ca.* 1875–1865 Sargon I of Assur *ca.* 1780 Rimsin of Larsa *ca.* 1757–1698 Shamshiadad I of Assur 1748–1716		
ca. 1830–1530 *Hammurabi Dynasty* Hammurabi (6th ruler) 1728–1686 Samsuiluna 1685–1648 Abieshuh 1647–1620 Ammiditana 1619–1583 Ammisaduqa 1582-1562 Samsuditana 1561–1530	*ca.* 1830–1715 *Ancient Assyrian* *settlement in Kanesh* Anitta of Kussara *ca.* 1715	after 1800 Hurrian invasion
		from 1670 Hyksos period Development of city-states
	ca. 1600–1500 *Old Hittite Kingdom* Labarna Hattusili I Mursili I *ca.* 1530 Hantili Zidanta	from 1570 Expulsion of the Hyksos. Revival of Egyptian influence
ca. 1530–1160 *Kassite period* Agukakrime *ca.* 1530 Karaïndash *ca.* 1420 Kurigalzu *ca.* 1390 Burnubariash II 1367–1346 Kurigalzu II 1336–1314	*ca.* 1500–1430 *Middle Kingdom* Telepinu Alluwamna Zidanta Huzziya	*ca.* 1530 Growth of Hittite power in N. Syria from 1520 Syrian campaigns by Tuthmosis III *ca.* 1500–1420 Heyday of Alalah
	ca. 1430–1200 *Hittite Empire* Hattusili II Tudhaliya III Suppiluliuma I from *ca.* 1380 Mursili II from *ca.* 1345 Muwatalli	*ca.* 1440–1360 Heyday of Ugarit *ca.* 1400–1350 Amarna period *ca.* 1350 Hittite supremacy in N. Syria
ca. 1380–1080 *Middle Assyrian* *Kingdom* Assuruballit I 1356–1320 Adadnirari I 1297–1266 Salmanassar I 1265–1235		

MESOPOTAMIA	HITTITE EMPIRE	SYRIA-PALESTINE
	from *ca.* 1315 Urhi-Teshub (=Mursili III) Hattusili from *ca.* 1280 Tudhaliya IV	1296 Battle of Kadesh
Tukultininurta I 1235–1198 Nebukadnezar I of Babylon (1128– *ca.* 1105) Tiglath-pileser I 1116–1078	from *ca.* 1250 Suppiluliuma II	1223 Death of Rameses II, exodus of Egypto- Hebrews from Egypt(?) *ca.* 1200 Iron Age begins. Sea People – Philistines Decline of Egyptian influence Israelite league from 1100 Aramaeans in N. and E. Syria *ca.* 1020–1000 Saul
	ca. 1000–711 Syro-Hittite petty kingdoms	*ca.* 1000–965(?) David 965–922(?) Solomon. Phoenicia dominated by Tyre 992 Secession of Israel from Judah
909–612 *Neo-Assyrian Kingdom* Adadnirari II 909–889 Tukultininurta II 888–884		

APPENDIX

MESOPOTAMIA	HITTITE EMPIRE	SYRIA-PALESTINE

Assurnasirpal II
883–859
Salmanassar III
858–824
Shamshiadad V
823–810
Adadnirari III
809–782
Tiglath-pileser III
   745–727
Salmanassar V
   726–722
   Sargon II 721–705
   Sanherib 704–681
Esarhaddon 680–669
Assurbanipal
   668–631

625–539
  Neo-Babylonian
   Kingdom
Nabopolassar
625–605
Nebukadnezar II
604–562
Amelmarduk
561–560
Nergalsharussur
559–556
Nabonidus
555–539

733
  Damascus becomes
  an Assyrian province
721
  N. Israel becomes
  an Assyrian province
701
  Sanherib's campaign
  against Judah
639–609
  Josiah king of
  Judah
598
  Nebukadnezar II
  takes Jerusalem
  1st deportation
587
  Destruction of
  Jerusalem. 2nd
  deportation
538
  Edict of Cyrus
  concerning
  reconstruction of
  Temple at
  Jerusalem
from 538
  Return of the
  Babylonian Jews

Bibliography

Akurgal, Ekrem/Hirmer, Max: *The art of the Hittites.* Thames and Hudson, 1962.

Alkim, U. Bahadir: *Anatolia I: from the beginnings to the end.* Barrie & Rockliff, London 1970.

Bardtke, Hans: *Bibel, Spaten und Geschichte.* Vandenhoeck & Ruprecht Verlag, Göttingen 1971.

Beran, Thomas: 'Die hethitische Glyptik von Boghazköy,' in: 76. *Wiss. Veröffentlichung der Deutschen Orientgesellschaft.* Verlag Gebr. Mann, Berlin 1967.

Bibby, Geoffrey: *The Testimony of the Spade.* Collins, London 1962.

Bittel, Kurt (*et al.*): 'Vorläufiger Bericht über die Ausgrabungen in Boghazköy im Jahre 1952,' in: *Mitteilungen der Deutschen Orientgesellschaft zu Berlin,* No. 86, Dec. 1953.
Grundzüge der Vor- und Frühgeschichte Kleinasiens. Tübingen 1950.
(*et al.*): 'Die hethitischen Grabfunde von Osmankayasa,' in: 71. *Wiss. Veröffentlichung der Deutschen Orientgesellschaft.* Verlag Gebr. Mann, Berlin 1958.

Blohm, Kurt Wilhelm: *Städte und Stätten in der Türkei.* DuMont Schauberg, Cologne 1971.

Bossert, Helmut Theodor: *Altanatolien – Kunst und Handwerk Kleinasiens von den Anfängen bis zum völligen Aufgehen in der griechischen Kultur.* Verlag Ernst Wasmuth, Berlin 1942.

Bray, Warwick/Trump, David: *The Penguin Dictionary of Archaeology.* Penguin Books, London 1972.

Ceram, C. W.: *Gods, graves and scholars.* Gollancz, London 1952.
Narrow Pass, Black Mountain. Gollancz, London 1956.

Cornelius, Friedrich: *Geschichte der Hethiter mit besonderer Berücksichtigung der geographischen Verhältnisse und der Rechtsgeschichte.* Wissentschaftliche Buchgesellschaft, Darmstadt 1973.

De Camp: *Geheimnisvolle Stätten der Geschichte.* Econ, Düsseldorf 1966.

Eggers, Hans Jürgen: *Einführung in die Vorgeschichte.* Piper, Munich 1974.

Fischer, Franz: 'Die Hethitische Keramik von Boghazköy,' in: 75. *Wiss. Veröffentlichung der Deutschen Orientgesellschaft.* Verlag Gebr. Mann, Berlin 1963.

Forrer, Emil: 'Für die Griechen in den Boghazköy-Inschriften,' in: *Kleinasiatische Forschungen*, Vol. I, No. 2, Weimar 1929.

Friedrich, Johannes: 'Werden in den hethitischen Keilschriften die Griechen erwähnt?' in: *Kleinasiatische Forschungen*, Vol. I, No. 1, Weimar 1927.

Hethitisches Elementarbuch – 1. *Teil, kurzgefasste Grammatik.* Heidelberg 1940.

Die hethitischen Gesetze. Leyden 1959.

Götze, Albrecht: *Kleinasien.* Munich 1957.

'Zur Chronologie der Hethiterkönige,' in: *Kleinasiatische Forschungen*, Vol. I, No. 1, Weimar 1927.

Grimal, Pierre (ed): *Mythologies.* Larousse, Paris 1963.

Hrozný, Friedrich: 'Hethitische Keilschriftentexte aus Boghazköi – in Umschrift. Mit Übersetzung und Kommentar,' in: *Boghazköi-Studien*, Art. 2, 1, No. 3, Vienna 1919.

Die Sprache der Hethiter – ihr Bau und ihre Zugehörigkeit zum indogermanischen Sprachstamm. Heinrichsche Buchhandlung, Leipzig 1917.

'Über die Völker und Sprachen des alten Chatti-Landes,' in: *Boghazköi-Studien*, Art. 3, No. 5, fascicle 2, 1920.

'Sumerisch-babylonische Mythen von dem Gott Ninrag (Ninib) – herausgegeben und umschrieben, übersetzt und erklärt,' in: *Mitteilungen der Vorderasiatischen Gesellschaft*, Yr 8, 5, Berlin 1903.

Kammenhuber, Annelies: *Die Arier im Vorderen Orient.* Carl Winter Verlag, Heidelberg 1968.

Kienitz, Friedrich-Karl: *Städte unter dem Halbmond – Geschichte und Kultur der Städte in Anatolien und auf der Balkanhalbinsel.* C. H. Beck, Munich 1972.

Kindlers Literatur Lexikon: 'Hethitische Literatur'. Munich 1974.

Klengel, Evelyn and Horst: *Die Hethiter und ihre Nachbarn.* Koehler & Amelang, Leipzig 1970, and Schroll, Munich 1970.

Klengel, Horst: *Geschichte und Kultur Altsyriens.* Koehler & Amelang, Leipzig 1967.

Zwischen Zelt und Palast – die Begegnung von Nomaden und Sesshaften im alten Vorderasien. Koehler & Amelang, Leipzig 1972.

Syria Antiqua. Edition Leipzig, Leipzig 1971.

Kündig-Steiner, Werner (ed): *Die Türkei.* Erdmann Verlag, Tübingen 1974.

Lange, Kurt/Hirmer, Max: *Egypt: architecture, sculpture and painting in three thousand years.* Phaidon, London 1968.

Mellaart, James: *Çatal Hüyük. A Neolithic Town in Anatolia.* Thames and Hudson, London 1967.

Mellink, M. J./Filip, J.: 'Frühe Stufen der Kunst,' in: *Propyläen Kunstgeschichte,* Vol. 13. Propyläen Verlag, Berlin 1974.

Metzger, Henri: *Anatolia II.* Barrie & Rockliff, London 1969.

Moscati, Sabatino: *Geschichte und Kultur der Semitischen Völker.* Kohlhammer Verlag, Stuttgart 1953.

Müller, Max W.: 'Der Bündnisvertrag Ramses' II und des Chetiter-königs – im Originaltext neu herausgegeben und übersetzt,' in: *Mitteilungen der Vorderasiatischen Gesellschaft,* 1902–1905, Yr 7, Berlin 1902.

Orthmann, Winfried: 'Der Alte Orient,' in: *Propyläen Kunstgeschichte,* Vol. 14. Propyläen Verlag, Berlin 1975.

Otten, Heinrich: 'Das Hethiterreich,' in: Schmökel, Hartmut: *Kulturgeschichte des Alten Orients.* Kröner Verlag, Stuttgart 1961.

'Kanaanäische Mythen aus Hattusa-Boghazköy,' in: *Mitteilungen der Deutschen Orientgesellschaft zu Berlin,* No. 85, June 1953.

'Die hethitischen "Königslisten" und die altorientalische Chronologie,' in: *Mitteilungen der Deutschen Orientgesellschaft zu Berlin,* No. 83, 1951.

'Die hethitischen historischen Quellen und die altorientalische Chronologie,' in: *Akademie der Wissenschaften und der Literatur, Abhandlungen der Geistes- und Sozialwiss. Klasse,* Yr 1968, No. 3.

Otto, Eberhard: *Ägypten – der Weg des Pharaonenreiches.* Kohlhammer Verlag, Stuttgart 1953.

Otto, Rudolf: *The idea of the holy* (2nd ed.). O.U.P., London 1950.

Pedersen, Holger: 'Hittitisch und die anderen indoeuropäischen Sprachen,' in: *Det. Kgl. Danske Videnskabernes Selskab* XXV, 2, Copenhagen 1938.

Rehork, Joachim: *Faszinierende Funde – Archäologie heute.* Lübbe, Bergisch-Gladbach 1971.

Riemschneider, Margarete: *Die Welt der Hethiter.* Kilpper Verlag,

Stuttgart 1954.

Roeder, Günther: *Ägypter und Hethiter.* Heinrichsche Buchhandlung, Leipzig 1919.

Schirmer, Wulf: 'Die Bebauung am unteren Büyükkale-Nordwesthang in Boghazköy,' in: 81. *Wiss. Veroffentlichung der Deutschen Orientgesellschaft.* Gebr. Mann Verlag, Berlin 1969.

Schmökel, Hartmut (ed): *Kulturgeschichte des Alten Orients.* Kröner Verlag, Stuttgart 1961.

Schuler, E.: *Die Hethitischen Dienstanweisungen für höhere Hof- und Staatsbeamte.* Graz 1957.

Weidner, Ernst F.: 'Der Zug Sargons von Akkad nach Kleinasien – die älteste geschichtliche Beziehung zwischen Babylon und Hatti,' in: *Boghazköi-Studien,* 6, Leipzig 1922.

'Politische Dokumente aus Kleinasien – die Staatsverträge in akkadischer Sprache aus dem Archiv von Boghazköi,' in: *Boghazköi-Studien* 8+9, Leipzig 1923.

Wolf, Walther: *Funde in Ägypten – Geschichte ihrer Entdeckung.* Musterschmidt Verlag, Göttingen 1966.

Zehren, Erich: *Die Biblischen Hügel – zur Geschichte der Archäologie.* Herbig Verlag, Berlin 1961.

Zimmern, H.: *Die Religion der Hethiter.* Leipzig 1925.

Index

313